NGOs, Africa and the Global Order

NGOs, Africa and the Global Order

Robert Pinkney
Visiting Professor of Politics, Northumbria University, UK

First published 2009 by
PALGRAVE MACMILLAN

Palgrave Macmillan in the UK is an imprint of Macmillan Publishers Limited, registered in England, company number 785998, of Houndmills, Basingstoke, Hampshire RG21 6XS.

Palgrave Macmillan in the US is a division of St Martin's Press LLC, 175 Fifth Avenue, New York, NY 10010.

Palgrave Macmillan is the global academic imprint of the above companies and has companies and representatives throughout the world.

Palgrave® and Macmillan® are registered trademarks in the United States, the United Kingdom, Europe and other countries.

ISBN-13: 978–0–230–54716–2   hardback
ISBN-10: 0–230–54716–8   hardback

This book is printed on paper suitable for recycling and made from fully managed and sustained forest sources. Logging, pulping and manufacturing processes are expected to conform to the environmental regulations of the country of origin.

A catalogue record for this book is available from the British Library.

A catalogue record for this book is available from the Library of Congress.

10   9   8   7   6   5   4   3   2   1
18 17 16 15 14 13 12 11 10 09

Printed and bound in Great Britain by
CPI Antony Rowe, Chippenham and Eastbourne

Contents

List of Boxes, Tables and Figures

Boxes

Tables

Figure

Glossary

BAe	British Aerospace
BiC	Bank Information Center
CBO	community based organisation
CNCR	Committee National de Concertation des Ruraux (Senegal)
CSO	civil society organisation
DENIVA	Development Network of Indigenous Voluntary Organisations (Uganda)
DFID	Department for International Development (UK)
DIY	do it yourself
ECOSOC	(United Nations) Economic and Social Council
EPAs	economic partnership agreements
EU	European Union
FES	Friedrich Ebert Stiftung
GATS	General Agreement on Trade and Services
GNP	gross national product
IFI	international financial institution
IMF	International Monetary Fund
IGO	inter-governmental organisation
INGO	international non-governmental organisation
IO	international organisation
JET	Journalists Environmental Association of Tanzania
KRC	Kabarole Research Centre (Uganda)
LEAT	Lawyers Environmental Action Team (Tanzania)
MAI	Multilateral Agreement on Investment
MDGs	Millennium Development Goals
MNC	Multi-national company
MSF	Medecins sans Frontieres
NAPE	National Association of Professional Environmentalists (Uganda)
NGO	non-governmental organisation
NPM	new public management
NRA	National Resistance Army (Uganda)
NRM	National Resistance Movement (Uganda)
PEAP	Poverty Eradication Assessment Programme (Uganda)
PRSPs	Poverty Reduction Strategy Papers

QUANGO	quasi-non-governmental (or near-governmental) organisation
RSPCA	Royal Society for the Prevention of Cruelty of Animals
RSPB	Royal Society for the Protection of Birds
SAP	structural adjustment programme
SAPRI	Structural Adjustment Participatory Review Initiative
SIDA	Swedish International Development Agency
TANGO	Tanzania Association of Non-Governmental Organisations
TGNP	Tanzania Gender Networking Programme
TNRF	Tanzania Natural Resources Forum
UN	United Nations
UNDP	United Nations Development Programme
US	United States of America
USAID	United States Agency for International Development
WTO	World Trade Organisation

Acknowledgements

The completion of this book has only been possible with the help and support of many individuals and institutions. The University of Dar es Salaam and the Makerere Institute of Social Research, Kampala, provided me with bases from which to carry out my fieldwork, and helped me to deal with numerous academic and administrative problems. NGO officers in Tanzania and Uganda, and in London, were happy to give up their time to talk to me and to provide me with much useful documentation. Of the individuals whose help stretched well beyond the call of duty, I would like to thank especially Maurice Barnes, Dr Frederick Golooba-Mutebi, Ineke Jongerius, Professor Max Mmuya, Nashi Mazava, Patrick Mulindwa and Sylvia Natukunda. Staff at Palgrave were a continuous source of support, and listened sympathetically to my excuses when the work got behind schedule. My wife Mary corrected much of the inelegant and ungrammatical English in the earlier drafts. To all those who helped I am very grateful, but I take full responsibility for any errors of fact or opinion.

1
Introduction

Over 30,000 competitors enter the London Marathon nowadays, and over 40,000 enter the Great North Run. Such levels of participation in British athletics were unheard of a generation or two ago. In politics, tens of thousands of groups, many of them based in small shacks or back room offices, and with a handful of paid staff, have emerged during the past 20 years. Many demand representation at global fora to give voice to the demands of the poor and underprivileged. Such participation in politics was unheard of a generation or two ago.

In the marathon, the winner collects a large pay cheque at the finish, and is almost invariably one of a small elite of international runners. For the amateurs who make up the vast majority of the field, each receives a cheap medallion and a bottle of mineral water. The satisfaction comes from having taken part, without any expectation of winning. In politics, the winners are also frequently members of a small international elite, but the losers may be less convinced that it is the taking part, rather than the winning, that matters. At stake may be the fate of particular communities such as peasants evicted from their land by a mining company or political dissidents suffering persecution, or of larger groups across the globe faced with continued poverty, debt and disease. To a growing extent the interests of these groups and communities have been articulated by non-governmental organisations (NGOs). Has this proliferation of NGOs affected the balance of political power substantially or has it, like mass participation in marathons, made for an impressive spectacle but without altering the identity of the ultimate winners?

Like a commentator in all good marathons, this book will leave such speculative questions hanging in the air at the start, and leave any assessment until the race is well underway. For the moment we shall simply offer an outline of the course to be followed. This book is concerned with the rise of NGOs and their impact on both the national and global stages. We shall look at detailed definitions and classifications later, and note here simply that an NGO is distinguished partly by the fact that it is a voluntary body with few, if any, statutory obligations, in contrast to state agencies whose functions are defined by law, and partly by the fact that it does not exist to make a profit like businesses in the private sector. For the most part NGOs are concerned with either providing services (ranging from offering advice to organic farmers to finding homes for street children) or with 'advocacy' (ranging from advancing the rights of hunter gatherers to campaigning for the cancellation of Third World debt). Although many governments now require NGOs to register their existence, their great asset is their flexibility in the absence of statutory functions or obligations to shareholders. NGOs can wax and wane as circumstances change. At one moment pressures to end authoritarian rule may lead to the emergence of 'democracy promoting' or human rights NGOs, at another NGOs may emerge to help the growing number of AIDs victims or to campaign against environmental pollution or 'unfair' trade agreements between rich and poor countries. Within Africa, it is from NGOs, rather than from parliaments, political parties or businesses, that many new ideas and pressures on authority have emerged, and it is NGOs that have become increasingly important in holding governments to account. In global politics, much of the challenge to policies that have allegedly contributed to Africa's continued impoverishment has come from NGOs.

Why Africa? Why NGOs?

Why should a study of NGOs focus on Africa? Apart from the author's own research interests, the main answer is that conventional politics and economics have found no solution to Africa's continued impoverishment, compared with most regions of the world. A variety of attempts have been made to stimulate development, notably through state socialism, military authoritarianism, neo-colonialism and *laissez-faire*, free market economics. The apparent failure of all these attempts raises questions as to what sort of political institutions, if any, might offer a way out of impoverishment, or at least mitigate the situation. Africa's plight is in contrast to much of Asia, where selective state intervention has produced flourishing 'tiger' economies, and Latin America where two centuries of independence from colonial rule have enabled states to work out their own salvation. Independence for most countries in Africa in the late 1950s and early 1960s was followed by two decades of falling export prices, with governments increasingly unable to deliver basic public services, or even security, to their citizens. Measured by such criteria as per capita income, literacy, infant mortality or life expectancy, the much sought after 'development' had not materialised.

The transition from authoritarianism to semi-democracy in the 1980s and 1990s brought benefits in terms of human rights and some ability to hold governments to account, but Africa remained at the mercy of forces it could not control. International Financial Institutions (IFIs) imposed retrenchment, privatisation and a market economy as conditions of aid; and the World Trade Organisation (WTO) demanded that Africa opened its markets to foreign imports while permitting Western governments to continue to subsidise agricultural production. The debts incurred by previous authoritarian African governments were cancelled only partially and grudgingly, and subject to further conditions of privatisation and retrenchment. Despite the nominal arrival of democracy, elected African governments had little freedom of choice in formulating social or economic policy.

Why should this study focus on NGOs? Certainly not because they offer a magic formula that has hitherto been overlooked. NGOs have no means of raising revenue, other than through grants or donations, no authority to impose new policies, and no automatic right to be heard by people in authority. In a better ordered world NGOs might be largely superfluous, with voters choosing their preferred parties and policies through the ballot box, and African governments fulfilling the popular will at home while fighting their corner in international negotiations. But in the real world, policies are more likely to be made in Brussels or Washington than in African capitals; and the answerability of African governments to their constituents is likely to be secondary to their answerability to elites, businesses and foreign governments. It is these bodies that provide African politicians with favours in terms of 'gifts' and promises of investment or increased employment, in the expectation that the politicians will repay them with policies that contribute to enhanced profits or to the advancement of Western foreign policy. Some of these policies may, of course, bring benefits to ordinary African citizens, but many will lead to continued poverty, pollution, the depletion of natural resources, the eviction of peasants from the land, and the diversion of resources into prestige projects which have little relevance to African development.

The formal political structure offers little defence against the process, often characterised as 'neo-patrimonialism', of African governments seeking to retain their power and wealth through a network of elite contacts. Individual academics, journalists, novelists, professional groups, or even occasional rebel politicians, may have their say, but to little effect. For the most part it has been NGOs that have gathered data, marshalled arguments, organised campaigns and lobbied politicians. The very fact that they do not occupy any formal position in the political system gives them more scope as 'wild cards', campaigning in different ways depending on the issues at stake, on the state of public opinion and on the possible receptiveness of the government. While they have lost more battles than they have won, it is difficult to see how the victories that they have achieved could have been won by any institutions other than NGOs.

The picture is similar at the global level. Many of Africa's woes may be traced to Western governments, IFIs and global businesses, yet there are few formal political mechanisms to enable African citizens or their representatives to campaign for fair trade, debt cancellation, the protection of the natural environment or the protection of workers from exploitation. African governments are frequently out-manoeuvred in negotiations with Western governments and institutions, which invariably have more resources and greater access to experts and lawyers. African Governments anyway have other pressing business to attend to, without devoting undue time to fighting losing battles around the negotiating table. NGOs, on the other hand, can make these campaigns central to their whole existence. Their successes so far may be modest, but they offer at least the possibility of the voice of the poor and the underprivileged being heard. We shall return to these matters in subsequent chapters, but for the moment we go on to focus on the question of how NGOs came to acquire their present role.

The transformation of politics and the rise of NGOs

In the final quarter of the twentieth century, three developments transformed politics in the West, in Africa and at the world level: the transition from mass society to post-industrial society in the West, the transition from authoritarianism to semi-democracy (or unconsolidated democracy) in Africa, and the transition from traditional international relations to globalisation in the wider world. Such a bald statement is obviously a gross simplification, and does not do justice to either the subtlety of all the changes or the extent to which aspects of the old order persisted, yet there is no escaping the fact that politics at all these levels was very different by the early 1990s from what it had been in the late 1960s, and that the new order in each case was much more conducive to the flourishing of NGOs than the old.

In the old order in the West, representative democracy existed as both a constitutional myth and a reality. Elections were contested by mass parties with deep roots in society, often based on social class, religion or ethnicity, and elected governments and parliaments were constrained by interest groups which also had deep roots in society, or which possessed professional qualifications that were widely respected. The groups included the representatives of business, organised labour, religion and the professions. Within such a tight political order there was little room for the sort of free spirits that subsequently formed the bases of many NGOs. In Africa the authoritarian rule that characterised most of the continent until the late 1980s was an even more obvious barrier to the rise of NGOs. African governments might bow to the pressure of stronger foreign governments, businesses or well organised ethnic groups, but there was little scope for groups claiming to represent the poor, the oppressed or the natural environment. In world politics the old order was characterised by interaction between national governments and their representatives, with little scope for groups pursuing causes which they regarded as transcending national interests.

There were, of course, some embryonic NGOs flourishing despite the rigidity of the old order. Amnesty International began campaigning for human rights in 1961, Oxfam's crusading for the poor goes back a further two decades, and religious and professional groups in Africa sometimes fought and won battles in a similar manner to modern NGOs. But for the most part the exercise of power and influence depended on various permutations of counting heads, threatening sanctions or wielding coercive force. The ways in which this power and influence was wielded obviously depended on certain underlying values. It might have been socially unacceptable to resolve a strike by shooting the workers, or to resolve an ethnic conflict by stripping tribal chiefs of their power and status, but the prevailing values might still leave little room for groups that were unable to demonstrate that they represented significant interests in society. If what we regard as 'advocacy NGOs' had difficulty in acquiring a role in the old order, would-be 'service delivery NGOs' fared little better. Charities and religious bodies went about their business of helping the poor and needy, and sometimes worked in tandem with state institutions, but they were not generally regarded as an integral part of the process of public service provision. That was the prerogative of central and local bureaucracies, answerable to politicians.

By the end of the twentieth century much of the political landscape had changed. In the West the decline of mining and heavy industry had had the effect of weakening traditional class loyalties and weakening the political parties and interest groups that gave expression to these loyalties. Organised professional groups, too, lost much of their formal influence as they were weakened by technological change, global competition and a greater willingness to challenge professional wisdom. Society had become more atomised. Politicians wanting to win or retain power could no longer rely on the automatic support of 'their own' people; and groups wanting to influence politicians could no longer rely on the easy access, based on common values, of earlier times. In Africa years of economic decline, and the loss of foreign patrons who had needed allies during the Cold War, had had the effect of undermining authoritarian governments by the late 1980s. A new order emerged over much of the continent which was democratic at least to the extent that relatively free and fair multi-party elections were held, and greater freedom of association and expression was conceded. Even if ruling politicians could use the advantages of incumbency and the powers of patronage to gain re-election, the effective exercise power now depended more heavily on attracting resources from the 'voluntary sector' at home or abroad.

The political processes in both the West and Africa were thus in a state of flux, as the older certainties about who wielded power and influence came increasingly into question. This did not necessarily mean that NGOs would fill the void. It could have been, and to some extent was, filled by populist demagogues, wealthy newspaper barons and footloose global businesses trading donations for governmental favours. There was also the possibility of the political sphere itself shrinking, as the state was no longer able or willing to provide such a wide range of services. There are no longer student grants in England or passenger railway services in Uganda. In other cases, services have been transferred to the private sector, sometimes with an obligation to continue to serve the public interest and sometimes not. But a major feature of politics in post-industrial Europe and post-authoritarian Africa has been the rise of NGOs both as service providers (a traditional role of the state bureaucracy) and as advocates of political causes (a traditional role of political parties and pressure groups).

What are the distinguishing features of these bodies? The term 'non-governmental' might suggest a residual category, defined more by what it is not than by what it is. It is not part of the public sector because NGOs do not normally have any statutory obligations beyond observing the law of the land. While a government department, a local council or a hospital trust is required by law to exist and to perform certain public functions, Oxfam, the Red Cross and Save the Children only exist because their members choose to keep them in being, and only carry out such functions as they choose to discharge. Neither is an NGO part of the private sector, as it does not exist to make a profit, and it is therefore dependent on funding from the other two sectors or from private individuals. This leaves NGOs with a largely blank canvas on which to make their mark, with their actual functions and effectiveness varying between different times and places, but a few generalisations will help to set the scene.

In the West the term 'NGO' is not used as widely as in Africa, and terms such as 'charity', 'voluntary group', 'third sector' or even 'pressure group' are often used, but organisations answering to the normal definition of NGOs now cover such diverse areas as the welfare of the disabled, social housing, the protection of birds, and campaigns to cancel Third World debt and to halt the building of new motorways. Sometimes NGOs provide services which were once provided by the state in a more social democratic era; sometimes they supplement state services. In other cases the emphasis is on advocacy rather than services, though the two are often difficult to disentangle. The advocacy groups might be seen as a mere continuation of pressure groups, yet they are more attuned to the current era than the mass-based or professional groups of yesteryear, such as political parties, trade unions, religious bodies or employers' associations. If advocacy NGOs have a large membership, which many do not, it tends (with a few exceptions) to be relatively passive. The activity of many members is confined to signing a direct debit form. Success depends more on the expertise and campaigning skills of the leadership, rather than on the ability to get the masses on to the streets. In these ways, the rise of NGOs reflects both the retreat of the state as a major service provider and the rise of 'post-material values', as many citizens have become sufficiently affluent to support causes that go beyond their own material well-being. While public sector bodies have their roles defined largely by statute, and the private sector is constrained by company law and the need to make a profit for shareholders, NGOs can alter their form or activity as circumstances dictate. Some, such as animal rights groups, may resort to direct action or even breaking the law, while others have a close working relationship with governmental bodies or businesses.

Some emphasise extensive public support for their cause as a major bargaining counter with the government, as in the case of debt relief, while others rely on quieter diplomacy over issues on which there is more limited public indignation, such as the recruitment of child soldiers or the illicit trade in diamonds. While each NGO has come to plough its own furrow, with little attempt to build any confederation of groups (at least in Western countries), the sum total of NGO activity has, one could argue, produced (or at least reflected) a radically different political system from that which prevailed for most of the twentieth century. Previously, representative democracy depended largely on votes and the counting of heads, mediated by the presence or threat of sanctions such as strikes or non-co-operation. While much of this representative structure obviously remains intact, the current political process now depends increasingly on other more subtle forces. NGOs, for the most part, do not claim a right to be heard on the basis of how many people they represent or on the extent to which they can help or hinder politicians by giving money or votes, or by disrupting the administrative process. Their claim is based much more on the conviction that they are right, and that they possess the expertise to support such claims. Their main weapon is not disruption but skill in campaigning, negotiating and persuading.

In Africa the sequence of events was somewhat different, but the end product was again one in which NGOs had acquired a much more extensive role. The relatively shallow democratisation since the 1980s has not, for the most part, given rise to political parties or pressure groups with mass support, and it is NGOs that exhibit the most visible manifestation of public challenges to the state. This is true in the physical sense of numerous signboards announcing the presence of a variety of NGOs in most of the larger and medium sized towns, but also in the analytical sense of NGOs frequently providing the most effective means of holding governments and their officials to account.

In world politics the context is different again. Here there has not even been any pretence at representative democracy. The most significant change, according to many observers, has been from a world order in which individual national governments sought to maximise their influence at the expense of other governments (international relations), to an order in which national governments, and national frontiers, count for less as more issues become 'global'. Businesses can shift investment or production from one part of the world to another with greater ease, and frontiers can be crossed more easily by migrants, diseases, mass media, religious sects and campaigners against global warming. This environment, like that within nations, is generally more conducive to NGO activity. Where citizens would once have expected their own governments to represent their interests and aspirations, they may now be represented by Oxfam, Friends of the Earth or the Jubilee Debt Campaign. Paradoxically, the very lack of democracy in world politics can strengthen the influence of NGOs. An individual government may dismiss an NGO's demands at the national level on the grounds that the government has been chosen by a larger constituency than the NGO has been, but the IMF, WTO or the World Bank can make no such claims. Here, NGOs may claim to represent the poor or the powerless against unelected technocrats and ideologues.

Matters arising

If the presence and greater effectiveness of NGOs is an observable fact, and if a strong case can be made that the rise of NGOs has been associated with the transformation of the working political process at the African, Western and global levels, how can we explore these changes in greater detail? Apart from their organisational form, what is it about NGOs that enables them to behave in different ways from other institutions, and possibly to produce different political outcomes? Should we take their 'distinctiveness' at face value, or should we ask whether they are merely the latest organisational fashion that will recruit similar personnel to other organisations, and ultimately succumb to the same bureaucratic routines? How easily do generalisations about NGOs travel when one looks at the distinctive politics of individual countries, each with its own history, culture and current power structures? If NGOs try to build links across and beyond national frontiers, how conducive is the current world order to this? Do the interests of national governments or the interests of global capital ultimately expose NGOs as the amateurs that they are – no match for those who wield such weapons as votes, money and physical force? Are NGOs, especially at the international level, as likely to be the agents of Western economic, cultural and strategic interests, as they are to be champions of the poor? And if we peer through the gun smoke of the major confrontations, what of the actual strategies being followed on the ground? What are the different means by which NGOs exploit the resources available to them, with whom do they co-operate, which centres of power can they lobby most effectively, and what sort of arguments are most likely to advance their cause? Even if we accept the thesis that the rise of NGOs has been more a consequence than a cause of major social and political changes, has the effectiveness of NGOs been so great as to transform the political landscape still further? If it has, how should one characterise this new landscape, and how far does it enhance, or detract from, democratic politics? Does it make for a more consensual style, or does it sweep genuine political conflict under the carpet, from whence it may spill over into undemocratic channels?

The individual chapters

Some of these questions can only be left as matters for speculation, but the individual chapters in this book attempt not merely to discuss what NGOs do, but to see them as part of an ever changing political process which shapes them and is shaped by them. Neither the questions, nor the answers (if answers exist), are capable of being easily categorised and put into neat self-contained blocks, like sheep herded into pens. Some questions can easily stray into what the reader might regard as the wrong pen; others have a disconcerting habit of reappearing in several different pens. But this book attempts to bring a degree of conceptual order to bear by beginning with the background history, and examining the debate on the distinctiveness or otherwise of NGOs. It then delves into the rough and tumble of NGO involvement in African politics before looking upwards at the different characteristics of the world political order within which NGOs seek to take on the most powerful institutions. Within this world order, we look at the potential power of international NGOs (INGOs) as either missionaries for global justice or agents of imperialism, before returning closer to ground level to look at the actual tools available to NGOs to make an impact on political events. While the chapter immediately after this one is largely concerned with questions of the 'how did we come to be here?' type, the concluding chapter is more interested in asking 'where are we?' At what sort of destination, or at least temporary resting place, have we arrived in terms of the current political order, and is it an order in which democracy is enhanced, weakened or rendered irrelevant?

Chapter 2 traces the rapid expansion of NGOs since the early 1980s. The exploration begins in the West, where the mass society of the mid-twentieth century was gradually transformed into a post-industrial society. The decline of heavy industry in the face of globalisation was a major driving force, and it wrought changes in society, the polity and, at least indirectly, in the natural environment. The net effect of these changes was to replace a tightly structured, hierarchical political order with one in which there were more diverse centres of power and influence. NGOs benefited from both the weakening of states that were now more willing to delegate areas of service provision to NGOs, and from a changing political agenda in which traditional conflicts between capital and labour were increasingly superseded by issues such as threats to the environment, and threats by global business to discrete groups, as opposed to whole social classes. While political parties and trade unions had been the primary vehicles for protecting the working class, NGOs were often better suited to pursue causes such as ethical trading, the employment of child labour or resistance to the building of dams that involved mass evictions.

The prevailing ideologies in the West by the late 1980s generally took a benevolent view of the rise of NGOs, even if they did not approve of some of their more radical campaigns. An 'enabling state' which left much work to the 'voluntary sector', and which was now much freer of the constraints of trade unions and the professions, went with the grain of right-wing ideology, while leaving the left with scope to mount a variety of campaigns through NGOs for causes which had previously been neglected. The general approval of NGOs in the West did not mean that they were then imposed on Africa, but it did mean that the rise of African NGOs, if conditions were propitious for their development, was less likely to be obstructed by the West. The initial driving force was often the need for self-help as African states became increasingly unable to deliver basic services in the face of economic decline. Self-help groups were soon joined by groups promoting democracy, human rights and the protection of various underprivileged groups, as authoritarian governments were increasingly unable to retain grip.

It suited the ideologies and interests of Western governments and IFIs to encourage development and service provision in Africa via NGOs rather than governments, and aid channelled in this way gave a further boost to NGOs. At the same time there were growing links, aided by new electronic communications, between advocacy NGOs in Africa concerned with human rights, the poor and the underprivileged, and like-minded NGOs in the West which were trying to promote 'global justice' through such means as fair trade, debt relief for Africa and end to Western support for oppressive regimes. Once again a fortuitous combination of free market forces on the right and radical campaigning on the left helped to consolidate a political order in which NGOs were now a growing force.

Having plotted the growing role of NGOs in politics and society in Chapter 2, Chapter 3 looks explicitly at the question of what is distinctive about NGOs as compared with other political institutions. It draws a contrast between the 'virtuous model' and the 'functional model'. In the former, NGOs possess a clear vision of moral causes to be won, especially on behalf of the poorest and least privileged groups in society. Their leaders possess distinctive expertise and skills, and their honesty, integrity and competence give them a public legitimacy which few other institutions can match. In contrast, the functional model emphasises the workaday role of NGOs. They are often created by opportunists seeking employment for themselves and grants from donors, they lack any mass membership base and are often controlled by a small clique. The dependency on contracts from African governments, or grants from Western donors, compromises the autonomy of NGOs, and at best they settle into a role not dissimilar from that of the state bureaucrats they have often displaced. At worst they are Trojan horses for the promotion of Western interests, having to conform to donors' demands as to what functions they perform and how they perform them. Both models, of course, are caricatures of reality, but they provide a useful guide to both the opportunities for, and constraints on, NGOs.

One body of opinion suggests that the late 1990s marked the heyday of anything approaching the virtuous model. Since then African states have begun to re-assert their authority, while Western security concerns since 2001 have made donors more discriminating as to which NGO activities to support, and where. Yet many NGOs have a resilience that enables them to adapt to changed circumstances and grasp new opportunities. Despite all the apparent powers of Western interests to impose their will, many NGOs continue to advocate a world order very different from the present one, and to advance the interests of groups that would otherwise be neglected. Political expediency may mean that would-be virtuous NGOs have to soil their hands by dealing with less virtuous institutions, and sometimes entering into less than virtuous bargains and compromises, but the end of helping the under-privileged, or maintaining a campaign for a more just order, may be regarded as justifying the means.

Chapters 4 and 5 examine the roles of NGOs in Tanzania and Uganda. While no two countries can be taken as 'typical' of the whole of Africa, Tanzania and Uganda do exhibit many of the typical features, including extensive poverty, economies dependent on a few primary products, dependence on the West, recent experience of authoritarian rule, and more recent attempts to establish pluralist democracy. Within this context NGOs are generally accepted in principle by state and society alike as having a legitimate role, but when it comes to practical politics the requirements of governments and NGOs are often difficult to reconcile. NGOs whose horizons extend beyond service provision, or meeting purely local needs, frequently envisage a political order in which the poor and underprivileged enjoy more secure rights and a larger share of the nation's resources. Such an order might imply a more open political system within which citizens participate more effectively and politicians are subject to greater scrutiny and accountability. Governments might accept much of this in principle, drawing on the socialist ideology of President Nyerere and the liberation ideology of President Museveni, but the practical requirement of holding on to power in Africa may require a different emphasis. In the absence of any appeal to distinctive class interests, politicians need to win votes by spending money, and acquiring that money requires dispensing favours to elite groups and businesses, both indigenous and foreign. When public resources are limited, the granting of such favours is difficult to reconcile with helping the disadvantaged. Politicians prefer the processes by which favours are granted not to be subject to the sort of democratic accountability favoured by NGOs. Corruption and open, democratic government do not go well together. There is thus a constant tug of war between NGOs seeking what they regard as social justice, and politicians paying lip service to such an ideal but in practice operating in a rather different system.

The restrictions on the existence of opposition parties until recently has meant that many of the traditional 'party' functions of representing different interests, and advocating policies which advance these interests, has been left largely to NGOs, many of which have displayed impressive knowledge and campaigning skills in presenting their cases. Many have also won impressive victories, and have encouraged civil society as a whole to put politicians and public officials under greater scrutiny. But unlike opposition parties, NGOs have no way of threatening to displace the government. We are left with a system of 'democracy without votes'. NGOs can perform such democratic functions as articulating public interests and concerns, stimulating informed debate, mobilising public opinion and holding the government to account, but their claims to legitimacy are not based on the counting of heads in terms of votes received, or even members enrolled. They are based much more on the possession of knowledge and expertise, and a conviction of the justice of their cause. In many respects democracy without votes has enhanced democracy in general in ways that would not otherwise been possible. NGOs have protected and advanced the interests of groups that would otherwise have had no voice, have pressed politicians and officials to account for their handling of public resources, have increased public awareness of a range of problems, and have developed lines of communication with otherwise remote politicians. Such actions are, of course, a feature of most democratic political systems. It would be a very impoverished polity that relied solely on votes in elections and parliament to determine political outcomes, without the wider civil society having a say. The major problem is that the effectiveness of 'democracy without votes' depends largely on it being inter-woven with 'democracy with votes' so that persuasion by NGOs can be reinforced by the sanction of voting out politicians who ignore public opinion too frequently. In most of Africa such a sanction does not exist for practical purposes. In the absence of social classes on which to build bases of support, and in the absence of many policy alternatives when donors, creditors and global economic forces limit the choices available, few opposition parties offer a serious prospect of 'turning the rascals out'. This means that while NGOs have achieved some remarkable results through deploying their expertise, knowledge and powers of persuasion, governments can in the end use their executive power, their domination of the legislative process, and their control of the means of coercion, to retain the privileges of the elites they serve.

In Chapter 6 we move from African to global politics. Does the rapid rise of INGOs, many of which are able to articulate the demands of African NGOs, imply a stronger NGO voice in the world? Is there a 'global civil society' which can uphold the values to which many NGOs subscribe? Much depends on how one conceives of the global political order. The chapter highlights six possible models of that order, constructed along the axes of democracy/authoritarianism and order/anarchy. No one model can capture the complex reality of constant shifts in power and influence, and we note the continuing rival pulls of 'power politics' on the one hand and 'global democracy' on the other. The economic strength of the West, and especially the United States, might suggest that power politics will win the day, with little scope for NGOs to advance the interests of the have-nots. There was certainly no consultation with any nascent global civil society to ask it if it wanted global capitalism, aid for Africa that is conditional on privatisation, free market policies that damage African economies, or investment decisions that benefit global businesses at the expense of indigenous businesses and citizens. One could argue that global decision-making is not based on democratic votes or consensus, but is generally by non-elected bodies dominated by Western powers, generally meeting in secret, without the effective participation of NGOs, and in the interests of wealthy countries and global capital. Yet power politics is not the same as totalitarianism. Some political actors may be weaker than others, but that does not mean that they possess no power at all. No global body is strong enough to deny NGOs the right to exist, to rally public opinion or to demand the right to lobby and negotiate.

Chapter 7 attempts to fill in some of the detail within the framework suggested in Chapter 6. It focuses on the role of INGOs. These bodies pursue a variety of objectives, from collaborating in the implementation of Western foreign and security policy, through advancing their own specific ideological or religious objectives, to campaigning for what they see as global justice. INGOs, like many NGOs in national politics, start from an apparent position of weakness, lacking the legislative, financial or coercive powers enjoyed by states, IFIs or businesses. Their strength depends partly on the legitimacy which is accorded to them by the political actors they are trying to influence, and partly on the vulnerability of these actors. We move into a political world in which there are few formal written rules, where what is important is often each actor's perception of what the other actors are doing, how they are doing it, and whether it is being done in the pursuit of acceptable ends. Some INGOs seek to influence African and/or Western governments, but they face the handicap not only of lacking sanctions to back up their demands, but of sometimes being deemed unrepresentative of any significant interest or body of opinion, in contrast to governments with their legitimacy based on popular election. In the case of African governments, INGOs face the additional handicap of being branded as outsiders, interfering in the business of a sovereign state. But in relation to international organisations such as the World Bank or the IMF, or indeed private business, INGOs may claim to represent a broad moral interest which these unelected bodies are neglecting. This does not, of course, guarantee their success. INGOs need to demonstrate not only their legitimate right to be heard, but the legitimacy of their objectives, their ability to work within accepted rules and conventions, the relevance of the skills and knowledge they possess, and their ability to achieve their stated objectives. An INGO that can demonstrate satisfactory credentials on some fronts may only be able to do so at the expense of others. Thus the production of impeccable reports and accounts, or pursuing goals that please Western governments, may be achieved at the expense of the ideals implicit in the INGO's 'mission', such as improving the lot of the poor or the sick.

Yet governments, IFIs and businesses would be weaker without the existence of INGOs. Not only would their absence create a huge gap in service provision which might result in economic and political chaos, but even apparently tiresome advocacy NGOs may provide useful warnings against the pursuit of unpopular or impractical policies. The apparently powerful institutions in global politics may feel more secure if they show a willingness to negotiate with, and make concessions to, INGOs.

While Chapter 6 looks down from the lofty heights of the global order as a whole, and Chapter 7 views the role of INGOs within that order, Chapter 8 looks more closely down on the actual arenas where contests are won or lost between NGOs and their adversaries. While it is difficult to set out any general explanations of NGO success or failure, certain trends may have strengthened the hand of NGOs. Governments, IFIs and businesses now seem less confident of the efficacy of the free market policies that were fashionable in the 1980s. They wish to preserve some legitimacy and respectability both by claiming to be concerned about the plight of the poor, and by consulting with NGOs that claim to represent the poor. While there has been a growth in the more militant groups which demand a transformation of the global order, and which have little time for negotiating or compromising with the enemy, many mainstream NGOs have become more willing to enter into dialogue with institutions that apparently have very different goals and interests from their own. The dialogue between NGOs and the World Bank over the impact of structural adjustment policies on the poor is but one example of apparently incompatible groups coming together. The gap between the groups is sometimes too wide to bridge, but there now appears to be a broader 'middle ground' where both sides leave their more controversial beliefs and demands in cold storage before entering into negotiation.

A greater NGO willingness to build links with decision-makers has been complemented by stronger links between different NGOs, from the purely local through the national to the global. It is not just a matter of Oxfam sitting down with representatives of the World Bank, but of Oxfam having established contacts with NGOs in Africa so that it can demonstrate clearly the plight of the local population. No magic formula has been found for producing more NGO successes, but a combination of the more ideologically insecure positions of global decision-makers, and a sharpening of NGO skills in mutual co-operation in bargaining with others, has helped to secure the righting, or partial righting, of a range of perceived wrongs. Much of this has been helped by a stronger sense of the injustice of the current global order with public opinion in the West. In campaigns on issues ranging from debt relief to cheap drugs for the treatment of AIDs, NGOs already have the fair wind of public opinion to help them on their way.

The concluding chapter reminds us that NGOs have not revolutionised politics, society or the economy. Indeed few of them, unlike many political parties, social movements or religious sects, ever set out to do so. Many governments continue to serve the interests of narrow elites, many businesses continue to exploit workers, consumers and the planet as a whole, and inter-governmental organisations continue to protect powerful governments and global capital. The poor are still with us, and in growing numbers, social inequality is probably greater than at any time since the dawn of industrialisation, and sickness and malnutrition are reflected in low levels of life expectancy in much of Africa.

The achievements of NGOs lie not in revolutionary changes, but in exploiting the range of opportunities created by the (often incomplete) transitions from mass society to post-industrial society in the West, from authoritarianism to semi-democracy in Africa, and from international relations to global politics in the wider world. Governments, IFIs and businesses have not generally been overthrown or radically transformed, but they have in many ways become more insecure, with weaker power bases, more limited capacity and diminished legitimacy. While the powers of money or naked force remain important, they are insufficient for the conduct of much day-to-day business. It is here that the resources of NGOs, such as knowledge, expertise, networking, persuasion, working with the grain of public opinion, and even claiming adherence to a higher set of moral principles, can make a significant contribution to the political process.

Whether the end product is a better political order is a matter of subjective judgement. The rise of NGOs was at least partly a consequence of the decline in the effectiveness of the institutions of representative democracy in the West, and the failure of comparable institutions to evolve adequately in much of Africa or in global politics. But the growth of NGOs has gained a momentum of its own, and pushed representative institutions aside still further. Where once decisions were based on counting heads or counting votes, much decision-making now involves what we have called 'democracy without votes'. It would be difficult, if not impossible, to revert to the old order of mass politics, but NGOs now face a major challenge not just as service providers or advocates, but as key actors in largely uncharted political waters.

2
From Mass Society to Post-Industrial Society and from Authoritarianism to Pluralism: The Context of the Rise of NGOs

In 1909 there were 176 international NGOs (INGOs) (Edwards 2000: 9); by 2003 there were 48,000 (Kaldor *et al*. 2003: 10). In the early 1980s there were only seventeen registered NGOs in Tanzania; by the late 1990s there were nearly 1,000 (Igoe 2004: 11). Current estimates, especially by foreign embassies, put the figure at 4,000. Uganda had 2,655 registered NGOs in 2000 and 5,200 by 2004 (Kwesiga and Namisi in Jordan and van Tuijl 2006: 82). Such figures can, of course, only be approximations, but no one would dispute that the twentieth century saw an enormous rise in the number of NGOs, and that there has been a particularly rapid rise from the late 1980s to the present. The figures depend on whether one is counting 'registered' or 'unregistered' NGOs. If the latter, how does one decide where NGOs end and other organisations begin. Salamon and Annheir (in Lewis 1999: 70–2) imply that registered NGOs are the tip of a much larger iceberg. In Ghana there were over 800 non-profit organisations in the larger urban areas alone, of which only a quarter were officially registered. There were also 114 'non-profit' hospitals, and 242 primary and 227 secondary schools linked to religious bodies. Beyond that there were innumerable village associations, and credit and savings associations. In Egypt, they reported, there were 17,500 non-profit organisations with a membership of six million out of a population of 53 million, together with a wide range of influential groups.

What should we be trying to count, and why? Governments, with a desire for both political and statistical order, might prefer to assert that an NGO is whatever they say it is, and that only those organisations that meet their criteria are qualified to register as NGOs. Other organisations may be variously described as civil society organisations (CSOs) with less formal structures, or sometimes 'community based organisations' (CBOs) or 'social movements' campaigning for radical causes, or merely professional groups defending their members' interests. For political scientists, rather than politicians, a broader definition of non-governmental organisations may be more useful, focusing less on legal niceties and more on the 'non' in the title. The interest is in the rapid growth of the 'voluntary sector' or 'civil society' which is neither part of government nor part of the private sector, yet impinges on the political process. Lines of distinction are invariably blurred and fluid. Some voluntary groups may be involved in charity, or sporting, cultural and recreational activities, without seeking political influence, and are therefore of little interest to this study. Others may come into politics intermittently when they seek funding or seek to defend their interests. Yet others are involved in constant campaigning, or in interacting with governments over policy or administration.

Choosing a broad definition of NGOs, we are likely to end up with an impressionistic picture rather than an accurate photograph, since one cannot identify and count all the 'voluntary' groups in existence, but our concern is less with precise statistics than with the growth of a sector which has no formal constitutional status or functions, yet which, by most accounts, wields growing political influence. What is distinctive about NGOs as political actors is a theme of the next chapter, but we can make a few preliminary observations. If NGOs are growing in numbers and scope, it is presumably at the expense of other political actors and institutions. They may attract activists who would once have joined political parties, they may provide welfare services once provided by the state, or they may provide a modicum of order and expertise in the world's trouble spots where governments are unable to act. In other cases they may have expanded the terms of political dialogue by raising previously neglected issues such as the plight of street children or endangered tigers, or by claiming new issues as their own, from climate change to the exploitation of child soldiers.

In all these ways the growth of NGOs matters because it affects the balance of political power, the content of political agendas and the outcomes of political conflict. Where once the study of politics focused mainly on political parties, elections, legislatures, executives and bureaucracies, with a brief digression into pressure groups, we now look more at 'civil society' as a major force in influencing, constraining and even sustaining governments. (We shall not, for the moment, pursue the question of whether 'civil society' is a useful concept. We merely note that it is often used to describe the universe which is populated by NGOs in the broadest sense).

Explaining the rise of NGOs: the old order crumbles

Is it the presence of a large 'non-governmental' sector that requires explanation at any time or place, or its absence? In much of pre-colonial Africa, states were limited in scope, and much human activity revolved around voluntary co-operation based on custom and practice. It was with colonisation that the state displaced much voluntary activity, using its coercive and bureaucratic power to constrain any activity that clashed with the interests of the colonial power. These might include attempts to promote African economic interests, such as growing cash crops which competed with European producers, or attempts to mobilise opposition to authority. With independence in the 1960s and the 1970s, the new nationalist governments were usually happy to leave the coercive state structures intact, and authoritarian rule was the norm until the late 1980s.

In Europe, too, one can go back to a time when most human activity belonged to the 'non-governmental' sector, with the churches and charities dispensing welfare, and gilds rather than governments regulating much economic activity. With industrialisation a range of new social and economic problems required state intervention, and the rise of an enfranchised working class led to demands for a welfare state which ultimately displaced many voluntary groups. While the concern of this book is primarily with Africa, the shadow of the West remains omnipresent in influencing, if not controlling, the scope of the 'voluntary' sector in Africa. We shall therefore look at the influence of events in Europe on the rise of NGOs before looking directly at Africa. (One can quibble about how far NGOs are purely 'voluntary', but the word is less clumsy than 'non-governmental'.) Does the scope of NGOs depend on ideological fashions, such as whether economic planning and welfare are preferred to *laissez-faire* and charity? Does it depend more on longer-term social and economic trends? How important are human choices, such as NGOs in the West forging links with groups in Africa, or Western decisions to reduce aid, leading to Africans resorting to self-help?

What sort of societies and polities are conducive to a thriving voluntary sector? In Table 2.1 we suggest, at the risk of over-simplification, a contrast between the 'mass society' of mid-twentieth century Western Europe and the post-industrial society of today.

Mass society was characterised by strong loyalty to one's social group, and in some cases one's ethnic or religious group. In Britain the Conservative Party had over three million members in the early 1950s

Table 2.1   Individuals and Groups in Mass Society and Post-Industrial Society

	Mass Society	Post-Industrial Society
Individual loyalties	Strong attachment to social, and possibly ethnic/religious groups	Weaker attachment. Greater individual choice
Membership of groups	Often influenced by social position e.g. high membership of political parties, trade unions; business and professional groups	Depends more on individual choice. Higher membership of single issue groups
Political issues	Redistribution; social welfare	More diverse, including many post-material issues
Nature of participation	Largely formal. Voting, striking, canvassing, fund raising, attending meetings, holding office.	Often confined to financial support. Or less structured participation e.g. demonstrations, direct action, solo activities

and the Labour Party over one million (Butler 1955: 107) compared with barely 320,000 and 214,000 by the twenty-first century (Hencke 2004: 4). Trade unions lost 40 per cent of their members in the 1980s and 1990s alone (Knight and Stokes 1996: 2). Mainstream churches, friendly societies, Scouts, Guides, Brownies, the Women's Institute and Round Tables have all suffered a similar decline (*ibid*: 2). We are not suggesting that these groups in their 1950s heyday had recruited members on the basis of some narrow class solidarity (and some of the groups were clearly 'non-political'), but one could argue that in many cases the act of joining was influenced by acquaintances of a similar social standing. Not many coal miners joined the Round Table, and not many stockbrokers joined friendly societies. In contrast, present day membership of the groups that have grown in size, such as Greenpeace or Friends of the Earth, is more likely to be the result of individual choice, less closely rooted in social networks. This in turn reflects the changing political agenda. The politics of the early post-war years was dominated by arguments about redistribution, social welfare and economic planning, which made for polarisation along class lines, whereas today political campaigns cover a greater heterogeneity of issues, including civil liberties, the environment, world poverty and animal rights, together with a range of narrower single issues from the plight of the mentally ill to the preservation of playing fields. At the global level, too, the political agenda looked very different by the twenty-first century from that of the 1950s. Kaldor traces the way in which changes in the dominant political issues have produced changes in the organisational form of political action. Before the 1970s the main issues included redistribution, employment, welfare and anti-colonialism, and the main organisations used to pursue demands in relation to these issues were formally organised parties, trade unions and pressure groups. By the beginning of the twenty-first century the issues had shifted to either major global matters such as climate change, world poverty and the functioning of global institutions, or to more discrete issues such as the building of large dams, the banning of land mines and the establishment of the International Criminal Court. These issues transcended the traditional social divisions, and were better pursued by NGOs with their greater flexibility and their ability to build coalitions and networks across national frontiers (Kaldor 2003: 79–84).

Participation in mass society was carried out in largely structured ways. People voted in much larger numbers in the 1950s than today – well over 80 per cent compared with barely 60 per cent – and we have seen that many traditional groups had a much higher membership. Participation was clearly structured, with party activists canvassing and attending meetings, trade unionists striking, and charities raising money. In post-industrial society, many groups are happy to build a large paper membership but to leave participation to a small number of professional campaigners. Greenpeace and Friends of the Earth are not as visible in the community as were the Young Conservatives or the dock workers in the 1950s. Putnam records a similar decline in participation in the United States. In 1973–4, 61 per cent of the 30–44 age group were involved in at least one form of participation in civic life. By 1993–4, only 31 per cent of the 30–44 age groups were involved (Putnam 2000: 242). Yet there is an argument that participation has taken on new forms rather than suffered a decline (see especially Inglehart in Norris 1999: 242; Norris 2002: 222; Pattie *et al.* 2003: 616–33; Whiteley 2003: 613). Protesters have turned out to support or oppose blood sports, oppose the building of new motorways, trample on genetically modified crops, and demand lower fuel taxes and an end to the poll tax. Most notably, they turned out in their millions all over the world to protest against the invasion of Iraq in 2003. In many cases the participation was less an expression of the objectives of specific groups, and more an expression of shared demands held together loosely, if at all, by umbrella groups such as the Anti-Poll Tax Campaign or the Anti-War Coalition. At the extreme end of the spectrum are acts of solo participation which require no organisation. These have included such expressions of political values as buying fair trade goods, boycotting McDonalds, refusing to pay the Council Tax and trespassing on US Air Force bases.

A key question for us is whether mass society or post-industrial society are more conducive to a flourishing voluntary sector in the West, which might in turn stimulate a comparable sector in Africa. A case could be made that mass society activities such as organising an election campaign, negotiating employment conditions, or even chairing a branch of the Women's Institute, require more sustained effort, and make more impact on society, than the immediate thrill of a protest march, a trespass or tax boycott. Indeed the latter activities might be seen as acts of desperation by citizens who can no longer maintain a dialogue with their rulers. In this view, the more stable institutions of mass society provided a means of interaction between the state and the citizen which has since been lost. Governments ignored at their peril the views of religious leaders, trade unions and professional groups, whereas today governments can survive through a mixture of crude populism and concessions to powerful financial backers and the media (this is discussed in more detail in Pinkney 2005: 49–54). Yet the sheer density of mass society left little room for the spontaneous emergence of voluntary groups responding to unfolding events. Where were the protesters to challenge the wisdom of the nuclear power lobby, the proponents of factory farming or motor manufacturers wanting more roads? Where were the voluntary groups to take some of the weight off the welfare state, to help the homeless or the mentally ill? It may be true that governments are now less responsive to 'leaders' of major sections of public opinion, but they may be more vulnerable to the ambush of an articulate group with the right expertise and campaigning skills. In that way, Jubilee 2000 was able to get many of the debts of poor countries written off, and the World Development Movement was able to get negotiations over the General Agreement on Trade in Services (GATS) halted until a thorough assessment had taken place of their likely consequences, most of which were thought to be harmful to developing countries (Timms 2004–5: 8–10).

All this leaves unanswered the question of why society in the West has changed in the ways described. Is it simply a matter of people choosing to change their loyalties, their political preferences and their methods of participation? Or are there deeper economic forces at work which have made the old order untenable? The former explanation might imply that people can shape a world in which the scope of NGOs can be expanded, contracted or transformed in such a way as to reflect either the wishes of the majority, or of a consensus in society. Chandhoke's review of the changes since the third quarter of the twentieth century suggests a substantial element of free will in changes in political behaviour and political horizons. In the first three-quarters of the twentieth century, she notes the success of political protest in such areas as opposition to the Vietnam War, the pursuit of racial and sexual equality, anti-colonialism and revolutions. People had been politicised through processes of sustained mass struggle. They had the vocabulary and the vision, articulating their views through such terms as imperialism, anti-colonialism, oppression, power struggle and emancipation. From the 1980s onwards the language changed: globalisation in place of imperialism, governance in place of politics, social capital and trust in place of struggle, community in place of class, and civil society in place of 'revolutionary imaginings', and NGOs in place of popular mobilisation. Members of global civil society needed to bring back the 'revolutionary imaginary' and think of contexts rather than isolated texts. Vocabularies that called for social capital and building networks 'conjure away the fact of political, social and economic oppression through semantic engineering ...' (Chandhoke in Kaldor 2003: 411–12).

Setting aside the question of how large a proportion of the population was ever involved in mass struggle or had 'revolutionary imaginaries', the article seems to imply that people have chosen, perhaps partly as a result of elite manipulation, to adopt a different language and a more blinkered view of what is possible in politics. But could one not argue that the new terminologies are used largely because they provide a better description of current reality? In such a view, 'globalisation' describes the impersonal forces which limit effective political activity, better than 'imperialism' which suggests exploitation by recognisable countries or rulers; and 'governance' describes the reality of diverse centres of decision making, as opposed to 'politics' (or simply 'government') where there was a clearer centre of authority where 'the buck stopped'. NGOs may frequently be a focus of interest, not because of some linguistic fad, but because defence of the underprivileged is often conducted better through such institutions than through trying to mobilise masses who will no longer follow their leaders.

Explaining the rise of NGOs: the economy, the environment, society and the polity

The argument is not that political actors have no free will at all, but that such freedom is circumscribed by the changed nature of polities, economies, the natural environment and societies in the West since the mid-twentieth century. Some of the changes, and their implications for NGOs, are suggested in Table 2.2.

The story of these changes has been told many times, so we shall confine ourselves to a very simplified account. By the 1970s there was an almost unbridgeable gap between voters' expectations of what politicians could do in terms of combining social welfare, full employment and stable prices; and politicians' ability to deliver in the face of rising oil prices and emerging competition from the Far East. Whether from conviction or necessity, politicians allowed unemployment to rise and welfare provision to fall. At the same time, newer technologies destroyed much traditional production. Not even the most powerful trade unions could have protected shipbuilders on Tyneside if customers chose to buy their ships from lower-cost producers in Korea. Indeed they could not even prevent the movement of Britain's newspaper production a few miles from Fleet Street to Wapping, using new technologies on the new site, which rendered previous agreements with unions obsolete. What became known as globalisation accelerated the processes further, as businesses were able to open or close factories in different parts of the world on the basis of changing costs, leaving workers as helpless bystanders and governments as supplicants offering financial incentives rather than trying to plan the economy.

Nearly four decades of these changes have left both politicians and citizens with radically altered priorities and interests. For citizens, many of the familiar landmarks of mass society have gone: the sense of class solidarity borne of employment in large factories, mines and shipyards, protected by effective trade unions; the expectation of a job for life and an equitable share of the national cake. Production has shifted increasingly from large-scale manufacturing to tertiary industries and to smaller factories servicing larger, often global, businesses. Success in life now depends more on individual than collective effort, and those who succeed in post-industrial society are more likely to vote for right-wing politicians who offer them lower taxes than for parties offering social equality. Despite the pain of industrial decline, higher unemployment and less protection for workers, the vast majority of people in the new post-industrial order are better off in material terms. For the

Table 2.2   **Forces Influencing the Rise of NGOs in the West**

Variable	Changes	Responses	Implications for NGOs
The economy	Globalisation. New technologies often made traditional industrial relations obsolete and weakened unions. Businesses less amenable to state control. But increased international control through IFIs	Greater penetration of society by business. More campaigns by voluntary groups against business activities in the absence of state action	Rise of NGOs concerned with ethical trading, fair trade, protection of child labour (Ethical Trading Initiative; Save the Children; Jubilee Debt Network)
The environment	Growing evidence, and awareness, of threats to the environment	More campaigns both on specific threats (e.g. against destroying a forest or building a dam) and on global issues (e.g. climate change)	Rise of large INGOs (e.g. Friends of the Earth, Greenpeace) often working with local NGOs in developing countries
Society	Weaker attachment to 'traditional' institutions. Reduced participation. Rise of post-material values	Fewer mass campaigns over social inequality and social injustice. Weaker unions and left-wing parties. But growth of voluntary groups concerned with specific disadvantaged groups, human rights and the environment	NGOs attract activists who might previously have worked for unions or parties. Focus often on global rather than purely national issues
The Polity	More limited state capacity and legitimacy	Privatisation, NPM. More 'governance' is delegated to agencies and contractors	NGOs can take over previous state functions (e.g. social housing), acquire state resources for voluntary work, or gain representation on statutory bodies

majority, the services and safety nets provided by the state have begun to matter less, and personal fulfilment can be sought in the pursuit of a wide range of goods and services from foreign holidays to new durable goods. 'Politics' is seen to matter less, except to the extent that it might provide the stability within which to enjoy growing consumption. 'Consumerism' has arrived, meaning not merely that people consume more, but that the pursuit of material wealth is, for many, an end in itself. The pursuit of this end has left less time for communal activities, or even for hobbies and interests unconnected with amassing material wealth.

> We have become a well-educated country with sophisticated tastes in terms of things like DIY and shopping (Jane Root, Controller of BBC2, quoted by Jacobsen 2001: 7).

While political participation, on most measures, has declined, material prosperity has also seen sections of the population pursue new concerns now that there is less of a struggle for survival. Concern with civil liberties, the environment, the welfare of animals, and the world's poor and disadvantaged generally, was encapsulated in the term 'post-material values' (Inglehart 1977; Inglehart in Norris 1999: 236–51). What we have come to call NGOs are, in many ways, tailor-made for the pursuit of these values. The institutions of mass society, such as political parties, trade unions and business and professional groups, had often been more concerned with protecting producer interests. They were not easily adaptable to post-material concerns which often implied producing and consuming less, as a means to a better quality of life or a more sustainable environment. NGOs, on the other hand, could be purpose built, either to campaign for environmental conservation in general, as with Greenpeace or Friends of the Earth, or for specific causes such as debt relief for poor countries or the plight of political prisoners. The appeal of these NGOs cut across traditional political loyalties. Would-be members and supporters were not required to subscribe to a complex ideology or set of policies, or to endorse the deals and compromises which often made political parties unattractive. They could bask in the glory of whatever successes the NGOs enjoyed, yet blame any failure on the remote world of devious politicians. In organisational terms, NGOs benefited from the technological aids that were new, or had become more widely available. The Internet made it possible for even a small organisation to keep its members informed of facts which governments might want to conceal, and to mobilise supporters and other NGOs in campaigns. The most celebrated success was the defeat of the proposed Multilateral Agreement on Investment (MAI) in 1998. The agreement would have enabled businesses to dictate to governments the terms on which they would invest in any country. A global campaign, using the Internet, enabled campaigners to expose the perceived injustice of the proposals (*Tanzanian Affairs* 1998: 10–12; Vidal 1998: 4).

What of the politicians themselves and their influence on the rise of NGOs? The passing of mass society weakened the largely class-based loyalties of their supporters, and the emergence of post-industrial society and globalisation reduced their ability to control events, as global capital could threaten to destroy jobs or withdraw investment if it did not get the tax concessions or the freedom to employ cheap labour, or to despoil the environment, which it demanded. As political choices narrowed, competition between parties became more a matter of public relations and projecting rival brands, rather than debating policy. This alienated voters still further, and increased the tendency of activists to prefer NGOs with distinctive ideals and objectives, to parties with few apparent ideals at all. As membership bases sank, and subscriptions shrank with them, parties relied increasingly on donations from business, which constrained still further their freedom to make policy choices.

But not even the best, most generously financed party campaign can save it from defeat if voters blame the party for policies that have worked to their disadvantage. Up to a point, voters might accept that uncontrollable global forces are to blame, but such an excuse can hardly be made for badly run schools or hospitals, accidents on the railways, misjudgements in manipulating interest rates, or for allowing prisoners to escape from jail. One obvious solution to the problem was privatisation, so that citizens' complaints could be redirected from politicians to private entrepreneurs, but much of the public sector did not offer any potential profit to private buyers. The alternative was a set of solutions which have come under the conceptual umbrella of new public management (NPM) (Turner and Hulme 1997: 229–40). As with many great rivers, the sources of NPM are many, and often difficult to trace, but they have converged to create a powerful force. One element was right-wing think tanks and ideologues who believed that public administration should be modelled as closely as possible on the private sector, with the creation of specific performance measures and targets, and rewards and punishments for those officials who succeeded or failed to achieve the targets. Another source was ruling politicians who could try to deflect responsibility for any unhappy outcomes to officials who failed to meet their targets. If policemen failed to catch enough criminals, if social security payments were delayed or inaccurate, or if the number of accidents on the railways increased, blame could be laid at the door of the relevant officials, rather than at a government which provided insufficient resources, or failed to create an environment in which people behaved in the expected manner. A third source was the administrator themselves, many of whom wanted a structure in which they enjoyed greater autonomy, free of 'interference' from politicians. This implied creating 'agencies' that enjoyed a corporate existence separate from the government. In some cases the agencies were still staffed by civil servants, in some they were private contractors, and in others they occupied the no man's land between the public and private sectors, as in the case of maintaining the railways, and running hospitals and further education in Britain. The term QUANGO (quasi non-governmental organisation, or quasi near-governmental organisation) became fashionable for the bodies created, and the title might suggest that they were near relatives of the NGO. There is usually, though not always, the distinction that NGOs are 'voluntary' bodies which can be created or dissolved as their members choose, whereas quangos are created by government edict and have statutory responsibilities. Yet the whole decentralised structure contributed another element to an environment in which NGOs were better able to flourish. The administrative structure was now treated more like a giant Lego set, in which different bits could be added, modified or dismantled as the need arose, rather than a hierarchy in which all the parts must conform to a central design. Within the new structure, NGOs (even if they were referred to as voluntary bodies, charities or even pressure groups) could more easily offer to complement state services, to deliver the services themselves, or take on a variety of advisory roles which enabled them to influence policy. Thus NGOs concerned with mental health could provide day centres for discharged patients (often with state financial support), gain representation on statutory health bodies, or campaign for reform of the law on the detention of patients.

None of the hopes of the different proponents of NPM was realised completely but NGOs, as largely silent bystanders in the debate on administrative structures, were among the obvious winners. Not only did they win at a 'micro' level, as in our example of mental health, but they won at a 'macro' level too. NPM implied 'governance' rather than 'government', that is decision-making through a diversity of (often decentralised) structures, rather than 'policy-making' at the top of a hierarchical structure. While a limited number of NGOs (or pressure groups) in the old order had enjoyed 'insider' status and would have expected to be consulted on decisions affecting their domain, the new order left the door more open to a diversity of NGOs. These groups often possessed the expertise, the public support and the legitimacy that enabled them to insist on a role in the policy process, which an increasingly ineffective and less legitimate state could not easily deny them.

The view from Africa

The relationship between the developments we have described and the rise of NGOs in Africa may still seem tenuous. The developments in the West were important in themselves in that they provided a model, or at least a rough guide, which Africa might follow even without any external pressure. While it would be unhelpful to seek an equivalent of 'mass society' in Africa, where the population is mainly rural and class structures are rudimentary, and even less helpful to look for 'post-industrial society' when there has been little industrialisation, some of the events in the West had parallels in Africa. The growing inability of governments to control economic events was clear. While African economies had always been dependent on uncontrollable external forces, the worsening terms of trade from the 1970s onwards exacerbated the problem and increased Africa's dependence on the conditions for aid offered by international financial institutions (IFIs), especially the International Monetary Fund (IMF) and the World Bank. The lesson was learnt that if governments took a fatalistic view of dependency, it was up to NGOs to shout more loudly. The Tanzania Gender Net-working Programme (TGNP) and the Uganda Debt Network provide examples of NGOs that tried to follow similar campaigns to Jubilee 2000 and Oxfam in Britain, in demanding a fairer global economic order (Chale in TGNP 2005: 6–15; Uganda Debt Network 2005).

Africa, like Europe, faced commercial threats to the natural environment, and NGO activity saw off plans for prawn farming in the Rufiji Delta in Tanzania, and for the destruction of much of Mabira Forest in Uganda in the interests of sugar growing (Journalists Environment Association of Tanzania n/d; Izama 2007: 1–2). The leaders of such NGOs were frequently attenders at international conferences where ideas could be exchanged. This is not to say that African NGOs were mere echoes of their Western counterparts, but the existence of well-established NGOs abroad was reassuring when so many other

Western institutions seemed to be on the side of foreign businesses or African governments, rather than the ordinary people.

As for the African state, its already inadequate capacity declined even more rapidly than that of the state in the West, in the face of economic decline and inadequate resources to buy precarious political support. A 'neo-patrimonial' system of ruling politicians providing contracts for businesses and local amenities for constituents, in exchange for funds and votes, was difficult to sustain in a shrinking economy. The scope for NGOs to fill the gap left by the retreating state was all too obvious. Again we do not want to play down the extent to which the rise of African NGOs was a spontaneous response to indigenous events. Yet it helped enormously that Western governments, which were the direct or indirect source of much foreign aid, had been largely converted to the orthodoxy of the 'enabling state', which set out general policy but left much service provision, scrutiny and public debate in the hands of the voluntary sector.

The West offered an 'enabling environment' in which it would generally approve, and support, a growing voluntary sector. This was in contrast to many aspects of African politics and society which Western governments have generally claimed (not always convincingly) to dislike. These include pretentious nationalist politicians, military dictators, corrupt and incompetent bureaucrats, tribalists, Islamic fundamentalists and Marxist agitators. But Africa had frequently produced many of these in the past despite Western disapproval. Why should it now turn to something more acceptable? We can focus on three inter-related developments: the long-term economic decline suffered by Africa which was beginning to threaten the survival of both the polity and society by the 1980s, the collapse or severe weakening of authoritarian governments, and the terms on which Western countries and IFIs were willing to offer aid for recovery. We shall look at some of these developments with particular reference to Ghana and Tanzania.

For most of the second half of the twentieth century, 'developing' countries in general and in Africa in particular suffered serious economic decline, fuelled largely by worsening terms of trade as prices of primary products fell. The decline was not helped by corrupt and incompetent governments, or by rising debts incurred by these governments, often in collaboration with Western lenders who had little concern for the viability of the projects they were supporting or the consequences of the debt burden on Africa. A few figures may illustrate the grim reality. In the late 1960s the distribution of per capita income between 'industrialised' and 'developing' countries was 15:1. By the late 1980s it was 20:1 (Kuhne in Brune *et al.* 1994: 16). Between 1964 and 1991 African exports and imports as a percentage of world trade halved from four to two (Brune *et al.* 1994: vii). Between 1982 and 1992 debts as a percentage of gross nation product (GNP) in Africa rose from 35 to 61, compared with a rise of only 22 to 25 in Asia, and no change in Latin America at 43 (Kreye in Chew and Denemark 1996: 118–19). Debt as a percentage of GNP in Africa in 1990 was 75.5, compared with 32.3 in all developing countries (Broad and Landi 1996: 12). In Ghana the terms of trade index fell from 100 in 1969–70 to 60 in 1982–3 (Kraus in Rothchild 1991: 127), reflecting the steep fall in the prices of primary products, and especially cocoa. Between 1979 and 1983 per capita income in Ghana fell by an average of 6 per cent per year (Frimpong-Ansah 1991: 95). Economic decline inevitably impinged on social provision. In Tanzania, although the economic decline had been less disastrous than in Ghana, primary school enrolment fell from 93 per cent in 1980 to 63 in 1991 (Gibbon 1995: 10), and the percentage of urban dwellers enjoying safe water fell from 90 in 1969 to 69 in 1993 (Tripp 1997: 77). The official figures on illiteracy showed a rise from ten per cent in 1986 to 16 by 1992, with a suspicion that the actual rise was greater (Raikes and Gibbon 1996: 291).

The rise of NGOs in Ghana

No 'law' in political science has yet been discovered that indicates a point at which economic decline triggers political upheaval. We do not know why people suffer in silence for long periods, only to respond at a certain point, whether through revolt or mutual self-help. We cannot even be sure that worsening economic conditions will produce a response, since people may have fewer resources with which to defend themselves. In the case of Ghana, it is difficult to reconcile different accounts of what happened to civil society in response to the economic disasters of the 1980s. According to Herbst (1993: 172) 'associational life' declined as the longer working hours necessary for survival, the shortages of fuel, spare parts for vehicles, and even writing paper, reduced the means of communication necessary for group activity so that 'every organisation in Ghana fell apart'. Azarya and Chazan, on the other hand, reported that the population became more self-reliant. Economic decisions taken in Accra, one infers, became less important as local groups organised their own production and distribution, including widespread smuggling, independently of state imposed price controls, marketing boards or customs posts (Azarya and Chazan 1987: 121–31). Chazan subsequently took the argument further. Civil society flourished in the early 1980s as the capacity of the state declined under the influence of political upheavals and economic decline. Economic, religious and communal networks served as vehicles for the expression of alienation from the existing political order (Chazan in Rothchild 1991: 26–7). It is possible that Herbst's account was relevant in the short term, but in the longer term Ghanaians found their way around the shortages, often working through a 'parallel economy'.

The emergence of a flourishing civil society against a background of economic decline may depend partly on what sort of history, if any, civil society had had in earlier times. Had its birth been virtually prevented by the authoritarian rule which followed, or had earlier regimes left room for civil society to flourish as long as it did not challenge the regimes directly? In the case of Ghana, Drah describes a 'nascent civil society' at the time of independence in 1957, covering occupational, self-help, recreational and political activities, which was largely destroyed as the ruling party centralised power and took control of groups such as the trade unions, co-operatives and farmers' organisations (Drah in Ninsin and Drah 1993: 76–7). Yet authoritarianism never silenced civil society in Ghana completely. Overtly anti-government chiefs might be de-stooled, outspoken bishops might be deported and party thugs might be sent to wreck university campuses, but the chieftaincy, the churches, academia, and the professions generally, survived as largely autonomous institutions. These and other groups, according to Chazan, evolved a liberal culture of resistance to interference in their affairs (Chazan in Diamond *et al.* 1988: 99–139).

The story of Ghana so far suggests a largely two-tier process, with the poorest sections of society seeking self-preservation, and traditional and professional groups seeking to preserve their autonomy. To these we should add a third group, overlapping with the other two, which was concerned with democracy and human rights. The military government under Flight Lieutenant Rawlings found it increasingly difficult to justify its existence on instrumental grounds as the economic saviour of the nation, and long-term opponents of the government were joined by a variety of business and professional groups and the urban poor in pressing for multi-party democracy. Encouraged by the collapse of authoritarian rule in Eastern Europe, the democracy movement eventually pressed Rawlings into setting up a Consultative Assembly to draw up a democratic constitution. The composition of the Assembly was itself indicative of the extent of civil society, containing not only representatives of chiefs and professional groups, but market women, bakers, hairdressers and canoe fishermen. The fairness of the 1992 election, held under the constitution proposed by the Assembly, was disputed with accusations of Rawlings using the power of incumbency in improper ways, but civil society continued to flourish and was indeed important in ensuring that subsequent elections were conducted more fairly. NGOs enjoyed sufficient legitimacy by 1996 to be able to confer with the main political parties and reach a consensus on the proper conduct of elections.

In very little of the literature cited on Ghana was the term 'NGO' used, but by the 1990s there was clearly a flourishing 'non-governmental' sector. Much of it, we have seen, had roots going back to colonial times, but we have hinted that many of the prototype NGOs had tried to hold aloof from the government, venturing into politics mainly when they felt their members or their values were under attack. By the 1990s NPM orthodoxy expected NGOs to be complementary to the government rather than aloof from it (with the exception of an American branch of the orthodoxy which remained suspicious of the state), and pressure of economic circumstances and donor demands helped to place NGOs in the complementary role. They provided services in lieu of the weakened state, and contributed ideas and expertise to the policy process. NGOs were not new to Ghana, even if the term was, but the indigenous factors of economic decline, an authoritarian government losing much of its legitimacy and capacity, and a populace that had never entirely succumbed to any of Ghana's authoritarian regimes, helped to forge a civil society which was more than a revival of the old traditional and professional groups, and which provided, as in so many parts of Africa by the 1990s, a 'third sector' more significant than anything seen before.

The rise of NGOs in Tanzania

Tanzania at independence did not have a 'nascent civil society' comparable with that of Ghana. In a country with many small ethnic groups and no large ones, the chieftaincy was not a significant institution in national politics. Business and professional groups did not enjoy the advantage of their Ghanaian counterparts of having a political party (originally the United Gold Coast Convention but re-emerging under several different names before becoming the New Patriotic Party which ruled from 2000 to 2009) which reflected their 'liberal' belief in limited government and a free market economy. From independence in 1961 to 1995 Tanzania experienced single-party rule, and the party was committed to a socialist economy until the mid-1980s. It certainly had no notions of 'limited government' which might shield sections of civil society. Indeed its policy of forcibly moving peasants into 'ujamaa' villages, on the grounds of making more external economies available, was hardly conducive to an autonomous civil society. Yet the civil society which had emerged by the 1990s was not radically different from that in Ghana.

If Tanzania did not possess a nascent civil society, how did the changes come about? The logical explanation might be that in common with Ghana, and with most of the rest of Tropical Africa, a major driving force was the economic decline of the 1980s and the concomitant loss of governmental capacity. Per capita income did not fall as dramatically as in Ghana, with an annual decline of 2.4 per cent between 1981 and 1985 (Barkan 1994: 22, 28). The ruling party enjoyed a greater reserve of legitimacy, having led the country to independence, and having established a reputation for non-violence, frugality and relative honesty, though not for tolerance of dissent. As in Ghana, some of the earliest stirrings of a potential civil society were found in simple acts of self-preservation and silent defiance of authority. Tripp describes how the state monopoly of public transport was challenged by passengers bursting into song on seeing a policeman, to pretend that they were a wedding party on a chartered bus rather than passengers on an illegal scheduled bus (Tripp 1997: 1–2). More generally, Tripp speaks of a 'second politics' emerging with the creation of voluntary neighbourhood groups and rural grassroots movements that produced alternative institutions of political decision-making and political obligation. New organisations and networks of self-reliance and co-operation were set up in activities such as farming, fishing and policing (Tripp 1997: 201).

Kelsall is more sceptical. Concentrating on rural Tanzania, he accepts that the growth of NGOs reflected the inability of the state to deliver social services or pay its employees, and that this led to greater self-help. But he sees NGOs as vehicles which could be used to facilitate exploitation of the poor in new ways. Local elites, often former party and state officials, continued to exploit the masses, and the patron-client relationship remained intact (Kelsall in Barrow and Jennings 2001: 141). It is difficult to reconcile these conflicting views, but there may be a distinction between NGOs which continued to carry out functions that had previously been under the control of state agencies, and NGOs which were breaking into new areas of activity, such as self-help and advocacy, where there was a greater break with the authoritarian past.

As in Ghana, the government eventually had little choice but to go with the grain of citizen activity and liberalise the economy. Would-be foreign donors would accept nothing less, and the succession of Julius Nyerere as president by Ali Hassan Mwinyi provided a 'natural break'. Where Nyerere had been a political idealist, Mwinyi was more of a technocrat, and he set about dismantling the command economy. Mwinyi was less of a political liberal than an economic liberal, and he resisted the destruction of the one-party state until the 1990s, but the fact of liberalising the economy itself had implications for civil society. The emergence of an indigenous business class created new independent centres of power, where people had less to lose in criticising the government, while at the bottom of the social scale the contraction of state welfare left a growing number of poor people who might resort to self-help in the ways we have described, or might become clients of any emergent service-providing NGOs. At the same time, cuts in the state bureaucracy led to redundant civil servants eventually finding self-employment as leaders of NGOs.

As in Ghana, sections of both the wealthy groups that had done well out of economic liberalisation, and the urban poor groups that had been adversely affected by a slimmer state, had an interest in political liberalisation (or perhaps we should say an 'objective interest'). Neither the masses nor the entrepreneurs took to the streets in large numbers demanding multi-party democracy, but they were potential beneficiaries if competition for votes could make politicians more sensitive to their demands. In the event, the main pressures for democratisation came from politicians who had fallen out with the ruling party, intellectuals who saw Western liberal values as superior to the apparently discredited socialist model, some socialists within the ruling party who saw the legalisation of opposition as a means of ridding the party of ideologically impure and corrupt elements, and ex-President Nyerere, who felt that the original rationale for a single party was no longer valid in a more mature country (Barkan 1994: 31; McHenry 1994: 51). Nyerere also took the practical view that if Tanzania did not reform its own polity, foreign donors would impose their own reforms. Even when a Presidential Commission set up by the government to examine the matter found that 77.2 per cent of the population favoured the continuation of the one-party state, the Commission recommended a multi-party system on the grounds that the minority who favoured this had a right to be represented (United Republic of Tanzania 1992: 7–8). As in Ghana, the incumbents won the subsequent electoral contest but, as in Ghana, the shape and size of civil society had changed radically despite the continuity of government. In Tanzania, the scope for change was probably greater, as the state and party had much larger burdens to shed. Just as state-owned stores gave way to thousands of independent shops in the economic sector, so 'wings of the party' covering areas such as women, youth and labour became largely autonomous NGOs in the voluntary sector. In other cases, new institutions emerged which would not previously have been permitted, such as independent newspapers and radio stations, and NGOs campaigning for human rights.

The government never lost entirely its instinct for regulating society. In 1997 it fought a long battle with the country's major women's NGO, and de-registered it for a time for being 'too political' (Tripp 2000: 203–12), and in 2005 it suspended an outspoken education NGO, HakiElimu, after it had drawn public attention to the discrepancy between official accounts of the state of education and the reality of misuse of funds, large class sizes, drunken teachers, schools without teachers and teachers without schools (HakiElimu 2005: 2–3). But the fact that such an articulate group had been able to document and publicise administrative weaknesses, which the government could not easily refute, was indicative of the progress which NGOs had made in a country where, twenty years earlier, there had been little tradition of groups standing up to authority. As in Ghana, a 'third sector' had emerged with a formidable range of political and administrative skills which politicians could not ignore.

The Washington consensus and other prescriptions

We have suggested that in both Ghana and Tanzania the inter-related factors of economic decline and a weakening authoritarian government paved the way for the rise of NGOs, aided by a general Western approval of this type of organisation. Kenya provided a somewhat rougher but still recognisable version of the Ghanaian and Tanzanian models, with an authoritarian government more reluctant to make concessions, but with NGOs still able to profit from the government's lack of competence and public support, and to acquire a larger stake in the political process (Pinkney 2001: 150–8). Similar trends could be seen in other parts of Tropical Africa where authoritarian governments made gradual concessions, first to permit an expansion of civil society and then to permit competitive elections. These countries were in the majority, but in a minority of cases the rulers insisted on retaining power by fair means or foul (notably the Congo/Zaire, Equatorial

Guinea and Zimbabwe), and in other cases conflict between government and opposition was conducted by violence rather than concessions and negotiation (notably Angola, Liberia, Sierra Leone, the Sudan, Somalia, Burundi and Rwanda). In the former cases the state was likely to clamp down on all but the most innocuous service providing NGOs, fearing that any others were potential sources of subversion. In the latter cases, it was often difficult for either governments or NGOs to function effectively, and the most prominent NGO activity tended to be in providing some relief for the victims of violence, starvation and displacement. Even here the relief was likely to come from INGOs rather than any home grown civil society.

But beyond indigenous forces, and broad hints of Western approval or disapproval, we still have to examine the cruder world of power politics, and the ideologies and interests that sustained it. For much of the Cold War years between the emergence of the first independent African states in the mid-1950s and the fall of the Berlin Wall in 1989, it is difficult to characterise Western economic policies towards Africa with any coherent ideology. The West obviously wanted to maintain the benefits it enjoyed from trade and investment, and would not have looked kindly on African governments that confiscated foreign property without compensation. It might have reacted cautiously to competition that adversely affected Western economies, as it did over the importation of Asian textiles, but for the most part African economies were not sufficiently developed to pose such a threat. Africa remained economically dependent, and the main threats it posed were political rather than economic, as the Eastern Bloc sought Cold War allies. Political leaders such as Nkrumah and Lumumba who were suspected, however erroneously, of Communist sympathies, were deposed with tacit or active Western support, and the victors in the 1964 revolution in Zanzibar were hastily incorporated into the new United Republic of Tanzania under the less revolutionary leadership of Nyerere. In Angola and Mozambique, the West gave support to rebel forces against Cuban and Soviet-backed national armies.

Insofar as there were any 'Western' views on how African economies should develop, these reflected the broad church of economic thinking of the period, from social democracy via Keynesianism to predominantly free market values. There were relatively few Western objections to the creation of state corporations to run large sections of African economies, or to attempts at state planning, especially when the private sector was weak and indigenous NGOs were still few and far between. The World Bank, which was later to rage against inefficient public enterprise, was quite happy to support the establishment of a state shoe factory in Tanzania, which was almost entirely dependent on imported raw materials and had little chance of paying its way. As long as the Eastern Bloc and Libya were willing to provide aid, and gain political influence in the process, Western donors could not be too choosy about what they supported, or impose over-rigorous sets of conditions which might drive potential recipients elsewhere.

> During the period in which most Asian and Africa countries came to independence, belief in the efficacy of development planning knew no bounds ... Plans would ensure that poor, agricultural countries would become rich, industrialised nations within a few decades (Turner and Hulme 1997: 133).

The mid-1980s appear to provide a watershed between the relatively permissive economic environment of the Cold War years and the tighter control over aid and debt which has continued to today. What became known as the 'Washington Consensus' replaced the 'hands off' approach to African economies of the Cold War years, although the consensus pre-dated the ending of the Cold War, and its ideological foundations could be traced back even further. We have noted the rise of the doctrine of NPM, and the election of Thatcher in Britain in 1979 and Reagan in the United States in 1980 provided the necessary missionaries to propagate the gospel. Both these politicians saw an overpowerful state, sustained by bureaucracies which had a vested interest in maintaining wasteful state activities, as an immediate target for attack. Where state activities could not be curtailed, they should be administered by autonomous agencies, preferably from the private sector or voluntary bodies, but if not by public bodies set free from their old bureaucratic masters. Whether the ideology made sense, or whether it was likely to be applied effectively in the West or Africa, is not our concern, but Africa in the late 1980s seemed to be a perfect laboratory for testing the ideas. African governments had generally been incompetent and corrupt, got themselves into debt, and maintained large bureaucracies to provide employment for favoured individuals. Their sins had now found them out, as they presided over economic decline and were not capable of providing such basic services as adequate roads, schools or hospitals, or of providing welfare for the poor. Privatisation and retrenchment were there therefore required, and Western aid, administered especially through the IMF and World Bank, involved structural adjustment programmes (SAPs) which depended on the application of the new economic dogma. African politicians were left increasingly sidelined as they could no longer choose their own policies, and left the complex administration of the new policies to the technocrats, while the poor became poorer still as public services were curtailed. Yet for NGOs, the new dogma had a silver lining. Wallace *et al.* suggest that mistrust of the state implied greater trust of the voluntary sector as a better means of service provision and a source of innovative development work, especially development for the poor. Hence the massive expansion of NGOs (Wallace *et al.* 2007: 19). For those with nostalgia for an imperial past, as well as those who wanted to save public money, this could be seen as harking back to the days when missionaries and charities looked after the poor and the sick.

Unfortunately the theory did not measure up to reality. There was little economic recovery in Africa, especially with its crippling debt burden; the poor remained poor, and it was still conceivable at the end of the 1980s that Africa's authoritarian politicians might cling to power despite the wreckage around them, or perhaps give way to general anarchy. Reagan departed in 1989, Thatcher in 1990, and their successors pursued a more pragmatic version of conservatism. Treating the fever of the African body politic was seen to require more than pouring icy water over it, or even tearing off some if its limbs. But changes in the White House and Downing Street were probably less important than changes in the views of the small number of technocrats (or changes in the technocrats employed) running the IFIs, and changes in the predominant voices among the much larger number of people who made up civil society (see especially Wallace *et al.* 2007: 1920). By the late 1990s the World Bank was acknowledging the persistence of poverty, and the need for safety nets and redistribution. African governments were no longer written off as obstacles to be avoided or bypassed, but as enablers which could stimulate the activities of NGOs and the private sector. NGOs should not only provide services, but hold governments to account and advocate on behalf of the poor (World Bank 1996: xii, xix–xx, 61, 63–7, 79; World Bank 1999: 26). Terms such as 'debt relief', 'participation', empowerment', 'human rights' and 'building civil society' came to be heard more, rather than simply fiscal discipline and retrenchment. By 1998 the World Bank was able to assert that

> The state is essential to economic and social development, not as a direct provider of growth but as a partner, catalyst and facilitator (World Bank 1998: 14).

The 'post-Washington consensus' had arrived. Why had this happened? It is tempting to believe that technocrats in the IFIs were merely following Keynes's dictum that 'When the facts change, I change my mind', but we might usefully turn to the voices of civil society, both in the West and in Africa. While technocrats might focus on 'what works', civil society might be more concerned with what sort of values should predominate, and then demand that Western policies be geared to the fulfilment of these values. We have mentioned the emergence of post-industrial society, and the rise of post-material values, and it seems likely that these sources, rather than technocrats at the World Bank alone, were instrumental in putting objectives such as debt relief, participation, empowerment, environmental conservation, human rights, and even social equality, on the agenda (Broad and Cavanagh in Broad 2002: 56–9; Kaldor 2003: 78–107; Scholte n/d: 6–11).

The post-Washington consensus, if that is an appropriate term for such a diverse range of ideas, was clearly not a return to the social democratic ideas of earlier decades. The state was not to be a 'direct provider', so there was no notion of state enterprise or state planning. The need to help 'the poor' was given prominence, but social inequality was not seen as a major problem. The range of ideas in the 'consensus', sometimes seemed incongruous. How was 'empowerment' to be reconciled with tight external control over aid and debt repayment? How could a sustainable environment be reconciled with the urgent need for export earnings to repay debt? Diverting scarce water resources, to grow flowers in Kenya for export to Europe, was likely to take precedence over organic farming. How could human rights be reconciled with giving ever more generous concessions to foreign mining companies in Ghana and Tanzania, leading not only to environmental degradation but to peasants being driven off their land with little or no compensation? How could human rights be reconciled with the well meaning conservationist idea of protecting animals in game reserves, by evicting humans from the land (Igoe 2004: 18–19)? As for the quest for 'participation', cynics might see this, as in national politics in post-industrial societies, less as a desire for citizen fulfilment, and more as a desperate attempt by those in authority to halt their declining capacity and legitimacy by giving the impression that decision-making now involved the active consent, or even the positive contributions of, the governed. The World Bank's attitude to NGOs might be taken as a case in point. It developed more formal relations with NGOs, as did the IMF (Kaldor 2003: 88–9). Participation was seen as a partial solution to ameliorate the effects of SAPs through the Structural Adjustment Participatory Review Initiative (SAPRI). Almost a thousand NGOs from all over the world worked together to draw the attention of the IMF and the World Bank to the hardship caused by SAPs, and to press for their modification. In the case of Uganda, the NGO Forum, representing 600 NGOs, drew attention to such issues as reductions in social services, rising unemployment, increased poverty and inequality, and the shift to non-tradition crops leading to a lack of food security (Avirgan 1997). It is difficult to point to any spectacular achievements by SAPRI, which might confirm the cynics' suspicion of token participation, but optimists might see another opening which puts NGOs, rather than African governments, in a position to claim to represent the people of Africa.

Before we attempt a general assessment of how the post-Washington consensus affected the development, we need to remind ourselves not only of the dubious compatibility of some of the objectives, but of the broad continuum of opinions, just as in the Cold War years. The United States remained closest to the free market end of the continuum, with Britain close by, with Scandinavia and the Netherlands closer to the social democratic end (Freres in Grugel 1999: 55; Howell and Pearce 2001: 39–40, 59–60). Indeed it has been asserted that the traditional American fear of the state as an over-powerful actor led to the US seeing Ghanaian civil society as a battleground between civil society organisations loyal to the government and 'democratic' CSOs (Hearn 2001: 16). At the other end of the continuum, a Swedish document on co-operating with Tanzania included in its goals 'economic and social equality', 'economic and political independence', 'environmental care' and 'gender equality' (Swedish International Development Agency (SIDA) leaflet, n.d.; see also Rylander 1998: 2–3, 10, 14; SIDA 1998: 4–5, 28). Even within individual Western countries, the range of ideological positions could be diverse. Semi-autonomous agencies such as the British Department for International Development (DFID) and the United States Agency for International Development (USAID) were often more welfare-minded, and ideologically and physically closer to African NGOs than their own governments and diplomats. Western INGOs such as Oxfam and ActionAid were often still further to the 'left', supporting or encouraging African NGOs, or even African governments, in protesting against the allegedly unfair conditions of international trade and aid.

Seen from an African perspective, there was also a diversity of ideological positions. As structural adjustment, retrenchment and debt re-scheduling became increasingly a matter of technocratic administration rather than politics, African technocrats sometimes adopted positions closer to Western governments and IFIs than to their own populations (see especially Costello 1996: 125; 141–4 on Tanzania). African politicians obviously preferred not to endorse openly policies that were harming their constituents, but frequently took the view that they had little alternative but to accept the prescriptions devised in Brussels or Washington, and brushed aside NGO demands for a more rigorous defence of the national interest as unrealistic. But even here there were exceptions, and African governments sometimes allowed NGOs to negotiate on their behalf at international conferences on the grounds that the NGOs had greater expertise, or could speak with greater authority on the hardships the people were suffering.

The opportunities and the constraints

It is beyond the scope of this chapter to go on to examine the impact of international events since 2001, as we are more concerned here with the evolution of NGOs from the mid-1980s to the end of the century, rather than with their current position. Focusing on this period how far, and in what ways had the policies of Western governments and IFIs contributed to the growth, role and effectiveness of NGOs in the African political process, whether by accident or design? Was there a flowering of civil society, as NGOs organised communities to defend their interests in the face of alleged foreign exploitation or the ineffectiveness of African political institutions? Or was the post-Washington consensus merely another chapter in the long history of neo-colonial exploitation, trying to give legitimacy to an unequal world order by talking about participation, empowerment, human rights and poverty eradication, but maintaining effective control over events and using NGOs as vehicles to this end?

On the negative side, we need to emphasise that the world economic order, which has seldom been generous to Africa, continues to put it at a severe disadvantage. In colonial times, Africans were not permitted to produce goods such as tea or coffee which competed with European producers, and were driven off land required by European farmers. Today similar ends are achieved by Western governments subsidising their agricultural produce heavily while prohibiting Africans from doing the same, and by foreign mining companies evicting with impunity anyone who stands in their way. While Europe, and more recently much of Asia, developed their economies by protecting new 'infant' industries, Africa is not permitted to do the same under World Trade Organisation (WTO) rules. If Africa wants to change the rules, it is severely handicapped by inadequate resources and personnel in the negotiating process, and by the fact that Africa wields less than 5 per cent of the votes at the IMF and World Bank. In earlier times, the slave trade drained Africa of much of its workforce. Today nothing as brutal exists, but Western countries can tempt many of African's most skilled workers away with offers of higher salaries, including doctors, nurses, teachers and academics.

Secondly, no amount of talk of participation or empowerment can disguise the fact that, in the last resort, it is Africa that is the supplicant, and African governments or NGOs wanting aid must comply with terms offered, or leave their people hungry, or even hungrier than they would otherwise be. Not only does this mean that public services are curtailed, workers are made redundant and development projects are abandoned, but Africans may be forced (or at least cajoled) into accepting 'aid' and investment they do not want as a price for enjoying the aid they do want. One example was the sale in 2002 of a £28m air traffic control system to Tanzania by Britain, which many critics felt was out of all proportion to Tanzania's needs and means (*Tanzanian Affairs* 2002, 72, May–August: 10–11; TANGO 2002: 6–7). Even INGOs, as we shall see in Chapter 6, are not always benevolent supporters of the African underdog, and can be used by Western powers as intermediaries in dispensing aid on Western terms.

Thirdly, Western governments, businesses and institutions have been able to enter into mutually beneficial deals with African politicians, the results of which at best divert resources away from Africa's basic needs, and at worst cripple African economies. Ghana, as the first independent state in Tropical Africa, was the victim of foreigners wanting to build luxury hotels, or cocoa silos that were incapable of preserving cocoa in the tropics, or a motorway from Accra to Tema when there was a crying need for short feeder roads to enable farmers to market their crops. In Tanzania, the processes involved in the air traffic control deal have yet to be unravelled, but it seems unlikely that beneficiaries will be the Tanzanian people. The construction of the Bujagali Falls Dam in Uganda might seem more justifiable. But the attempted and actual deals between foreign businesses and politicians made it difficult for any impartial assessment to be made of how far the project would benefit a population needing adequate electricity, rather than politicians wanting business contracts (Majot in Jordan and van Tuijl 2006: 211–28; Rice 2007: 21).

Finally there is the question of how far NGOs themselves are really part of an autonomous civil society, and how far the emergence, survival and focus of attention of NGOs depends on the carrots and sticks provided from abroad. In financial terms, there is little doubt that most African NGOs would collapse without foreign support. In Uganda, Barr *et al.* estimated that 80 per cent of the revenue of Ugandan NGOs comes from (mainly foreign) grants (Barr *et al.* 2005: 666, 671). Beyond that is the argument that foreign donors will have their own ideas on what NGOs should be doing, and skew their support accordingly. Dicklitch and Lwanga complain that in Uganda donors are more interested in civil and political rights than social and economic rights, although the latter are more pressing. Donors are happy to support civic education, election monitoring and constitutional development, but shy away from NGOs too critical of the regime or too 'political'. They were reluctant to look at corruption, military spending or military involvement in the Congo (Dicklitch and Lwanga 2003: 508–9). Maina presents a similar picture in Kenya. Donor support for civil society concentrated on a few areas of activity which reflected the donors' perceptions of what was important in their own countries. Donor emphasis was on Western liberal rights, with less concern for radical groups defending the interests of the poor (Maina in Van Rooy 1998: 157–60). Hearn takes a much bigger swipe at foreign influence. Aid for 'civil society groups', she argues, is largely a means of promoting free market economics, and isolating those who oppose such a policy. In Ghana, USAID feared that a change of government might lead to alternative policies, and it therefore tried to avoid supporting any activities that might help the promotion of such policies. Advocacy NGOs concerned with human rights and election monitoring were acceptable, but a vast array of non-elite social groups were excluded from support. The emphasis was on strengthening 'a new African elite' which continued to support 'procedural democracy and structural adjustment-type economic policies' (Hearn 2001: 43–53). In South Africa, too, Hearn saw foreign aid as a means of shoring up electoral democracy, while steering clear of groups that might provoke public discontent by pursuing greater equality and social democracy (Hearn 2000: 815–30).

On the more positive side, we need to remember that the unequal power relationship between the West and Africa does not mean that the West can always get its own way, whether through threatening to withdraw aid or by despatching a gunboat. Governments can drag their feet over retrenchment programmes, and NGOs can spend funds, or embark on activities, in ways not intended by donors. One can read annual reports of African NGOs in which they condemn the current global order and all its works, yet print a list of donors (whether governments or foreign NGOs) whose political sympathies would almost certainly lie in a different direction. The donors might tolerate such heresies in the belief that 'sticks and stones may break my bones', and that they will not be adversely affected by mere words. But it is also possible that they recognise a groundswell of African opinion against policies that have allegedly impoverished Africa, and feel powerless to halt this even if eventually words are turned into actions against Western policies. There is also the importance of a climate of opinion in the West which is critical, perhaps more critical than many African NGOs, of the current global order and which has been channelled into increasingly effective campaigning. While there is a strand of liberal opinion in the West, going back at least to the 1930s, which campaigned for the independence of the colonies, there was less concern before the 1980s with the practicalities of removing immediate injustices in the global order. Now campaigns for debt relief, fair trade and equitable investment policies, are well organised, well publicised, frequently attract substantial public support from people who are otherwise politically inactive, and often gain access to ruling politicians. The results do not always match the expectations, but politicians have been forced on to the defensive, and to concede the justice of many of the demands. In this atmosphere, African NGOs can plug into the activities of the more powerful INGOs outside, both in briefing them on local conditions and in using the INGOs' expertise and resources in their own campaigns. Similarly where the perceived injustice is national rather than global, African NGOs concerned with human rights, press freedom or corruption can enlist the support of bodies such as Amnesty International, Human Rights Watch, Reporters without Borders or Transparency International. Even foreign embassies, which might sometimes be regarded as agents of the unjust global order, are at least on paper converts to the causes of democratisation and human rights, and may be useful allies for an NGO trying to challenge abuses of power by an African government.

Finally there are the benefits of modern technology which may have narrowed the degree of inequality between the underdog and the elite. Even modestly endowed NGOs can now use computers to produce campaigning newsletters, to maintain communications with like-minded organisations, and even to join in worldwide campaigns such as that against the erstwhile Multilateral Agreement on Investment. Local radio stations, too, can put NGOs in touch with both potential supporters in the community and with their adversaries. In Ghana, listeners to a phone-in programme were treated to a dialogue between a representative of the IMF and citizens who were on the receiving of its policies. The policies may not have changed dramatically as a result, but again the power holder was put on the defensive.

Conclusion

By the mid-1990s NGOs had acquired a prominence in many African political systems which few people would have expected, and possibly few would have wanted, a decade earlier. They were providing many essential services, pursuing research on policy, and fighting a range of campaigns on issues from the local through the national to the global. In the process they had built links with INGOs which enabled them to punch above their weight and to tap into the growing body of public opinion in the West concerned with 'global justice'. African governments find themselves increasingly under scrutiny, whether directly from NGOs or from citizens who have been encouraged by NGOs to stand up for their rights. None of this detracts from the fact that Africa is poor, dependent, and subject to rules of world trade which it had no hand in choosing and which it has little opportunity to change, but politics is a matter of exploiting whatever opportunities come along rather than bemoaning the fact they do not come along in greater abundance.

In seeking explanations for this rise of NGOs, we have followed some tortuous routes. The fact that a 'non-governmental' area of political activity is significant at any time or place might be attributed to the fact that either the government is too weak to prevent it, or is confident enough of its own position to permit or even encourage it. In much of Africa in the 1980s, weak government was the obvious explanation, and many NGOs (often very informal groups rather than 'registered' NGOs) were established out of desperation as governments were unable to maintain basic services. One can only speculate as to how these informal NGOs would have survived or evolved if there had been little African contact with the outside world. In the event knowledge of, and contacts with, the outside world enabled African NGOs to draw strength from 'NGOs' in the West (even if they were not always called 'NGOs'), but Africa's relationship with the outside world was also subject to constraints on what could be done.

We dwelt on the importance of 'post-material values' in the West because these were important in both pushing global, as opposed to more parochial, concerns nearer to the top of the political agenda, and in frequently making the NGO the most useful vehicle for pursuing the relevant political demands. Whether the issue was a 'narrow' one of protecting child soldiers or helping AIDS victims, or a broad one of world poverty and debt, NGOs enjoyed the flexibility in campaigning and mobilising support which political parties generally lacked. As African civil society groups moved beyond the informal stage, the NGO was the obvious model to adopt, especially if opposition parties were still prohibited. The NGO did not seek to destroy the government (at least not explicitly) but to complement its work. If the support of INGOs could be enlisted directly in helping such developments, so much the better.

One observation which has recurred in this chapter is that the emergence of NGOs was often the outcome of circumstances over which NGOs had little control, and which they did not necessarily seek to influence. NGOs grew in strength in the West (and were thus able to demonstrate their virtues to Africa) with the rise of post-industrial society, as many people felt that political parties were no longer offering clear choices or taking moral stands. New public management added to the momentum, as a hollowed out process of governance left more scope for groups outside the formal hierarchy. NGOs emerged in Africa partly on account of economic decline and a weakening of authoritarian governments, and partly because the Washington consensus believed that the voluntary sector was administratively and morally superior to the state sector. When the post-Washington consensus succeeded its more rigid predecessor, NGOs were handed yet more opportunities which they had probably not anticipated, as they were expected to scrutinise and monitor government and administration, and act as advocates for the poor (see especially Jordan and van Tuijl 2006: 10–12 on the effects of changes in Western political and economic orthodoxy on the role of NGOs). Is the existence of all these openings favourable to NGOs merely fortuitous, or does it tell us something about the nature of NGOs? Are they the answer to a whole range of political and administrative problems which the world has only belatedly discovered, or is it that enlarging the role of NGOs appears to be the most innocuous way of meeting new challenges? Many people hate politicians, political parties, bureaucracies and armies for a variety of reasons, but few people hate Oxfam or the Tanzania Gender Networking Programme. Are NGOs a 'catch-all' solution which is likely to offend the fewest people, or do they possess distinctive virtues which will stand the test of time? It is these questions to which we shall turn next.

3

A Third Sector or a Second Preference? What is Distinctive about NGOs?

Can one be a non-smoker in a community that has not discovered tobacco? Can an organisation be 'non-governmental' when there is no government? The notion of being 'non-governmental' assumes implicitly the existence of a government from which NGOs can be distinguished. And the notion of NGOs constituting a 'third sector' assumes that the other branch of the trinity, the private sector, is also flourishing. We shall look briefly at the presence, strength or weakness of this trinity before pursuing the question of how far NGOs are able to manifest themselves as distinctive entities.

The relevance of the private sector need not detain us for long. Governments that have eliminated such a sector for ideological reasons are unlikely to look kindly on any other independent centres of power. Few countries, if any, in the Soviet Bloc had anything resembling a network of NGOs, believing that most human activity should take place within the party/state structure. In Africa, Tanzania between 1961 and the mid-1980s approximated to this model, but did not eliminate charities or churches. In other parts of Africa the rhetoric of socialism was not normally matched by the existence of an all-powerful state.

While the private sector can be expanded, contracted or eliminated by governmental fiat, the position of the state, as the 'first sector', is more complex. Some pre-colonial communities have been regarded as 'stateless'. Somalia in the late twentieth century was similarly regarded, but generally the existence of states is a matter of degree rather than a question of 'present' or 'absent'. States in some rudimentary form existed in Liberia and Sierra Leone even at the height of civil wars, though their writ did not necessarily run throughout the country, and their capacity to provide the normally accepted range of public services was very limited. At the other extreme, no one could doubt the existence of effective states in Egypt or South Africa over the past century.

What bearing does this have on NGOs? In countries with weak or non-existent states there may be charities to relieve poverty and suffering, often externally based and administered; and there may be informal self-help groups in the absence of any public provider of basic services, as in the years of chaos in Uganda between the fall of General Amin and the rise of President Museveni. But there are unlikely to be many formally structured NGOs in an environment where public order is largely absent. One possible exception is where NGOs precede the nation state rather than evolving under its umbrella. DeMars suggests that the International Africa Association, created in 1876 by King Leopold to develop the Congo, was 'essentially a shell NGO', and that the Congo Reform Association created in the early twentieth century 'was really a working NGO' that served as the nucleus of the reform movement against Leopold's personal colony (DeMars 2005: 73–4, 77). Perhaps the work 'personal' gives the game away. If a country is ruled as the personal property of a king, with none of the normal political and administrative structures, any 'non-governmental' organisation may become an element of *de facto* government, rather than an NGO in the normal sense of a body largely autonomous from the governmental apparatus.

Our search for authentic NGOs, then, begins with the premise that there need to be recognisable states and private sectors for a third sector to exist, just as an organised football match requires a marked pitch within whose boundaries the game can be played. Our task in this chapter is to examine the extent to which NGOs can be regarded as distinctive entities, whether in terms of their underlying philosophies, their capacity to shape events or their autonomy from other institutions. Have they altered, or could they alter, the shape of African politics in significant ways? There are wide divergences of academic opinion in these matters, some of which are highlighted in Table 3.1.

Table 3.1 suggests a 'virtuous model' of NGOs as institutions with strong moral convictions, attending to the needs of otherwise ignored or disadvantaged groups, and enjoying the freedom and flexibility to pursue whatever causes they regard as most deserving. They possess distinctive expertise and campaigning skills, and enjoy growing legitimacy as state institutions are increasingly tainted by political failure, corruption and remoteness from their constituents. The functional model, in contrast, sees NGOs more as workaday institutions, emerging and functioning to meet the requirements of other institutions, rather than as crusaders for social justice. NGOs often come into being for reasons of expediency, such as the availability of grants or the need to provide employment for redundant bureaucrats. Their claims to

Table 3.1   NGOs: The Virtuous Model and the Functional Model

Virtuous Model	Functional Model
Distinctive objectives, often rooted in strong convictions	Creation and functioning are based on expediency e.g. the need for employment, the availability of grants
Pursue radical causes which would otherwise be neglected	Often co-opted by governments, or compromised by being brought into consultative processes. Attempts are made to de-politicise NGOs
As voluntary bodies, NGOs enjoy freedom to pursue whatever causes they regard as most important	NGOs are heavily dependent on foreign funds, or on contracts with African governments, which makes them subordinate to other institutions
Ability to represent the most disadvantage sections of society	Claims to representation are often unsupported by evidence. Internal structures are often undemocratic, with little accountability
Possess distinctive expertise and campaigning skills. Enjoy a flexibility which state bureaucracies do not	Leaders are often ex-bureaucrats or party officers who carry on their work under a different name. NGOs acquire the features of state bureaucracies as they expand
Enjoy greater legitimacy than many other institutions, less tainted by political failure, corruption or remoteness from the population	Legitimacy is difficult to sustain when NGOs acquire greater political and administrative responsibilities
Globalisation and NPM have increased the scope of the voluntary sector. NGOs can acquire the right to consultation with national and global bodies	Neo-colonialism and Western security interests remain intact. NGOs are captured by the forces that continue to exploit Africa

representation, accountability, internal democracy and legitimacy are unsupported by evidence, and any moral virtue is compromised by co-option by governmental (and sometimes business) institutions, and by heavy dependency on external funding. Rather than challenging national or global elites, they are exploited by them.

The virtuous model

At first sight the distinctive moral pedigree of NGOs might seem self-evident. The Red Cross, as an early NGO, went into the battlefields with very different objectives from the belligerent governments or the private arms manufacturers. The Anti-Slavery Society took on the mantle of virtue against governments and businesses colluding in human trafficking; and Oxfam acted and spoke for the poor in a world where governments often had other priorities. DeMars recognises the distinctive philosophies of NGOs, though he is sceptical about the consequences of their attempts to do good. They frequently fail to consider adequately the consequences of their (often narrowly focused) demands. Thus Amnesty International demands the release of political prisoners as a matter of principle, but is not concerned about, or responsible for, any consequent threats to law and order. NGOs assume that their demands and actions will create only the intended consequences and no others. They claim to adhere to norms 'above governments' on issues such as human rights, and to represent the people in advancing their interests, even though NGOs have not necessarily been elected by, or become accountable to, any identifiable group (DeMars 2005: 8–25). In DeMars's world, NGOs are apparently the rogue elephants of politics, gentle giants that mean well but which can usurp the processes of representative government and the rule of law in their pursuit of their self-proclaimed objectives. The side effects of implementing their demands are not always what the NGOs, or the rest of society, might have wanted. Greater freedom of the press may lead to the spread of rumours or untruths which threaten national security; debt relief for poor countries may mean that the money saved goes into the pockets of African elites, and the pursuit of animal rights may mean that pastoralists are driven off the land to make way for game reserves.

Other writers take a more charitable view of the distinctive virtues of NGOs. Boli claims that they enjoy legitimacy based on their openness of membership, their democratic structures, and the importance of the qualifications and expertise of their members. They are also helped by the moral fervour and commitment of their members (Boli in Boli and Thomas 1999: 267). Rugendyke shows a similar enthusiasm. NGOs enjoy the advantages of flexibility, the ability to work through local institutions, and in remote areas neglected by governments, and the benefit of better links with the neediest groups (Rugendyke 2007: 5). Collingwood emphasises NGOs' claim to legitimacy based on their belief in universal moral standards. They uphold legal norms which states and businesses ignore, possess distinctive expertise, and give a voice to the poor and marginalised. She acknowledges NGOs' frequent lack of distinctive constituents, and their lack of accountability and democratic procedures, but argues that states in recent years might be subject to comparable criticisms. State institutions have lost public support as they have surrendered increasingly to business interests at the expense of democratic accountability. As states have failed to meet liberal democratic standards, NGOs have gained public support and legitimacy (Collingwood 2006: 439–54).

Hard evidence of the legitimacy and public esteem enjoyed by NGOs is difficult to obtain, but Logan et al. found that in Uganda only 10 per cent of voters believed that NGO leaders were corrupt, whereas the percentage perceiving corruption in other institutions was 32 for government officials and the police, 22 for judges, 20 for MPs and 18 for the President. Only teachers and religious leaders were regarded as more honest than NGOs (Logan *et al.* 2003: 36). This may be partly a reflection of the nature of the work carried out by each office or institution. Postmen, 'lollipop ladies' and in-store Father Christmases tend to be more popular than traffic wardens, rent collectors or tax inspectors. NGOs enjoy the advantage of being able to demonstrate the beneficial results of their work in promoting development, relieving poverty or sickness, or the worthiness of the causes they have promoted, without generally being held responsible to the unpleasant things in life. Unlike governments, NGOs do not have to make cuts in public services, attack civil liberties or sacrifice national interests to foreign exploitation. The consequent public perceptions of NGOs and other institutions may be unfair, but higher public confidence, however unfairly earned, may be a useful asset in a world where this commodity is increasingly scarce.

The functional model

One immediate criticism of the virtuous model is that NGOs frequently fail to practice what they preach. Rather than NGOs articulating the ideals of the people they claim to represent, Anderson and Rieff (in Anheier *et al.* 2005: 29) claim that they 'invite people to become constituents of their ideals'. In terms of practical politics NGOs are said to be handicapped by lacking mass memberships and lacking the sanctions enjoyed by traditional pressure groups (Chandler in Baker and Chandler 2005: 148–70). They are allegedly weak in articulating interests, and especially in speaking for the poor and marginalised. They fail to do so in terms of national interests which might appeal to states. They lack understanding of decision-making processes, and lack the necessary contacts and influence (Cohen 2003: 126; Michael 2004: 1).

Individual nation studies highlight the remoteness of NGOs from the people, especially the poorest (Barr *et al.* 2005: 657–79 on Uganda;

Igoe in Igoe and Kelsall 2005: 115–46 on Tanzania), and their failure to facilitate democracy, consultation or communication. Decision-making is in the hands of a few members, and clients cannot select leaders, influence decisions or hold the management to account (Igoe in *ibid*: 115–46; Abdelrahman 2004: 196, on Egypt). Leadership is drawn from narrow graduate and professional elites, who claim to know what the poor need (*ibid*: 173: 98; Barr *et al.* 2005: 670, on Uganda).

Defenders of NGOs might plead that many of these criticisms could equally be levelled at political parties, and that it is the failure of parties to perform their textbook roles of providing political vision, and representing diverse interests, that has stimulated the rise of NGOs. When particular types of party are outlawed, such as Islamists in Egypt, it is NGOs that may be able to provide alternative means of advancing their interests (Abdelrahman 2004: 197). And in most of Tropical Africa NGOs had a head start over opposition parties, many of which were not legalised until the 1990s.

Parties can, at least in theory, be voted out if they fall short of people's expectations, whereas NGOs can continue their alleged inward-looking, elitist existence to the detriment of any possible democratic advance. This however implies that there is some golden road to participatory democracy and social justice that both parties and NGOs are wilfully obstructing. Without digressing into the varied explanations as to why democracy is not being 'consolidated' in much of Africa, and why it is probably declining in the West, we may note that poverty, debt, dependency, and the desperation of African elites to cling to their disproportionate share of the limited wealth available, have all played a part. The best equipped party or NGO in the world is not going to be able to alter these circumstances, although the circumstances may well constrain the room for manoeuvre of parties and NGOs.

African NGOs might, within limits, be able to establish more democratic structures, and consult more widely with their varied stakeholders, though problems of communication in largely illiterate societies, and the degree of deference accorded to educated elites in African culture, could limit any progress. Beyond these limited reforms lie the more formidable obstacles of dependence on a hostile world. While NGOs might like to see themselves as knights in shining armour who have come to right a range of injustices, other institutions may see NGOs as a useful means of perpetuating the *status quo*, or at least as a means of limiting any damage to it.

DeMars suggests that NGOs are everyone's second or third choice. Authoritarian rulers would prefer to torture or execute their opponents, but pressures from civil society or the outside world may force them to allow NGOs to lobby for more humane policies. Human rights campaigners themselves would prefer to arrest authoritarian leaders and bring them to justice, but if this is not feasible they may settle for pressure via NGOs. Religious groups might prefer to concentrate on spreading the faith and saving souls, but they are more likely to be permitted to operate if they carry out charitable or developmental work under the banner of NGOs (DeMars 2005: 47). One could pursue the argument further. International Financial Institutions (IFIs) might prefer to dictate the economic policies to be followed by African governments, but public resistance might be softened if they bring NGOs into a consultative process. Businesses might prefer to maximise their profits without regard for the plight of their workers, but adherence to the principles of corporate social responsibility, and a willingness to allow NGOs to inspect their factories, may improve their image. Once NGOs become 'the lesser evil' rather than means of pursuing high ideals, they have to face a world where many political and administrative constraints stand between them and their objectives. While the political and the administrative obviously overlap, we can make a rough distinction between the practical (administrative) problems of surviving in everyday life which are not, for the most part, the result of any calculated attempt by other groups to gain advantage over NGOs, and the (political) problems of African and Western governments, businesses, international NGOs (INGOs) and IFIs advancing or protecting their interests at the expense of African NGOs.

Administrative constraints

One immediate problem confronting NGOs is that few of them have adequate independent sources of income. They can seek to enter contracts with African governments for the provision of services, such as caring for discharged hospital patients, or they can seek external funding, whether from foreign governments and their agencies, INGOs or charities in the narrower sense. In the former case, the nature of the contract will normally specify narrowly what an NGO can do, rather than leaving it as a free spirit. With the latter, it is statistically unlikely that the range of activities which NGOs wish to pursue will dovetail with the range which donors are willing to support. While the reasons may sometimes be 'political', as with donors not wanting to support radical causes, in many cases it is simply a question of which donor interests have evolved most over the years. If, for the sake of argument, many donors have as their objective the advancement of women's rights, and few exist to support animal rights, would-be animal rights advocates may have to carry out their work on a shoestring or consider a different line of activity (Igoe in Igoe and Kelsall 2005: 296–300; Sadoun 2006: 49; Vincent 2006: 22–8). This deviation from original intentions might be seen as nothing more than the unfortunate consequence of being a supplicant, but we need to remember that not all NGOs are created for purely altruistic reasons. In many cases they are a potential source of refuge from unemployment, especially for redundant public servants, so that donor funding becomes the main consideration, with the actual activities to be funded secondary. In Egypt, Abdelrahman describes how the attractions of donor funding led to the creation of unwanted day centres for pre-school children, in a society where most families looked after their own children; and campaigns to persuade more people to seek modern medical facilities, even though the underuse of such facilities was not the result of ignorance but of lack of money (Abdelrahman 2004: 182–5).

If NGOs lose some of their distinctiveness and autonomy through the need to work within the limits set by African governments and donors, the actual process of applying for funds constrains them still further. Here groups which started off as either idealists seeing the needs of their fellow beings at first hand, or as entrepreneurs seeking to put their talents to use, have to enter what is for many an alien world. In the West it is a world that people have learnt to adapt to in recent years, even if it gives rise to much grumbling and cynicism. Whether one is working in local government, a university, a sports club, a museum or a charity, one learns that applying for funds is more likely to be successful if one tells the funders what they want to hear, and in the esoteric language in which they want to hear it (Maina in Van Rooy 1998: 162). To obtain funds for your new pavilion, your new laboratory, or your gallery for exhibiting dinosaurs, you need to be familiar with performance targets, measurable outputs, stakeholders and partners. This is the world of new public management (NPM) which we touched on in the previous chapter.

While applicants for funds in the West can generally learn to negotiate their way through this system, and employ additional staff or resources to cope with it where necessary, African NGOs are not so fortunate. To begin with there is the physical process of writing an application in what is not one's first language, when one has only a small staff, and when computer facilities are limited or non-existent, and subject to the vagaries of regular power cuts. If the initial application is successful, similar problems then have to be faced in writing reports in a style that will please donors sufficiently to attract further funds, all of which diverts time and resources from the actual activities which are the NGO's *raison d'etre* (Bornstein 2006: 57). Objectives frequently have to be expressed in quantitative rather than qualitative terms, and this is said to reduce the emphasis on longer-term achievements in terms of innovation, participation, sustainable development and transforming people's attitudes (Bornstein 2006: 55). A human rights NGO might have to measure success in terms of the number of cases taken up successfully with the police, but not in terms of improved public confidence in the police as a result of its activities.

The whole process of report writing, on which further funding depends, is said to distort the ways in which an NGO's achievements and problems are presented. Not only do quantifiable successes have to be highlighted more than (possibly more significant) qualitative successes, but exaggerating (if not openly lying about) successes is more likely to attract further funding than a realistic appraisal of the problems encountered, and an attempted dialogue with donors as to how they might be resolved (Bornstein 2006: 55–61; Ebrahim 2003: 158–9; Prato 2006: 12; Sadoun 2006: 49; Vincent 2006: 22–8). This in turn means that donors remain unaware of the problems, and that money which might have been used to resolve them is instead used to support unsound activities.

Two further aspects of the consequences of donor funding need to be touched on briefly. Firstly, the procedures we have described put a particularly heavy burden on the smaller NGOs, which may find it difficult to survive if they have to divert their meagre resources into competing for funds and justifying their existence (Morena 2006: 33). While one should beware of idealising the small NGO as either the authentic voice of the common people, or as the repository of radical campaigning, unsullied by the compromises which larger NGOs have made with the forces of reaction, there is an understandable fear that the tendency towards fewer, larger, more bureaucratised NGOs might lead to greater conformity. In some cases, what start off as 'grassroots' movements, close to the people, have been transformed into formal NGOs in order to attract funds, only for leaders to lose touch with their roots as answering to donors takes precedence over answering to constituents (Kelsall in Barrow and Jennings 2001: 140; Igoe 2004: 110–18; Igoe 2003: 863–85). Secondly there has been a trend since around the mid-1990s towards greater co-ordination of aid by donors. This is perfectly understandable as a means of avoiding waste and duplication, but the fear of some recipient NGOs is that this trend is increasing the influence and hold of donors still further, not just in administrative terms but as part of a general revival of neo-colonialism (Community Development Research Network 2005: 27–8).

How can one respond to all these charges of unwarranted bureaucracy, the diversion of NGO activities into channels that please donors, and the crushing of NGO imagination and initiative? Given the chance, would NGOs develop long-terms plans, innovate and utilise their alleged rapport with local communities, with few acting dishonestly or putting individual interests before the common good? Would Africa benefit in terms of greater development, democracy and social justice if NGOs were given large sums of money and left, within generous limits, to spend it as they saw fit? One immediate answer is that many of the restrictions were imposed or tightened because experience suggested that funds had been misused corruptly or because money had been poured into ill-thought out schemes which yielded few benefits. Given the enormous expansion of NGOs from the mid-1980s which we plotted in the previous chapter, it would have been remarkable if a proportion of NGOs had not been corrupt, incompetent or simply over ambitious. In principle it seems reasonable for any funder to have the right to judge whether the funds requested would be put to sensible use, and whether the recipient had accounted adequately for the disbursement of the funds. Whether such judgement has been used in the best way, whether in terms of procedures or actual decisions, is of course another matter.

The argument that the trend towards fewer, larger, more bureaucratic NGOs is harmful is also one that should not pass without questioning. Morena (2006: 33) suggests that a lack of diversity is a threat to the pursuit of global justice, yet diversity has not always been regarded as an essential feature of radical causes. In earlier times, few people demanded a diversity of left-wing parties or a diversity of trade unions to fight for the underprivileged. Then the call was for 'solidarity'. Perhaps a diversity of NGOs could be harnessed by some invisible hand in pursuit of a greater good, but a case has not really been made.

On the converse argument that size and bureaucratic organisation are often equated with conservatism, ineffectiveness or remoteness from constituents, one wonders what alternatives are available. There are even hints that there is something un-African about replacing informal, local groups with bodies that seek formal registration, keep accounts and minutes of meetings, take votes and invoke constitutions to resolve disputes, in contrast to the African tradition of meeting in the shade of the palaver tree and allowing everyone to speak until a consensus has been achieved. Some formal procedures may, of course, be used by more articulate and educated members to bamboozle the underprivileged. Garland complains of Africans serving on NGOs in Namibia having to use 'Western' bureaucratic procedures such as formal speeches, motions and votes before any notice will be taken of them (Garland in Comaroff and Comaroff 1999: 89–92). We can also acknowledge that too cosy a relationship with African governments or donors is always a danger, but these are hardly arguments for retreating from the reality of modern politics. While Igoe and Kelsall lament the transformation of local groups defending local rights into remote NGOs talking more to donors than constituents, Cameron laments the inability of a Tanzanian pastoralist NGO to grasp the opportunities the political system afforded for articulating demands in a way that might influence the ruling elite (Cameron 2001: 55–72). The leaders lacked training in 'participatory forms of community empowerment' (*ibid*: 59). Such jargon might conjure up a picture of bewildered pastoralists being sent off on courses to learn how to understand their own communities, but there is a serious general point that NGOs might devote more effort to exploiting the opportunities available to them rather than bemoaning their weaknesses.

They could begin by noting that donors are not all-powerful. As Ebrahim points out, NGO 'success' enhances the reputation of the donor. Donors depend on NGOs to demonstrate that the release of their funds has resulted in successful projects (Ebrahim 2003: 155). Just as bakers can only survive by selling bread at a price people can afford, so donors can only survive by donating on terms that are generous enough to enable NGOs to make successful applications. Just as the survival of many NGOs depends on donor funding, so the careers of many employees of donor groups depends on dispensing the funds. This may mean that they are often willing to turn a blind eye to NGOs that fail to follow all the bureaucratic requirements to the letter, or do not always spend their money in the specified way. Although writing mainly about India, Ebrahim's observations are relevant to Africa. NGOs cannot ignore the current priorities of the outside world. They must adapt to new 'global discourses' on the environment, development, gender, participation and professionalism, but they may test and try to re-shape the discourses. An NGO may have to appoint a 'gender specialist' to appease a donor, but it will not necessarily employ the specialist in the manner specified (Ebrahim 2003: 44). In other words, NGOs can 'play the system' in a variety of ways, writing the sort of reports that will keep donors happy, but not telling the whole truth, and taking their own decisions on priorities. Donors may want NGOs to deliver services rather than indulge in radical advocacy, but can they always detect a women's NGO that claims to be counselling battered wives while actually campaigning for women's land rights? Can they prevent an NGO that is nominally looking after the welfare of displaced peasants from campaigning against the policies that allowed new game reserves or foreign mining companies to displace them? Even if one recognises that the global order has dealt Africa a poor hand, NGOs can still play their hands to maximise whatever opportunities exist.

Political constraints

We now move on from constraints that are mainly the result of the rough and tumble of everyday life to those that reflect the desire of other institutions to secure or advance their own interests at the expense of African NGOs. To begin with, we need to emphasise that the lines of conflict are not necessarily between Africa and the West, but that African governments are often wary of their own NGOs and frequently impose severe restrictions on what they may do. In both Tanzania and Uganda, NGOs have fought long, and largely unsuccessful, battles against legislation to curb their freedom action (Kajege in Friedrich Ebert Stiftung (FES) 2003: 98–9). In other cases, African MPs or governments have created their own NGOs to try to retain some control over the 'informal' sector. Cohen describes the way in which the widening of access to the United Nations Economic and Social Council (ECOSOC) has led to (often authoritarian) governments sponsoring their own NGOs (Cohen 2003: 45–8) – effectively quangos representing governments rather than NGOs representing communities. Maina reminds us that the African state is not necessarily neutral between different civil society groups and, especially in the case of Kenya, it may heighten ethnic divisions by deciding which NGOs to favour (Maina in Van Rooy 1998: 135–7). In the case of Zambia, Rawlence suggests that NGOs are run by people who derive their authority from the state, so that nominal attempts to 'strengthen civil society' actually give more power to unelected state nominees (Rawlence in Igoe and Kelsall 2005: 147–65).

If the hazards of a state takeover can be avoided, there is still the hazard of co-option, whether by the African state or by global bodies. We shall consider the global aspect in more detail in Chapter 6, but we can note here the age old ploy of luring protest movements off the streets and into plush offices where their opinions will be heard respectfully, though they will frequently go unheeded (Chandler in Baker and Chandler 2005: 163–5; Scholte 2004: 211–33). In the case of Madagascar, Duffy explores the concept of the 'governance state' where policy is formulated largely through a mixture of government, indigenous NGOs and donors. There is less emphasis on donors laying down rigorous conditions for funding because they have managed to get their feet under the table in the offices where policy is actually made. This does not necessarily mean that NGOs have been reduced to the role of powerless collaborators, because the donor consortium is not always sufficiently monolithic to impose its will (Duffy 2006: 713–49) but such arrangements clearly take us a long way from the autonomous NGO pursuing distinctive ideals. Co-option of this sort does not seem to have gone so far in English-speaking Africa, with its tradition of leaving more autonomy with civil society, and Kelsall implies that Tanzanian attempts to get NGOs to follow a 'governance agenda' have failed (Kelsall in Barrow and Jennings 2001: 133–4). Indeed such an orderly arrangement seems alien to much of Africa, where government (or even governance) is more of a piecemeal process, but that does not preclude a range of *ad hoc* devices for seducing NGOs into the corridors of power, from the World Bank to the State House in Dar es Salaam or Kampala.

Beyond the gentle prodding implicit in co-option lies the harsher reality of Western governments, and sometimes INGOs, using their superior power to impose their will on Africa. Duffield asserts that from the mid-1990s, NGOs have been increasingly under the control of donors. They find it increasingly difficult (especially in countries devastated by war) to separate their traditional non-governmental development and humanitarian activities from the wider aims and implications of 'the new security framework' (Duffield 2001: 80–1, 259). Agg suggests that NGOs wanting partnerships with the Department for International Development (DFID) must prove that they contribute to the British government's priorities and targets (Agg 2006: 15–21), and Barr *et al.* speak of the Ugandan NGO sector acting 'as a relay for international governmental and non-governmental agendas ... The activities of Ugandan NGOs largely reflect the agenda and concerns of these international actors' (Barr *et al.* 2005: 675).

Of the specific Western preferences most frequently cited is the preference for 'service provision' or 'development' over 'advocacy' or 'campaigning' (Chandler in Baker and Chandler 2005: 63–4; Ebrahim 2003: 70–1; Makumbe 1998: 305–17; Mercer 2002: 5–22; Morena 2006: 29–33; Prato 2006: 11; Sadoun 2006: 49; Tomlinson 2002: 27). Variations on this theme include a preference for 'safe' groups not involved in human rights activity, and a reluctance to support 'global justice' groups, especially in the post-2001 political climate. As Western countries develop a sharper perception of their ideologies and interests, NGOs in Africa, and in poor countries generally, can expect little support if they challenge these.

While it is difficult to dispute the broad thrust of the arguments, there remain some nagging doubts. Firstly, what constitutes a 'safe' area of activity? While Makumbe suggests that human rights activity is something that donors avoid, we noted in the previous chapter that Hearn criticised donors for supporting bourgeois human rights while ignoring social and economic rights (Hearn 2000: 3–4). It may be that donors are happy to support NGOs that organise conferences on the virtues of free and fair elections, but are more wary of NGOs that challenge military or police abuses of human rights if such challenges are seen to weaken a friendly, if illiberal, government. Similarly with other areas of NGO activity, what is important is less the job description than the impact of the activity on Western interests. Anti-corruption NGOs may be fine if they bring dishonest public officials to book, but not if they start asking questions about dubious arms or timber deals involving Western businesses or governments.

Secondly, there is the need to avoid perceiving a monolithic entity such as 'donors' or 'the West'. As we have already noted, there is a broad spectrum of Western opinion from the free market United States to the social democratic Scandinavia, and within each country there may also be wide divergences. As much aid is channelled through semi-autonomous agencies such as DFID and USAID, many of them largely staffed by Africans, or by Europeans with social democratic persuasions, the ideological position of Western political leaders may become increasingly remote. Apparently radical NGOs may be supported if only because their activities, and the publicity they receive, might suggest that donors are getting a positive return on their investment. Much praise from donors and foreign embassies has been heaped on HakiElimu, the education NGO in Tanzania, for its ability to embarrass the government by revealing the gap between official pronouncements and the reality of life in Tanzania's schools. Even HakiKazi, which is more like one of the 'global justice' NGOs allegedly out of favour with donors, is able to obtain foreign support. It might be objected that donor attitudes would change if alliances between radical groups in Africa and global campaigning groups mounted a serious challenge to the global order, but a more 'rational' donor response might have been to strangle such groups at birth rather than risk their subsequent growth.

Thirdly, how easy is it to put 'service provision' and 'advocacy' into separate pigeon holes, and to argue that donors are discriminating against the latter? There are some think tanks in Africa that are 'advocates' in the sense that they politely present sets of policy recommendations to their governments without providing services to anyone but, over much of the NGO world, advocacy and service provision are difficult to disentangle. The Latin American priest who said 'When I help the poor they say I am a Christian; when I ask why they are poor they say I am a communist' was a case of someone straddling the two activities. Providing services to the poor, the disadvantaged, the victims of discrimination or the victims of human rights abuses, is normally going to lead the providers to forming opinions on what politicians or the outside world should do to alter the conditions which have led to the need for the services. Helping the victims of domestic violence may lead on to campaigns for amendments to the law on rape; providing legal aid to peasants faced with eviction may lead to a questioning of the current land laws, and helping the poor generally may lead to a questioning of the current world trade regime. Just as many individuals give donations to the Salvation Army 'because they do a lot of good', without necessarily subscribing to the theology that motivates the Salvationists, so donors may have little choice but to support the service provision while turning a blind eye to the advocacy, or remaining ignorant of it. Donors that become too fastidious might find dwindling outlets for their funds, and we have suggested that a donor without recipients is like a baker without customers.

Finally on the political constraints that are implicit in the desire by other institutions to secure or advance their own interests at the expense of NGOs, we come almost full circle. NGOs can be hijacked by African governments, co-opted by international bodies or be squeezed into activities that do not threaten other institutions; but the final ploy used against them may be to try to persuade NGOs that what is happening is not really 'politics' at all. What is required in poor countries is sound administration, with a minimal role for politicians and political campaigners. Lipschutz suggests that 'elites' are trying to 'depoliticise' society and human activity generally, as market forces take over. He cites the example, admittedly in Asia rather than Africa, of the sportswear firm Nike accepting the need to regulate working conditions, in response to pressure from NGOs and public opinion, but without society or its elected representatives deciding on a framework of working conditions or trade union rights (Lipschutz in Baker and Chandler 2005: 171–85). Ebrahim suggests a greater emphasis on managerial capacity, which is difficult to reconcile with public participation and sensitivity to local conditions and needs (Ebrahim 2003: 49–50). This takes us back to Chandhoke's argument about the whole language of politics being doctored in order to avoid words that imply conflict, exploitation, inequality or injustice (Chandhoke in Kaldor *et al.* 2003: 411–12).

One can certainly argue that, without a single law being passed or a single decision on the allocation of resources being altered, more competent administration and management in Africa would relieve a great deal of poverty and suffering, and even perhaps right a lot of injustices or human rights abuses. Indeed a common refrain among NGO officers in Tanzania and Uganda is that there is little wrong with government policy, and the problems lay with inadequate implementation. One might also argue, as we suggested in the previous chapter, that the changes in terminology condemned by Chandhoke are at least partly a reflection of a world where governance, networking, co-option and consensus may do more to relieve the plight of the poor and oppressed than militancy, confrontation or appeals to class solidarity. Yet depoliticisation and an emphasis on sound management, if that is what is taking place, do seem to mean that NGOs, and Africans generally, have to accept a national order and a world order on terms dictated by more powerful institutions. Nike employees may obtain better pay or shorter working hours, but they still have to accept the principle of work contracted out to countries where the workers are most defenceless, and accept that their own contribution to any improvement in their lot will be minimal.

It may also be the case that those INGOs which resist calls for depoliticisation are often the ones to achieve significant successes, often working in co-operation with indigenous NGOs: Oxfam on poverty, Jubilee 2000 on debt relief, Amnesty International on human rights, and Friends of the Earth and Greenpeace on conservation. The causes they have pursued have not been about carrying out the same activities more efficiently, but about persuading governments and international bodies to depart, at least partially, from previous practices.

This leads us on the question of the ability of at least a minority of NGOs to break out of the political constraints we have described, and to take on some of the characteristics of the 'virtuous model' in Table 3.1: distinctive philosophical positions, the ability to pursue radical causes, to represent the most disadvantaged sections of society, to utilise their distinctive expertise and campaigning skills, and to enjoy legitimacy amongst both the highest decision-makers and the lowliest peasants and workers. Such literature as we have is stronger on description than analysis, but it may give us some clues as to why it is sometimes possible for groups to play to their strengths and win.

Pommerolle takes the case of the Kenya Human Rights Commission, though purists might regard it as a quango rather than an NGO. It has, she says, carved out a distinctive role for itself, and maintained a wide range of contacts, especially with the poor. It has campaigned effectively for social and economic rights as well as constitutional rights (Pommerolle in Igoe and Kelsall 2005: 93–112). In Tanzania, the Tanzania Gender Networking Programme (TGNP) has many admirers, and has a happy ability to blow its own trumpet. It has campaigned for 'progressive NGO laws', lobbied Parliament on land issues, and pressed for the scrapping of the oppressive laws highlighted by the Nyalali Commission on the Constitution. It offers courses in social analysis for transformation and development (Chachage in Bujra and Adejumobi 2002: 129-83), and it has campaigned against European and American trade practices seen to be damaging to Tanzania (Mbilinyi and Rusimbi 2005: 627–30). Its strength was demonstrated by President Mkapa begging for its support in convincing IFIs of the damage which their policies were doing (TGNP 2004: 2). Such issues clearly go beyond traditional women's issues, and it is difficult to find explanations of the group's high profile other than extremely efficient organisation and the ability to research subjects thoroughly before expressing an opinion. It is possible that the fact of being a women's NGO is also important. Politicians may be more reluctant to attack women's groups that go beyond their nominal terms of reference (with one notable exception in Tanzania) than they would other NGOs, given the reputation that women's groups generally enjoy as friends of the underprivileged. There is a rough parallel with the Catholic Church in Latin America in the twilight of authoritarian rule, where bullying the church might produce a stronger backlash than bullying a trade union or an underground political party.

Also in Tanzania, Shivji describes the attempts by Maasai pastoralists in defending their land rights through a combination of traditional leadership and accountability structures, with modern NGOs and other means of 'national and international campaigning' to publicise their plight (Shivji in Semboja *et al.* 2002: 111–12). In Senegal, McKeon takes up the case of the Committee National de Concertation des Ruraux (CNCR) which has won a negotiating place for peasants and made a major impact on rural policy. It is a confederation of farmers, pastoralists, fishermen, horticulturalists and rural women, with a membership of three million, which aims to promote dialogue and exchange of experience among members, and to act as a spokesman for the peasant movement *vis-à-vis* the state and donors. Under the influence of the CNCR, Senegal was one of the few Sub-Saharan African countries in which farmers' organisations were seriously involved in determining the content of the World Bank's Agricultural Structural Investment Programme. It gained cuts in interest rates, tax concessions and a five year moratorium on the repayment of farmers' debts. McKeon explains the CNCR's success in terms of a carefully crafted strategy, taking advantage of the new spaces and political opportunities afforded by state retrenchment. It constructed alliances with a range of actors at different levels and made disciplined use of protest and social mobil-isation. 'Vision and skilled leadership' were important (McKeon in Ghimire 2005: 190–214).

Good leadership and the 'right strategies' are the themes running through these descriptions. Are there any other possible explanations of their success? In Kenya in the later years of the Moi regime, the govern-ment was strong enough to violate human rights but not strong enough to suppress criticism, and this probably helped the Human Rights Commission to build a broad base of support. In Tanzania the ruling party has been electorally secure, with over 60 per cent of the vote in rel-atively free and fair elections, and it is therefore confident enough to give a wide degree of latitude to civil society, so that sufficiently determined NGOs can flourish. Senegal, too, has a more tolerant political tradition than most African states, and relatively few ethnic tensions. Under more authoritarian regimes, such as the Egyptian, or in countries with greater ethnic tension, such as Rwanda, it would have been difficult for even the best organised NGOs to have made such an impression. Secondly, one could look at the ability of the NGOs to deliver benefits to a wide range of clients, such as the farmers, pastoralists and Tanzanian women. The common caricature drawn of NGO leaders – that they sit in air con-ditioned offices pontificating on political issues without having any real contact with ordinary people (Igoe in Igoe and Kelsall 2005: 115–46) – did not apply in these cases. Finally, the NGOs were often seen by their gov-ernments as complementing the work of the governments, especially in the cases of TGNP and CNCR, and they were sometimes able to represent national interests better than the governments themselves, whereas many NGOs are seen as confrontational, or as political parties in disguise which pose a threat to the current order.

Yet we must reiterate that these success stories are greatly outnumbered by 'failure stories', or at least partial failures where NGOs have suc-

cumbed to internal mismanagement, domination by African governments, co-option by international bodies, diversion of objectives
by donors and a general capitulation to global capitalism. The current
Western rhetoric about the virtues of democracy, pluralism, governance and participation may be difficult to reconcile with blatant
attempts to suppress any NGO that begins to get ideas above its
station, and the obstacles in the way of the virtuous model remain
many and persistent.

The global context

We have looked in general terms at the impact of conflict between the
strong and the weak on NGOs, but we now look specifically at the
arena within which this conflict has been fought out over the past
decade or more. We have noted that NGOs enjoyed a rapid expansion
from the mid-1980s in response to both the inability of African governments to cope with the basic demands which the process of government requires, and the ideology of Western governments which saw
states as largely an encumbrance, and favoured an expansion of the
voluntary sector. In retrospect, the years to the late 1990s may now be
regarded as a golden age for NGOs, as they attracted more personnel
and funds, provided a widening range of services, and acted as initiators of ideas, and scrutineers of politicians and administrators. What
has happened since then? Several developments have affected the role
of NGOs, including the 'revival' or resilience of states, the Western perception that Africa, and the 'developing' world generally, is still in a
state of near-chaos; and the emergence of security issues after 2001.

Most African states, unless ravaged by civil war, made some recovery
after the nadir of the mid-1980s. Economic conditions improved, if
only marginally, as aid was provided in the form of structural adjustment programmes (SAPs), and the most incompetent or corrupt rulers
either departed or were forced, often under pressure from donors, to
mend their ways. The emergence of at least a minimal form of pluralist
democracy provided some checks on the behaviour of rulers. All this
meant that there was now the semblance of a political process in
which governments attended, however inadequately, to the needs
of the population; and in which population was willing, by and large,
to accept their authority rather than retreating into illegal activities.
At the same time, we have seen that the post-Washington consensus meant that Western powers acknowledged the need for a greater
role for the African state. Paradoxically, NGOs may actually have

contributed further to the revival of the African state. Their growing provision of services in the late 1980s contributed to a modicum of order and stability, without which states might have disintegrated further. But it is not NGOs but governments, in collaboration with donors, that have the power to allocate resources, raise taxes, control the bureaucracy and initiate changes in the law, and governments could now wield their authority more effectively. Cohen suggests that NGOs have reinforced the resilience of states still further by pressing them to intervene more in areas such as the economy, justice, development and human rights (Cohen 2003: 178–83). None of this means that the role of NGOs has become insignificant, but they have become relatively smaller fish in a bigger pond. The NGO role is clearly visible at times of economic collapse, famine or civil war, when states appear largely powerless. As order returns, governments can start legislating to clip the wings of NGOs, to change the zoological analogy, or to insist that administration is the prerogative of the state, with NGOs left to fill the gaps in service provision or to act as scrutineers of the administration.

While people within Africa might have felt by the late 1990s that some progress had been made over the previous decade, despite the continued problems of debt, poverty and economies that had ever growing difficulties in competing in world markets, the external perception was often different. Moves towards pluralist democracy were welcomed, as was the stability of countries like Ghana, South Africa and Uganda compared with the 1980s, but it was felt that there must be something wrong with Africa if it could not achieve the progress made in much of East Asia or even parts of Latin America, especially when the West had poured in so much aid. The ability of former dictators such as Moi, Rawlings and the military leaders in Nigeria to retain power, through allegedly fraudulent elections, suggested that much of the old order remained intact.

Jacoby writes of a Western, and especially a United States, perception of a barbaric world which had failed to adopt the cultural norms of the West. The failure to tackle poverty, human rights abuses and environmental degradation was the fault of poor countries, not the fault of the world order. Major donors have therefore pressed the (international) NGO sector to bear more of the moral responsibility for international action. This is a more effective means of ensuring Western domination than 'blatant imperialism', which may cost lives, lose votes or damage Western trading interests, but the unifying assumptions are still that Western powers have a right to impose their will on lesser breeds

(Jacoby 2005: 215–33). Duffield, too, sees Western policy by the late 1990s as driven not just by the desire to relieve poverty and promote development, but to impose 'liberal governance'. Aid was designed to change societies and behaviour. The autonomy of NGOs has been reduced as they are caught up in global governance, applying remedies prescribed by Western governments and international governmental organisations (IGOs) (Duffield 2001: 44–74). Berman takes an even more critical view of the American attitude towards the wider world.

> In the American case we have a military and economic empire that views the world as one big happy market, and believes that every-body needs to come on board. We – that is global corporate con-sumerism – are the future, 'progress'. If the 'barbarians' fail to share this vision, they are 'medieval'; if they resist 'evil' (Berman 2001: 2).

Many of the Western attitudes described above pre-dated the security issues that emerged after 2001, so these cannot be explained simply as adjuncts of the 'war on terror', yet they mark a departure from the earlier attitude that African states should be left largely to their own devices as long as they did not threaten Western trade, investment or Cold War interests. The literature cited does not offer many explana-tions as to why there was now a greater concern with the internal ordering of African politics and society, but the ending of the Cold War appears to be one factor. Fukuyama's 'end of history' thesis both reflected and probably influenced the views of Western politicians. With the collapse of communism, he argued, Western-style liberal demo-cracy, reinforced by free market economics, was now the only viable type of political order (Fukuyama 1991: 659–63). Other types of polit-ical order, one inferred, were eventually doomed to oblivion, but the West could do the people living under such regimes a good turn by has-tening the process, hence Berman's observation about bringing everyone on board. The execution of this civilising mission was not always as easy as its propagation, and regular visitors to Africa may wonder how far pol-itics and culture have really changed. Formal democratic institutions are now the general rule, and some countries have been persuaded through a mixture of carrots and sticks to make more effort to tackle corruption, electoral fraud and human rights abuses, but few observers have ques-tioned the appropriateness of 'neo-patrimonialism' as a term for charac-terising African politics. Politics, for many, is less a matter of taking democratic choices, than of seeking patrons in higher places to dispense political resources.

Yet for many NGOs the post-Cold War environment, combined with the other constraints we have examined, has restricted their room for manoeuvre, and the new more interventionist ideology has given a greater legitimacy to the more restrictive conditions and procedures for donor aid. The sort of de-politicisation we have described leaves many NGOs, other than most courageous or foolhardy, to concentrate on the everyday problems of poverty and development, without asking too many questions about why Africa is in its current condition, or what might be done about it.

The relevance of the post-2001 security issues might not seem immediately relevant to NGOs in Africa, much of which has been largely a backwater in the 'war on terror', though backwaters are often affected by ripples from the mainstream. The United States is certainly trying to increase its military presence in Africa as an aspect of the 'war on terror', with increased military aid held out as an inducement to governments that are willing to accept an American military presence (Berrigan 2008: 7–8; Mutahi and Kagwanja 2008: 22–3), but this has not yet had any obvious effect on NGOs.

If we take the Middle East, Afghanistan and Pakistan as the mainstream, there is little doubt that the West, and especially the United States, need NGOs to deal with the social disruption caused by invasion and occupation, but do not expect them to express any opinions on the merits of the invasions or the policies for dealing with their consequences (Ali 2006: 34; Klein 2003: 16). Indeed Klein claims that the United States is openly proclaiming that NGOs are, or should be, an arm of the US government, bringing food and health care on its behalf to a grateful population. This leaves NGOs with the choice between working as best as they can because the poor and the sick need them, or withdrawing because they find it intolerable to be treated as agents of an unpopular and, they would say, immoral government. As far as the backwash in Africa is concerned, one obvious effect is the 'those who are not with us are against us' mentality. Islamic groups are an obvious target for suspicion, but this can spread to radical groups that are critical of American foreign policy. After 2001, according to Igoe and Kelsall, donors began to redistribute aid money from NGOs to African states 'to combat the terror threat'. What does not happen may be as significant as what does. NGO protests against the invasion of Iraq, and broader critiques of American imperialism, have generally been muted, with a desire not to jeopardise funding by making futile gestures. Some African governments, notably the Ugandan, made it clear that they would not tolerate such protests anyway, especially if they threatened relations with a powerful ally.

> The NGOs are no substitute for genuine social and political movements. In Africa, Palestine and elsewhere, NGOs have swallowed the neo-liberal status quo. They operate like charities, trying to alleviate the worst excesses, but rarely questioning the systemic basis of the fact that five billion citizens on our globe live in poverty (Ali 2006: 34).

Pursuing the theme of what has not happened, the frequently lamented absence or weakness of 'genuine' social movements may have been another casualty of the 'war on terror'. At best, according to this argument, some NGOs can campaign for a different global order as a sideline while providing services that meet with Western approval, but anything beyond that is generally precluded by the notion of avoiding lost causes, or by a fear of what African governments would do to stamp out any 'anti-Americanism' that threatened the flow of aid.

Conclusion

Could one ever discover a 'virtuous' NGO with the characteristics described in Table 3.1? Its characteristics would include distinctive objectives based on strong convictions, speaking up for otherwise neglected causes and disadvantaged groups by using its distinctive expertise and campaigning skills; enjoying legitimacy amongst the high and lowly alike, yet remaining untainted by bureaucratic rigidity or political expediency. Political reality suggests a negative answer. The pursuit of virtuous objectives generally requires interaction with less virtuous people. One may have to soil one's hands by accepting their money and having to make unpleasant compromises, especially in the event of being co-opted on to formal bodies which share little of the NGO's idealism. This may mean being implicated in unpopular decisions, which may then erode the support and legitimacy the NGO once enjoyed. Pursuing the end of virtuous outcomes may mean using means which are less than democratic, with decision-making concentrated in the hands of a few leaders. This then leaves NGOs open to the rhetorical question 'Whom do you represent?' and, by implication, 'What right have you got to demand that your wishes prevail?' As the number and scope of NGOs increases, they are more likely to employ, or even be led by, people who see their work as just another job, rather than a higher calling. They may simply choose to work in the voluntary rather than the private sector because the funding, or government support available, make this a more rational decision. In the global arena, many of these problems are likely to be even more acute, as idealism comes face to face with the struggle for economic and political supremacy.

Much of this assumes that the founders of NGOs do start off from an idealistic position. In practice the NGOs may be created to meet an immediate need, whether through self help or by providing services to others, with little thought given to any longer-term principles. In a minority of cases the NGOs are simply created to obtain whatever funds they can, and are never seen again – the proverbial 'briefcase NGO'. There is no reason to look down on those NGOs that are created by people looking for useful employment, or to trying to plug a gap in service provision, but the existence of such groups suggests that one should not expect all (or even most) of the distinctive qualities implicit in the virtuous model. Compromises have to be made, not just with the national and global political orders, but with the reality of everyday life in societies where social and economic problems are many, and employment opportunities are few. As for the national and global orders, our discussion suggests that there are no outright winners or losers. NGOs can hardly expect to triumph over African governments, Western governments and the forces of global capitalism; and their final resting place in terms of their functions, freedom of action and expression, and internal organisation, is often remote from the destination they had initially envisaged. We have also noted the arguments about the impact of relatively new forces such as the rise of NPM, the revival of and strength of African states, the pressure for cultural and political conformity in the wake of post-Cold War triumphalism, and the post-2001 security concerns. These have all had the effect, it is said, of pushing the roles of NGOs back towards charity or service provision, rather than campaigning for the disadvantaged and for a more just social order. On the whole these arguments, while important in emphasising that NGOs now have to face a more uphill struggle, do seem to gloss over the actual opportunities available, and do not always square with the diversity of NGO activity on the ground. Many NGOs are, of course, content to work within the existing, constricting, order as best as they can, without questioning the fairness of that order or seeking to test its vulnerability. But we have seen that, like many people and groups in subordinate positions the world over, those that dare can exploit the disunity, indecision, survival requirements, finite resources, and even the better nature, of their nominal superiors. Funds can be diverted for purposes not strictly specified by donors, and applications for funds and reports can be economical with the truth. Criticisms of African and Western governments, and campaigns for a more just order, may be tolerated or overlooked by donors because the donors do not want to lose the credit they enjoy for supporting NGOs which otherwise carry out important functions. As for post-Cold War attempts by the West to impose greater political and cultural conformity, Africa has a long record of absorbing what it wants from alien cultures and discarding what it does not. It may be necessary to go some way towards echoing modern managerial techniques or claiming to pursue whatever objectives are fashionable in the outside world, but no one can be looking over the shoulder of an NGO all the time. The post-2001 security climate may mean that it is imprudent to risk the wrath of the United States by challenging the morality or logic of the 'war on terror', and African governments may restrain NGOs or any other groups that make such challenges, but Africa is no longer the explicit campaigner against Western imperialism that it was in the days of Lumumba, Nkrumah and Nyerere. Africa realises that it has few means, if any, of changing American foreign policy. NGO criticism of the West focuses much more on the economic policies of the IFIs, and to a lesser extent the European Union, which have a much more direct impact than anything happening in Afghanistan or Iraq. And this African NGOs have many allies both amongst INGOs and within Western public opinion generally.

We have looked at cases of successful NGOs in Kenya, Senegal and Tanzania which did seem to come close to the virtuous model. While one cannot generalise from such a small number of cases, these NGOs appeared to enjoy the advantages of efficient, perhaps visionary, leadership; and an ability to build goodwill and legitimacy by defending and advancing the interests of their constituents. This, in turn, enabled them to build a platform from which they could campaign effectively for what they regarded as just causes, and negotiate with governments and international bodies from a position of strength. Such NGOs are, of course, the exception, and we have cited numerous examples of NGOs that possessed many of the converse characteristics and remained subordinate to the whims of donors and African and foreign governments. The lesson to be learnt may be to avoid too much determinism. The current world of post-industrialism, post-communism and governance, and of global forces which can push NGOs and societies this way and that, yet cannot control them in detail, all makes for a degree of indeterminacy. Against this background, NGOs are far from masters of their own fate, but those with sufficient determination can exploit a variety of opportunities. In an ideal world, political parties, broad-based social movements or elected governments might be better vehicles for promoting alternative visions of society or representing disadvantaged groups, but the failure of such institutions either to materialise or to perform the requisite roles makes the argument academic. One has only to imagine an Africa without NGOs to recognise the significance of the roles that they actually perform.

4
Democracy Without Votes I: The Background to NGOs in Tanzania and Uganda

---

Box 4.1 A Letter from an African NGO

Anytown
Africa

To: Department for International Development, London.

Dear Sir/Madam

I am establishing an NGO whose objectives include defending the land rights of Africans against foreign mining companies and indigenous game reserves; protecting workers exploited by multinational companies; ensuring that African produce can be sold fairly in European and American markets; and abolishing global capitalism. Could you please send me details of the government agencies and international NGOs which might support such an NGO?

Yours sincerely

A. Rebble

Box 4.2 A Reply from London

Department for International Development
London

Dear Mr Rebble

In response to your letter, and thousands of others like it, I am pleased to enclose a long list of government agencies and international NGOs that will be able to help you.

Yours sincerely

I. Makepeace

In a world where supply responded to demand, the letters in Boxes 4.1 and 4.2 might correspond more closely to reality. While we obviously cannot be certain of the priorities of the people across the whole of Africa, it seems plausible to believe that security of tenure on the land, a living wage earned under humane conditions, and an opportunity to trade fairly in world markets, would all be among the highest priorities. Critics might note the absence of references in the correspondence to health and education, but the resources generated by economic changes might pay for such provision. What of democracy, human rights and competent, honest government? Few Africans would object to such additions. Neither would be they be averse to the tackling of man-made environmental problems which have contributed to floods, drought, soil erosion, and polluted air and water.

But does the existing distribution of NGOs in Africa reflect the continent's wants and needs? Is the balance tilted more in favour of NGOs pursuing democracy and human rights in the narrow sense, as some of the sources cited in previous chapters suggest, rather than towards access to land, the rights of African labour and the right to trade freely? If it is so tilted, why? A partial answer might be that NGOs and the voluntary sector in general are not the best vehicles for pursuing 'economic rights'. Is it not up to governments to secure these rights, often in negotiation with foreign governments and businesses, rather than leaving it to well meaning voluntary effort? Yet this view is hardly convincing when one looks at the inept record of governments in developing countries on these matters, in contrast to the at least sporadic successes of NGOs where *ad hoc* deals have been struck to protect specific groups such as Tanzanian land holders, Pakistani sweatshop workers, Ghanaian cocoa growers or Indians living near proposed dams.

To dependency theorists and those occupying similar ideological positions, the dearth of radical NGOs is merely a reflection of the current world order. The strong continue to exploit the weak because their superior economic power allows them to do so. If the lot of the poor can be ameliorated by NGOs continuing in the tradition of nineteenth century charities, so much the better, but there is no reason to expect any serious effort to prevent the poor from being poor, whether by NGOs or governments. For others, the problem may go beyond the unequal relationship between rich and poor countries. One might want to spell out more clearly the institutional relationships between NGOs, African governments, donors and citizens. Given the power and resources of these different elements, what can one reasonably expect NGOs to be able to do, and subject to what limitations?

Tables 4.1 and 4.2 set out the main types of NGO interviewed in Tanzania and Uganda in research for this book, and their principal functions (many NGOs obviously performed more than one function,

Table 4.1   NGOs Interviewed in Tanzania and Uganda, 2007

	Tanzania	Uganda	Total
Indigenous NGOs	28	26	54
International NGOs	5	6	11
Total	33	32	65

Table 4.2   The Principal Functions of NGOs Interviewed in Tanzania and Uganda

Principal Functions	Indigenous NGOs in Tanzania	International NGOs in Tanzania	Indigenous NGOs in Uganda	International NGOs in Uganda	Total
1. Service delivery; development	5	0	4	1	10
2. Poverty eradication	2	0	3	0	5
3. Enabling, mobilising, empowering	10	1	12	1	24
4. Advocacy	15	2	11	2	30
5. Promotion of democracy, human rights, civil society, good governance	4	3	5	3	15
6. Women's rights	6	0	5	2	13
7. Environment; wildlife	2	1	0	0	3
8. Global issues	3	2	5	0	10
9. Research; think tank	1	0	4	0	5
10. Umbrella organisation	4	0	6	0	10
11. Professional; interest group	3	1	2	0	6

so the totals in each column add up to more than the total number of NGOs). I can make no claim that the NGOs are typical of those in Tanzania and Uganda as a whole, especially as the sample is biased in favour of NGOs in the capital cities and the provincial towns of Arusha, Fort Portal and Mbeya, but the sample includes the most accessible NGOs in the towns and cities concerned.

Even after allowing for ambiguity in exactly what the 'functions' may cover, the tables suggest that only a small minority of NGOs were concerned with the sort of fundamental issues raised in Mr Rebble's letter in Box 4.1. 'Land rights' were covered by environmental groups (paragraph 7 in Table 4.2), and by 'interest groups' (paragraph 11) which included pastoralists. Concern with fair trade was covered by groups pursuing global issues (paragraph 8).

This still left the vast majority of NGOs more concerned with trying to ameliorate existing conditions than with challenging the existing distribution of power, even though exceptions might be found in some unlikely places. Some women's NGOs (paragraph 6) were willing to make such a challenge, and some research groups (paragraph 9) asked searching questions about the persistence of poverty. 'Enabling, mobilising and empowering' (paragraph 3) frequently went no further than encouraging communities to ensure that they received their allocated share of the budget, but there were occasional cases of questioning the effectiveness of government policy as a whole. As for Mr Rebble's concern about the exploitation of workers, one might argue that we should look to trade unions rather than NGOs, but we hinted in the previous chapter that, in the current global order, the limited victories that have been won for workers have frequently owed more to campaigning by NGOs than by unions.

These observations suggest than any search for 'democracy without votes' in Africa should set itself modest targets. We are not likely to witness, in the foreseeable future, a titanic struggle between the 'haves' and the 'have nots', but there is the possibility of making governments more accountable and more responsive to their constituents, and of some of the worst abuses of power being curbed. For the more distant future, we can only speculate that the minority of NGOs that campaign for 'social justice' at home, and 'global justice' in the wider world, might gradually make an impact on those who wield power.

These somewhat lengthy preliminary observations lead us in to the purpose of this, and the next, chapter. Using examples drawn mainly from Tanzania and Uganda, we are concerned with the extent to which NGO activity can be a supplement to, or a substitute for, the democratic process provided by formal 'electoral' or 'representative' democracy. We noted in the previous chapter that NGOs are not always on safe ground when they claim to 'represent' a specific group or cause, but has the formal democratic process in Africa done much to turn the wishes of the voters into reality, or to uphold their rights? The transition from the authoritarian political systems, which covered most of Africa until the 1980s and 1990s to the democracies that cover most of the continent today, has obviously brought many benefits. Few people are now tortured or imprisoned for their beliefs. Political opinions can, for the most part, be expressed freely, and may even make an impact on ruling politicians. Incompetence and dishonesty in high places can be revealed more easily, and may sometimes be remedied. Yet if democracy is seen more in terms of voters being able to choose between competing political parties offering rival policies, and of the knowledge on the part of governments that an inadequate performance is likely to lead to defeat at the polls, the picture is somewhat different. Peaceful transfers of power through the ballot box have taken place in a few countries such as Benin, Ghana, Malawi and Senegal. In Kenya and Zambia, governments have also been displaced through the ballot box, but with the new rulers (many of them former members of the old order who had jumped ship) treating their opponents and the electorate as a whole in a similar way to that of the previous authoritarian regime, with widespread disregard for the spirit and letter of the constitution. In most of the remaining countries where democratic transitions have occurred, power remains in the hands of the rulers or parties that presided over the earlier authoritarian regimes. This does not necessarily mean that elections have been rigged, and there is nothing intrinsically undemocratic about voters deciding that their country is best left in the hands of former authoritarians, now subject to more checks and balances. But it does mean that the traditional democratic opportunity of being able to 'turn the rascals out' is frequently not available for practical purposes. Even if elections are free and fair, the advantages of incumbency, and the inability of opposition parties to offer serious policy alternatives or to mount serious election campaigns, leaves most voters with only the hope that the existing rulers will pay some regard to their needs.

It is against this background that we look at the contribution to democracy of NGOs in Tanzania and Uganda in this chapter and the next. We shall offer a brief profile of the two countries, and then examine the context within which NGOs are working. We shall look at the broader civil societies in which NGOs are rooted, at the nature of the NGOs themselves, at the states within whose laws and policies they have to operate, and at the impact of external forces. We shall then try to assess the ability of NGOs to compensate for any democratic deficit that exists.

Tanzania and Uganda: a brief profile

Tanzania and Uganda cannot be treated as 'typical' of Africa as a whole any more than any other two countries, but they do share many of the characteristics of the rest of the continent that may have a bearing on the scope for NGO activity. Like most of Africa, both are amongst the world's poorest countries, heavily dependent on foreign aid and limited by global forces in their ability to compete in world markets. Like most of Africa, both have made the transition from authoritarianism to nominally democratic government, but with the same rulers or their successors retaining power through the ballot box. Some of the major social and economic characteristics of the two countries, and the contrast between their poverty and the wealth of Britain, are indicated in Table 4.3. Most of the figures are self-explanatory. While levels of school enrolment and literacy in Tanzania and Uganda are high by African standards, the relatively short life expectancy is indicative of the levels of poverty and inadequate health provision. The share of the already small national cake going to the poorest 20 per cent of the population in each country translates into each of the poorest Tanzanians each receiving $53 per year and the poorest Ugandans $83.

Poverty, illiteracy and a short life expectancy are not insuperable barriers to democratic political participation, as the experience of India shows, but one would not normally expect democracy to flourish

Table 4.3   Figures on Development in Tanzania, Uganda and the United Kingdom

	Tanzania	Uganda	United Kingdom
GDP per capita ($s)	744	1,454	33,228
Percentage of GDP going to the poorest 20%	7.3	5.7	6.1
Life expectancy at birth (years)	51.0	49.7	79.0
Adult literacy (%)	69.4	66.8	99.0
Net primary school enrolment rate (%)	91	77	99
Net secondary school enrolment rate (%)	N.A.	45	95

Source: UNDP 2007: 229–83.

easily when resources are sparse, and those enjoying a disproportionate share of the limited wealth available use whatever (usually undemocratic) means available to retain or increase what they have. To that extent,

Table 4.4   The Politics of Tanzania and Uganda Compared

	Tanzania	Uganda
Political stability	Extensive, with rule by the same party since 1961	Largely imposed after 1986 insurgency. Prolonged rebellion in the north
Government claims to legitimacy	Electoral	Liberation and electoral
Ethnic/regional conflict	Very little	Dissent and civil war in the north. Continued disputes over Bugandan autonomy
Role of the army and police	Largely depoliticised, though some harassment of opposition	Loyalty is largely to the regime rather than the state
Government attitudes to criticism and dissent	Extensive tolerance, though much criticism is ignored. Largely free press	Government remains sensitive to criticism of army and police, who sometimes act outside the law. Cases of violence against journalists
Government attitudes to NGOs	Generally tolerant, but some areas of NGO criticism are regarded as illegitimate. Restrictive legislation	NGOs are probably less effective in challenging government, but are sometimes seen as a security threat. Restrictive legislation
Political position of NGOs	A few proclaim radical challenges to the existing national and global orders. The majority take the current order as given	Very few radical NGOs, though some specific issues have led to NGO confrontation with government
Strength of civil society	Generally believed to have grown stronger in twenty-first century	Has probably grown stronger, but challenges to the state are less effective than in Tanzania
Subordination, or receptiveness, to external influence	Debt, conditional aid, concessions to foreign timber and mining companies. Concessions to foreign hunting groups	Debt, conditional aid. Fewer mineral, timber or game resources, but dependence on military aid

Tanzania and Uganda are not untypical of Africa as a whole, but there are subtle differences between the two countries that have affected the role of NGOs and their contribution to the democratic process. Some of these are indicated in Table 4.4.

Both Tanzania and Uganda gained independence from Britain in the early 1960s and were, for a time, part of the same East African Community which administered many common public services, but their histories soon diverged. Tanzania comprised a large number of small ethnic groups, none of which was strong enough to dominate the others, or to act as a focus of opposition. The ruling party won almost every seat in the pre-independence election and was never seriously challenged subsequently. It was quick to proclaim itself as the only legal party, as was the case with many ruling parties in Africa at the time. But, unlike most other ruling parties, it enjoyed genuine mass support and permitted a wide degree of internal democracy. Putting aside the more troubled history of the island of Zanzibar, which was incorporated into Tanzania in 1963, the country has enjoyed a degree of stability rare in Africa, with little ethnic or regional conflict. The ruling party has ridden the transition to democracy with little difficulty, and has won three competitive elections with ease. Uganda, in contrast, has suffered a history of violence and instability. The first President, Milton Obote, had to rely much more on force than consent than did his counterpart President Julius Nyerere in Tanzania, especially in crushing the Kingdom of Buganda and its King, the Kabaka, who demanded more autonomy than the President was willing to concede. Even today, the question of Bugandan autonomy remains in dispute.

Obote's growing reliance on military force left more and more power in the hands of the army, which took control in 1971 under General Amin. Amin's brutal regime was ended by an invasion from Tanzania in 1979, and there followed years of near-anarchy until an insurgent movement built up gradually under the leadership of Yoweri Museveni who took power in 1986. This was not a mere military coup, but the victory of a broadly based revolutionary movement which had steadily won the support of local communities that had grown weary of incompetent, self-seeking and violent governments. The National Resistance Movement (NRM, sometimes referred to simply as 'the Movement') has remained in office since 1986, converting itself from a revolutionary army into a political party.

Uganda now appears to have acquired some of the stability which Tanzania has always enjoyed, yet the stability has not been institutionalised in the same way. Initially the fact that the Movement had liberated the country from chaos was sufficient to give it widespread support and legitimacy, without too much concern for the niceties of elections and constitutions, but the pre-1986 political parties were never willing to recognise that legitimacy, and nor were many intellectuals who demanded the same sort of constitutional democracy as other African states were beginning to acquire. There also remained armed rebel groups whose political ideologies were unclear and which often treated banditry as more of a means of acquiring wealth than as a means to any political end. The absence of freedom to contest elections gave them a (somewhat flimsy) pretext for continuing their violence, and the Lord's Resistance Army kept the north of Uganda under siege for well over a decade. Dissent in the north was not confined to armed rebellion. There has continued to be a sense that it has been neglected deliberately. Not only does the north elect a disproportionate number of opposition MPs, but survey evidence suggests a greater dissatisfaction with the working of the political process. According to Logan *et al.*'s survey, 72 per cent of all Ugandans were satisfied with the working of democracy, but the figure was only 39 per cent in the north (Logan *et al.* 2003: 11).

Constitutional democracy was restored by 2003, with a court ruling that opposition parties had the right to contest elections, but the rift between the pro- and anti-Movement sides has never been healed completely. The Movement and its supporters see themselves as morally superior as liberators of the nation and see opposition as, at best, a necessary evil, while opposition parties and much intellectual opinion see the Movement as a democratic government in authoritarian clothing, looking after its own, and intolerant of anyone who challenges the propriety of anything it does. This emerges especially when it comes to the position of the army and police. Whereas in Tanzania these institutions have been largely depoliticised, despite the occasional banning or disruption of opposition rallies, the loyalty of the army and police in Uganda is often to the regime rather than to any larger entity such as the state or the nation. The police have been used to abduct journalists, or even to use tear gas to break up an innocuous student meeting because it was to be addressed by an opposition MP, and the army has been the subject of various alleged human rights abuses

against civilians in the north. As the Movement originated as the political wing of the insurgent National Resistance Army (NRA) the army
has never entirely abandoned its belief that it is the judge of the
nation's security requirements, and that mere laws and constitutional
provisions should not stand in its way.

All this gives the rules of the political game in Uganda, let alone the
observation of the rules, greater uncertainty than in Tanzania. Uganda
has a livelier and more irreverent press than Tanzania, but it also has
journalists who have been taken away in the night. It has high levels of
political participation, stimulated by the need for co-operation and
self-help after the chaos of the early 1980s, but it also has a constitution that has been largely shaped by the President to ensure his
indefinite continuation in office. At election times, citizens promoting
apparently harmless local causes have been the victims of police harassment. In Tanzania, the worst that normally happens when the government is upset by criticism is that an NGO is suspended temporarily,
and for the most part the government is sufficiently confident of its
own position after nearly 50 years of continuous rule to treat criticism
as water off a duck's back. In Uganda, the porcupine might be a better
symbol than the duck, prickly when it fears that the material and sym-
bolic gains of the post-1986 years are under threat.

Turning from tolerance in general to tolerance of NGOs, the position
of the Tanzanian government has generally been one of acceptance
unless an NGO is regarded as pursuing Political objectives with a
capital 'P' in such a way as to embarrass the government, as opposed to
campaigning politically (with a small 'p') on matters that may be con-
tentious but which merely reflect differences of opinion or priorities
between the NGO and the government. It is thus possible for NGOs to
demand greater rights for pastoralists, the repeal of allegedly repressive
laws, or a halt to privatisation, but not to suggest that the government's education policy has been a disaster. The latter type of criticism
might be regarded as something that should be the prerogative of
opposition politicians, and prudent NGOs will strive to avoid looking
like opposition parties in disguise. In Uganda, NGOs have not generally had comparable skill, or perhaps the courage, given the more
'prickly' government, to mount aggressive public critiques of government policy. If anything the government's belief in a significant role
for NGOs is more positive than that in Tanzania, as the whole post-
1986 structure of politics and society required an active 'voluntary
sector' while the state was still convalescing from the chaos of previous
seven years (Hansen and Twaddle 1998: 147). The government's main

fear is not so much political embarrassment, as threats to the security of both itself and society. In a country with a recent history of violence and civil war, there is the possibility that an NGO might really be a front for a violent group, able to raise money once it has official recognition. The fear of 'political' NGOs in Tanzania and 'terrorist' NGOs in Uganda helps to explain why parliaments in both countries have passed legislation to monitor and restrict NGOs, details of which we shall examine in the next chapter.

As to the perspectives of the NGOs themselves, we have suggested that whatever representative function they are deemed to perform, they do not for the most part claim to represent the toiling masses against their oppressors. A minority, especially in Tanzania, are critical of the current global economic order, and campaign actively on matters such as debt relief and fair trade; but the majority are more pragmatic, taking the current order as given and doing what they can to improve the lot of the people within that order. In both countries access to the government appears to be remarkably easy, though access does not, in the majority of cases, mean that the NGOs get what they want. In Uganda, informal relations with politicians and bureaucrats are probably stronger, reflecting the smaller size of the country and the compactness of the educated elite. An NGO leader lobbying the government will often find an old school or university acquaintance on the other side of the desk. Yet the inchoate nature of the political system sometimes leads to more aggressive forms of confrontation, notably over the construction of the Bujagali Falls Dam and the proposal to destroy a large area of Mabira Forest to grow sugar. The latter case saw a rare demonstration in the streets of Kampala, with NGOs unable to contain the violent fringe.

The nature of 'civil society' is something we shall return to presently, but for the moment let us take it to mean the sum total of NGO and other 'non-governmental' activity, as opposed to the individual parts. It is now commonplace to hear observers of the political scene in Tanzania remark that the strength of civil society has grown rapidly since around 2003. By this they generally mean not merely that individual NGOs have become more effective but that the combined effect of NGO activity, possibly aided by academics and even the much maligned opposition parties, has been to make the state at all levels more accountable and sensitive to public scrutiny. The form of scrutiny may include local communities demanding to know why they had not received the resources allocated to them in the budget, or angry crowds heckling their MP over corruption in the local hospital. In

Uganda the trend appears to be in the same direction, but a few steps behind Tanzania. Uganda has not enjoyed the longer period of stability within which scrutiny and accountability could be institutionalised, though at a local level there was a sense in which civil society actually preceded formally structured local government, and elected councillors and public officials continue to face critical publics. At the national level the performance has been patchier but, as in Tanzania, there has been a noticeable tendency for citizens to stand up for themselves when they feel that their needs have been neglected. To take just one example, when a Chinese agency re-surfaced the main street in Fort Portal in a slipshod manner, there was an immediate protest from residents who insisted successfully that the work be done again. In earlier times, citizens would have been more likely to adopt a fatalistic attitude to such inadequate provision.

On subordination, or responsiveness, to external influence, Beetham *et al.*'s checklist on criteria for the effectiveness of democracy includes the question 'How free is the governance of the country from subordination to external agencies, economic, cultural or political?' (Beetham *et al.* 2002: 66). In the case of both countries, it would be tempting to answer 'not very'. Both face restrictions imposed by creditors and donors, and are frequently required to pursue free market policies such as privatisation and retrenchment of public spending, even though there is little public support for such policies and little evidence that they bring any benefits to society. Tanzania's apparent subordination is more visible in the sense that its timber, mineral and game wealth leave it open to deals with foreign businesses which often pay scant attention to the needs or wishes of local communities, as forests are destroyed, people in mining areas face eviction and suffer the effects of pollution, and the rights of foreigners hunting for 'sport' may conflict with the basic needs of hunter gatherers. Uganda has less to tempt the foreign investor, but the problems of establishing and maintaining order, especially in the north, has left the government heavily dependent on military aid. While it may merely have reflected President Museveni's personal preferences, his consistent support for United States foreign policy, including the invasion of Iraq, might also be seen as a necessary price to pay for resources to fight his own 'war on terror'.

Yet a more optimistic interpretation might be placed on the situation. East Africa is not on the front line of any global conflict, and there is therefore no need for external powers to impose rigid controls over what East African governments do. On issues such as the search for peace in the Congo and the Sudan, and for the settlement of ethnic conflicts in Burundi and Rwanda, there is no obvious divergence of views between the governments of Tanzania and Uganda and the Western powers; and when Uganda struck out on its own to invade the Congo, the West did little to stand in its way beyond admonition and hints of cuts in aid. One of Uganda's main cards has been its claim to have been a force for stability in Central Africa once Museveni had restored stability in his own country, and this has made Western governments reluctant to jeopardise that stability. They would have preferred an earlier return to multi-party politics, a constitution that limited presidents (and especially the current incumbent) to only two terms, tougher action against corruption and breaches of human rights, and the exclusion of Ugandan troops from the Congo. Some influence was wielded successfully through quiet diplomatic meetings, but a perusal of the actual outcomes might suggest that Uganda's 'subordination' was a lot less than total.

In Tanzania there have been fewer explicit divergences of ideas and interests than in Uganda. Sceptics might attribute this to a governmental acceptance that there is little alternative to subordination, and that the best that can be hoped for is to press as effectively as possible for whatever concessions are feasible. Politicians are as critical as any others in Africa of the current world economic order, but Tanzanian politics since the retirement of Nyerere in 1985 have had a somewhat 'bureaucratic' tinge as the country has grappled with the transition from a centralised socialist economy to a market economy sustained by foreign aid. With the failure of the former model, there has been little room for any ideological debate on any attempt to 'go it alone' or to stand up to global capitalism. Yet many Tanzanians would be affronted by the idea that politics is a matter of a subordinate country simply implementing whatever its masters imposed on it. Indeed the fact that so much of the time of politicians is taken up with negotiating the terms of aid and debt relief, rather than with any more rarefied political debate, may mean that political skills are honed more sharply in order to maximise whatever advantages can be gained.

We should also note, in the case of both Tanzania and Uganda, that subordination may be mitigated by politically correct notions of dependent countries becoming 'partners' in development, with donors now referred to as 'development partners'. Critics may argue that none of this makes any difference to the reality of dependency, and that some donors will continue to be explicit as to the limits of what they will support – Save the Children will continue to save children, but not support other projects outside that remit, no matter how worthy or popular. Neither can one wish away the continuation of aid with strings. What penalties will a country suffer if it rejects an arms deal that suits the donor country? Yet if donors (or 'development partners') continue to insist that they encourage African governments and NGOs to work out their own priorities, this may open the door to greater autonomy in reality as well as rhetoric.

One final problem with the 'subordination' issue is the philosophical question of what happens when it is the external agency that is seen as the supporter of democracy, and the indigenous government is defending its right to rig elections, intimidate the judiciary, abuse human rights or siphon off public resources into private pockets. This problem has manifested itself in the case of disputed elections in Zanzibar, where in 1995, 2000 and again in 2005 most observers agreed that the ruling party had lost, yet the Electoral Commission decreed otherwise. Foreign powers protested at what they saw as this violation of democracy, not only in the counting of votes but in the partisan use made of police power, and nominal cuts were made in aid as a punishment. The Tanzanian government responded that no outsider had a right to interfere in internal politics. Is the survival of the ruling party in Zanzibar a triumph for resistance to external control, or defeat for democracy? Broadly similar questions could be posed about President Museveni's ability to get the constitution amended to allow him to stand for a third term, in the face of widespread Western disapproval. Was his success a triumph for Ugandan autonomy or a defeat for democracy because it allowed an unhealthy concentration of power in the hands of one man? Perhaps the questions posed by Beetham *et al.* could be re-phrased along the lines of 'How receptive are the government and society to external attempts to enhance democracy?' or 'How far are the government and society able to resist external actions that diminish democracy?' Such questions would not resolve the problem of the variations placed on the term 'democracy', especially by interested parties, but it would allow for the fact that external powers may be promoters of democracy on some occasions, while undermining it on others. A strong case could be made (if one believed in democracy) that external pressure was justified in the case of Zanzibar because the wishes of the majority of the electorate were being flouted. On the other hand, Western demands that free market policies should be imposed regardless of the wishes of African governments or voters, or that public resources should be distributed in a particular way as a condition for aid, might be regarded as incursions on the democratic rights of voters and their elected representatives. If we re-phrased the questions in the ways suggested, how would Tanzania and Uganda fare? Tanzanians generally claim that they have been willing to explore the experiences of other countries in building multi-party democracy, but have not been the subject of external pressure. This is true up to a point, but it was ex-President Nyerere who was one of the first to realise, with the collapse of the Soviet Bloc, that if some form of pluralism was not adopted, it might well be imposed from outside. Western governments made no secret of their preference for multi-party politics. Mmuya and Chaligha recorded that in 1992 a meeting was held with would-be opposition politicians and representatives of most Western embassies to search for a common opposition front, with financial support provided by 'Western foreign agencies' (Mmuya and Chaligha 1992: 146). No explicit Western threats were made as to what would happen if the one-party system was preserved, but a mixture of prudence, and a feeling that the one-party regime had run its course, led to a transition to multi-party democracy. Tanzania was receptive to external influence to the extent that it now saw little alternative to the liberal democratic model. This was in contrast to the position of President Moi in Kenya who saw party competition as a recipe for violent ethnic conflict and clung to power for another decade, and to President Mugabe in Zimbabwe who appeared to equate opposition parties with Western imperialism.

In Uganda the receptiveness to external influence was more qualified. The period after 1986 was seen by political actors and observers alike not as a transition to democracy in the conventional sense, but as a completion of the process of liberation. Political participation was encouraged as a contribution to development, especially at the local level, but not as a means of criticising the regime or advocating its removal. The ruling politicians, we have suggested, saw their legitimacy as stemming from their role as liberators, and saw no need to confirm that legitimacy by holding multi-party elections. Western powers confined their criticisms mainly to demanding that any referendum on maintaining the no-party order should be conducted fairly, rather than to demanding that the order should give way to pluralism. In the event the consensus of observers was that the referendum was rigged, yet no effective external sanctions were brought to bear. When multi-politics were finally restored in 2003, it was the result of a High Court ruling rather than any immediate external pressure.

The nature of civil society

Having outlined the nature of Tanzanian and Ugandan politics, we now go on to look at the institutions with which NGOs interact, and at the relevance of this interaction to the scope for democracy. We shall look first at civil society as the arena within which NGOs operate, then in the next chapter look at the activities of NGOs themselves, and at the impact of the state and of external forces on NGO activity.

We begin with the crude assertion that NGOs are to civil society what political structures are to the political system. Structures such as political parties, legislatures, judiciaries or health authorities do not float in mid-air, but derive their character largely from the political system as a whole. Whether the system is authoritarian or democratic, centralised or decentralised, stable or unstable, will have an important bearing on how each institution works. Political parties in the centralised, authoritarian Soviet system clearly worked differently from parties in the federal, pluralist American system. The major problem when we examine the parallel relationship between NGOs and civil society is that while there is general agreement on what a political system is, civil society is much more of a contested concept. Like the wood carver who said he produced carved elephants by chipping away all the parts that did not look like an elephant, we could begin by chipping away all the parts of the social, political and economic order that 'are not civil society', and then hope to discover the fine detail. We can chip away most of the state and private sectors (though with some significant exceptions), as by definition they do not belong to the 'third sector'. We can also remove those parts of society which are not 'civil' society because they have little direct political significance, in that they do not seek to influence political events except intermittently. Families, sporting and cultural bodies, and customers in bars, generally belong to that part of society which is beyond the bounds of 'civil' society. But this negative approach still leaves us with many questions unanswered. Who belongs to civil society, and by what criteria do we include or exclude them? Having established who belongs to this entity, we then have to ask 'what does it do?'

Some of the arguments about qualifications for membership of civil society are suggested in Table 4.5. To begin with, there are challenges to the traditional notion that only voluntary groups qualify. This was for a long time the accepted view of civil society in the West, where commentators from de Tocqueville onwards celebrated the fact that

Table 4.5   Who Belongs to Civil Society?

Voluntary and/or non-voluntary groups?
Formally structured and/or informal groups?
Groups autonomous from the state and/or quasi-state groups?
Conservative and/or radical groups?

democracy rested on the willingness of citizens to participate in institutions that gave coherence to society. Flourishing churches, co-operative movements, residents' associations, Rotary Clubs, trade unions, youth groups and cultural groups ensured that there was an intermediate layer of activity between the state and the individual. Without it, the state would either rule in an arbitrary manner, in the absence of any groups to influence it or moderate it, or the state would be unable to rule at all in the absence of any means of public co-operation.

If one searches for an African civil society based on the Western 'voluntary' model, it is immediately obvious that Africa does not possess the proliferation of groups described above, which generally require a relatively educated, urbanised population with sufficient wealth, leisure and means of communication to keep voluntary groups functioning. This might lead to the conclusion that there is therefore no such thing as civil society in Africa, but merely traditional non-voluntary groups based on ethnicity, together with NGOs sustained by donor funds. Religious and professional groups might qualify as voluntary, but they would hardly be sufficient to sustain a civil society. But this puts an emphasis on what civil society is rather than what it does. If one is searching not for a replica of civil society in the nineteenth century United States but for whatever significant intermediaries exist between the state, in the narrow sense, and the individual, one could accept Lewis's view that civil society should not just comprise religious and professional groups, but also informal self-help groups which mistrust the state, and non-voluntary indigenous structures which were co-opted by the state in colonial times (Lewis 2002: 569–86). Karlstrom (in Comaroff and Comaroff 1999: 104–23) makes the point that the monarchy and clan system in Buganda was not part of any 'voluntary' sector in the sense that anyone could join or leave at will, yet it was the functional equivalent of a voluntary group in the West, to the extent that it contributed to the stability of the political process. Similarly the local government structure in Uganda is constitutionally part of the state, but the legitimacy of different councils depends heavily on the attitudes of local communities towards them. The distinction between state and society thus becomes blurred, as indeed it has in the West with the growth of quangos and similar bodies.

Much of the confusion might be avoided if there was less obsession with the word 'voluntary', and a recognition that there is a continuum between completely free choice and involuntary commitment. Anyone is free to join or leave Friends of the Earth at any time, whereas Baganda citizens living in the Kingdom of Buganda have no choice as to their ethnic identity, but there are many intermediate positions. Did citizens in medieval Europe have any choice as to whether they belonged to the Catholic Church? Did coal miners in mid-twentieth century Britain have any choice as to whether they belonged to the National Union of Mineworkers? In both cases a mixture of social pressures for conformity and sanctions against deviation (eternal damnation or the loss of one's job respectively) made membership less than purely voluntary.

In Africa much human activity tends towards the non-voluntary end of the continuum, though genuine voluntary NGOs obviously exist alongside this. In Tanzania, Gibbon suggests that the components of civil society include lineages, clans, age sets, elders' committees and women's credit groups, as well as more formalised entities that have shifted between the state and civil society such as co-operative societies, branches of political parties, village vigilante groups and local development organisations (Gibbon 2001: 819–44). What emerges in a search for African civil society is thus a mixture of the voluntary and involuntary, the structured and the informal, and the autonomous and the semi-autonomous. The key question in assessing whether a group or institution qualifies for membership of civil society is less 'What is its status?' than 'Does it contribute to the functioning of the political process between the state and the individual?'

This leads us on to the question 'What sort of contribution?' Howell and Pearce highlight the distinction between what we might call the conservative view of civil society as a means of maintaining an equilibrium in the political order, and the dynamic view of civil society as an institution for transforming the social and political order (Howell and Pearce 2001: 222–60). The conservative, and probably more widely accepted, view is that civil society acts as a 'societal invisible hand' where a moral order emerges. The free market and a minimal state are maintained, but civil society helps to keep capitalism socially responsible and checks any excesses of state power. The alternative model rejects the assumptions of harmony between state, market and society, and sees civil society as a means of mobilising populations to challenge global capitalism, especially by demanding debt reduction and fair trade. In reality, many civil society groups ignore these distinctions, and a given group may questioning the mis-spending of public money at one moment, while urging the government not to sign unfair trade agreements with the EU the next, but the distinction is useful in that it raises questions about one's expectations of civil society. Is it to be welcomed as a means of creating new democratic openings, or condemned as providing a front for the imposition of bourgeois democracy and free market economics? Or should radicals welcome it as the first instalment of political and economic emancipation which can eventually develop into something more ambitious? Within that civil society, are NGOs hamstrung by their dependence on donors, their elitist leadership and their alleged remoteness from the daily grind faced by the poor, or are they the only realistic means by which the lot of the ordinary citizen can be improved, taking one step at a time?

Both Howell and Pearce's and Lewis's models assume that civil society does have a collective impact on the political order, for good or ill. Whatever the background of the varied groups involved, they have the welfare of their constituents, or preferably the whole community, at heart. But if civil society is taken to cover the range of political activities between the state and the individual, does this not include tribalists, religious fundamentalists, party thugs, terrorists and criminals who channel bribes from foreign businesses to African politicians? There is a largely irresolvable disagreement between purists who take the word 'civil' to imply some sense of public duty, and who therefore believe that civil society should include the 'goodies' but exclude the 'baddies' (see especially Cox in Amoore 2005: 103–23), and those who accept that, in an imperfect world, the distinction is often a blurred one. Governments often have to negotiate with the baddies in order to keep the ship of state afloat, and circumstances sometimes make violence or criminality the only available means to desirable ends, as with the struggle against apartheid in South Africa. Apart from questions of vice and virtue, the inclusion of the elements hostile to the rest of the community challenges the notion that civil society performs a 'functional' role, whether in upholding a free market, pluralist order or in replacing it with something more equitable. A broader conception of the membership of civil society suggests that it can often be dysfunctional. Civil society in Kenya was often given credit for establishing multi-party democracy in the 1990s, as NGOs and churches pressed steadily for free elections and constitutional reform, but a darker side of civil society was seen after the disputed 2007 election when ethnic violence erupted and political parties were unwilling or unable to control events. In Uganda, the dispute over the destruction of a large area of Mabira Forest for sugar growing was not just a gentlemanly debate over conservation, but had some ugly and violent anti-Indian overtones, as the project was seen as an example of the government's willingness to give generous concessions to Indian businessmen.

How, then, are civil society in Tanzania and Uganda relevant to the different characteristics we have considered? Neither country, given their poverty and the smallness of the urban elites, possessed many voluntary, formally structured groups, in the Western sense, before the 1980s, and such formal 'autonomous' activities as existed depended heavily on the goodwill of the state. Indeed Tanzania between 1961 and the mid-1980s came close to the 'no such thing as civil society' model. Chiefs and ethnic groups had never been as powerful as in many other parts of Africa, and the centralised one-party regime was not philo- sophically inclined to encourage group activity outside the party struc- ture. The compulsory movement of most of the rural population into ujamaa villages weakened any incipient group activity still further. Uganda was a more difficult country on which to impose conformity, with Buganda seeking autonomy and other kingdoms and chiefdoms wanting some recognition if Buganda was to have special privileges, and the north often acting as a semi-detached part of the nation. With the breakdown of order in the early 1980s, civil society manifested itself in the form of self-help groups and, if one stretches the definition of civil society to the limits, in the form of the NRA and NRM taking the law into their own hands long before they captured the presidential palace.

Events after the mid-1980s suggested some convergence between the two countries. In Uganda the informal *de facto* wielders of local power became incorporated into the local government structure, though we have seen that the effectiveness of this still depended heavily on the extent of public consent, and not just constitutional power. In Tanzania the ruling party divested itself of most of its 'integral wings' with the approach of multi-party politics, and many of these were transformed into NGOs. In both countries, the Western demand for a larger non- governmental sector as a condition of aid led to a proliferation of NGOs, so that it was now tempting to see civil society as a territory occupied mainly by formally registered, donor-dependent, urban-based NGOs, with rural groups at the proverbial grassroots now having only a marginal importance. Why ask the question 'In what ways has civil society contributed to the nature of NGOs?' when for practical pur- poses NGOs are civil society? Yet we have cited enough local studies to suggest that the picture is not so simple. Within local communities a variety of groups have always found ways to defend and advance their interests. As political structures in Uganda have changed, from insur- gency to liberation under the Movement, to a nominally constitutional order, and from one-party rule to pluralism in Tanzania, there has always been an underlying civil society which has been sufficiently autonomous to use whatever means are to hand to fight political battles. Sometimes the battles are internal, as in the case of former party and state officials in Tanzania creating or hijacking NGOs to defend their previous gains, and sometimes they have been against the outside world, as pastoralists or people displaced by foreign mining companies, or opponents of the Bujagali Falls Dam have created, or enlisted the support of, NGOs.

At the national level at least three aspects of civil society can be highlighted as shaping the framework within which NGOs operate. First, unlike more troubled parts of Africa, there is almost unanimous acceptance of the existence of the nation and its boundaries, or at worst virtually no opposition to it. Uganda, with its disputes over the status of Buganda, or the alleged neglect of the north, might be expected to harbour secessionist tendencies, yet Logan *et al.* found that 96 per cent of the population believed that 'Uganda should remain united as one country' (Logan *et al.* 2003: 46). In Tanzania outside Zanzibar, such a question is hardly worth asking, given the absence of regional or ethnic conflict. The acceptance of national boundaries means that NGOs can focus on lobbying their own government without the complications of trying to subvert it at the same time, or of building links with a foreign government with which they have a greater affinity. One could contrast this with the position of NGOs in the Southern Sudan, which may have little respect for the government in Khartoum, and be accorded little respect by it.

Secondly we can look at the process by which the evolution on NGOs was facilitated. While it is tempting to see them as alien bodies that have appeared as a result of Western demands for a slimmer state, and donor offers of cash, their evolution and survival needs to be examined at least partly in terms of the extent to which political actors were willing to develop NGOs as the best means of advancing their interests or the interests of their perceived constituents. In Uganda we have noted that civil society, in the sense of informal groups fighting for day-to-day survival, largely preceded both the formal local government structure created by Museveni, and the rise of formal NGOs which could build on the earlier experiences of self-reliance and improvisation. In Tanzania the rise of NGOs owed less to self-help groups in the bush and more to the dismantling of the all-embracing one-party state. This was not simply a matter of decreeing that a women's group or a youth group that is a wing of the party today shall be an NGO tomorrow. It also required a collection of attitudes, beliefs and skills that existed within society. The society that evolved over the previous

30 years had, for all its faults, left the country with a tradition of public participation, public service and a range of administrative skills. Some of the participation was based on noble motives, some on thoughts of status or material gain. Some of the personnel running NGOs had previously held office in the party; others had not. But one could argue that an established civil society provided a culture on which NGOs could build.

Our third consideration is the sort of attitudes to authority that civil society had fostered. Tanzania under one-party rule had a reputation as a well ordered country where people fatalistically accepted whatever was decided from on high. Van Donge and Liviga describe the public response to the radical shift in the early 1980s from a centrally planned economy to a free market.

> [The policy changes] were never presented as diverging from the road to socialism that Tanzania had taken. There was very little public debate about them nor any recriminations about what had happened in the past. These major changes were made in a political culture of consensus that is so typical of Tanzania (Van Donge and Liviga 1989: 48).

Yet if there was little challenge to national policy, Tanzanians had acquired by the 1980s, if not earlier, an ability to bend or break the law if it stood in the way of their immediate needs. No party ideologue prevented the emergence of a flourishing black market when the planned economy failed to meet the people's needs, and few private bus conductors have been inhibited by safety regulations from cramming their buses to the physical limit. What has been more interesting in recent years has been the willingness of civil society, in its various manifestations, to demand accountability from the state. There may still be little challenge to actual policies, but there have been growing demands that communities should receive the budgetary allocations voted by Parliament, and that those politicians and officials who have diverted these allocations elsewhere should be pursued. While it is a common complaint that the bigger corrupt fish never get caught, the pursuit of corruption had by 2008 actually brought charges against a major participant in the Tanzanian purchase of the expensive air defence system from British Aerospace (BAe) (*Tanzanian Affairs*, January–April 2008: 3). At a lower level, there were vocal protests against alleged corruption in the police service and in a local hospital, and against the eviction without compensation of residents to make way for a foreign mining firm (*ibid*: 8). These assertions of citizen power did not, for the most part, come from NGOs, but either from spontaneous protests from citizens or from opposition parties. This would suggest that while NGOs have done much to encourage citizens to stand up for their rights, there is also an underlying trend in the wider civil society to demand that the state and its officials act within the law, and in the interests of the citizens they serve. If that interpretation is correct, then civil society now provides a more propitious base from which NGOs can use their distinctive skills to press for yet more accountability.

In Uganda similar trends can be detected. Again NGOs have often set the pace in challenging authority, and a wider civil society has responded by gaining confidence and learning the necessary skills; but again there has been a change in public attitudes that cannot simply be attributed to a mechanical process of applying the guidelines set out in an NGO instruction manual. Society as a whole, and not just the minority who belong to NGOs, has become more assertive, whether it is over street repairs in Fort Portal or the preservation of Mabira Forest. A recent survey found that 81 per cent of Ugandans had participated in at least one form of collective community activity during the previous year, and 80 per cent had attended community meetings (Civicus 2006: 27). The reasons for this greater assertiveness in the two countries are largely a matter for speculation. We might be witnessing the much trumpeted but seldom seen 'democratic consolidation' that is supposed to follow the initial transition to democracy. If voting is a useful safety valve against arbitrary government, but produces few changes in policy or administration, citizens may at least press their masters to carry out what they have said they will do, and to apply the laws they have passed and the budgetary allocations they have voted.

The greater assertiveness might be explained partly in terms of learning from experience, so that groups learn which strategies to adopt on the basis of past successes and failures. There may also be a feeling on the part of ruling politicians that, despite the current electoral arithmetic, indefinite electoral success is not guaranteed, and that they must therefore be more responsive from pressures from civil society. This view came across in many interviews in both countries. Modern technology helps, as computers can be used to produce campaign material and email can be used to alert activists. Local radio stations, which have proliferated over the past decade, have also been important, with phone-in programmes enabling citizens to grill politicians and officials, and even NGO leaders.

Our explanation of (or search for) civil society has, like the search for the Loch Ness monster, presented us with a dual problem. We have to persuade the sceptics that it exists, and then we need some notion of what it looks like should we find it. The argument has been that the creature will not necessarily look attractive, and will not necessarily correspond in appearance with apparently similar species on other continents, but that it nonetheless exists and its existence is important to the whole political ecology. We argued that a range of groups comprise civil society, and that it is not helpful to exclude some of them because they are not 'voluntary', not 'autonomous from the state' or generally unpleasant because they hold divisive, extremist views or indulge in crime or violence. If our concern is to understand the ways in which the scope for NGOs may be advanced, constrained, or diverted in some directions rather than others, we need to look at civil society in the round. Using a broad interpretation of the term, we have suggested that it includes self-help groups, age sets and elders' committees as well as registered NGOs; quasi-state institutions as well as voluntary bodies, sinners as well as saints, and (though many would disagree) the Lord's Resistance Army as well as Save the Children.

Civil society in Tanzania and Uganda begins with some negative advantages from the point of view of facilitating the rise of NGOs. There are few widely held political or religious dogmas that question the legitimacy of NGO activity in general, or of particular types of NGO. Few Muslims question the rights of Christian NGOs, or *vice versa*, the rights of women to organise their own NGOs is generally accepted, as are the rights of NGOs that criticise the current global order, even if it allegedly means biting the hand that feeds Africa. On the more positive side, despite the contrasting history of the two countries, there is a long tradition of political participation which can be harnessed by NGOs. Even at the height of one-party rule in Tanzania, intra-party elections could see the incumbent MP, or even ministers, defeated if they neglected their often vociferous constituents. Such issues as the neglect of local social services or permits for corrugated iron sheets for church roofs could determine the fate of an MP (Mvungi and Mhina in Othman *et al.* 1990: 103–20; Migiro in *ibid*: 182–201). With the end of one-party rule, the participation could flow into other channels and especially into NGOs. In Uganda the participation had been more diffuse, with an almost collapsed state in the early 1980s, rather than a centralised party-state, driving people to work together to ensure survival, and then development. When donor pressure subsequently called for more formally structured NGOs, these were not imposed from outside, as in Iraq, but were constructed from the foundations which civil society had provided. There was then, to change the analogy, a danger of the NGO tail wagging the civil society dog, with NGOs acting as the primary intermediary between state and individual. NGOs certainly gained a momentum of their own, both in holding the state to account and in encouraging the wider citizenry to participate, but donor funding and skilled leadership alone would not explain the success of NGOs. While competitive elections have provided a nominal outlet for democratic participation, the survival of the ruling party has seldom been in doubt, and the limited alternatives opposition policies offered have seldom fired the imagination. Such influences as civil society has on political outcomes have been more in scrutinising the executive and, urging it to implement its declared policies and enforce the laws it initiated. Here, there has been a largely spontaneous growth in the pressures that civil society has exerted since the early years of the twenty-first century. NGOs, like a surfer, have ridden the wave with some panache, but the wave has come from civil society.

An obverse consequence of civil society's emphasis on scrutinising the executive rather than voting or campaigning for alternative policies and parties, has been that NGOs operate in an environment in which the ends of government policy are taken as given. This is in contrast to much of Europe in the early twentieth century when large sections of civil society, including trade unions, co-operatives, learned societies and social democratic parties envisaged a different social order, while other sections of society showed equal enthusiasm for defending the *status quo*. Such a contrast with present day Africa is understandable, given the nature of the current global order and Africa's dependence on it, but it means that African politics consists largely of the scrutiny of the executive we have described, patron-client relations to extract such resources from the state as are available, and a series of single issue campaigns on matters as diverse prawn farming, forest conservation and the welfare of street children. The first, and more especially the third, of these are very much NGO territory. Some NGOs, we have seen, do have views on social justice and the global order, and may even have opportunity to lobby international institutions, but seeking limited influence is still a far cry from seeking power to serve the needs of the poor. As we go on to look at the NGOs themselves in more detail, we need to bear in mind not only the positive aspects of civil society which have encouraged political participation and a vigorous defence of citizens' rights, but also the constraints of an apparently immutable political order. Civil society for the most part accepts the current government and its policies as given for the fore-seeable future. There are few political parties or social movements, if any, with which NGOs could link to campaign for radical change. Civil society has furnished NGOs with many advantages, but in the last resort it is a base from which they can advance, rather than an infantry that can advance with them.

5
Democracy Without Votes II: NGOs, Governments and the Outside World

The nature of NGOs in Tanzania and Uganda

There is no lack of literature on the shortcomings of NGOs in Tanzania and Uganda. It is said that they are, for the most part, non-political and concentrate mainly on service provision (Chachage in Bujra and Adejumobi 2002: 145; Mercer 2002: 5–22). The urban-based NGOs which might be expected to have broader horizons are inadequately organised to have any great impact in rural areas (Kelsall in Barrow and Jennings 2001: 140; Michael 2004: 73). NGOs are heavily dependent on donor funds, which amount to 80–86 per cent of their income (Barr *et al.* 2005: 675; Bazaara in Ghimire 2005: 132–61; Dicklitch and Lwanga 2003: 482–509; Oloka-Onyango *et al.* 1996: 194). Dicklitch and Lwanga spell out a detailed argument that the activities of human rights NGOs in Uganda are distorted by donor dependence, so that the focus is more on innocuous activities such as conferences on the virtues of fair elections, than on getting to grips with the reality of human rights abuses.

Donor dependence in the literature often shades into dependence on African governments. These are able to tame NGOs through their ability to award or withhold contracts. It is often implied that African governments and foreign donors are on the same side of the ideological fence. Governments accept aid and loans which may benefit politicians but are detrimental to African society, and donors are willing to ignore the more illiberal activities of African governments rather than risk losing allies or outlets for trade and investment. Beyond governments and donors lies the spectre of international financial institutions (IFIs) which, even if they have moderated their free market fundamentalism, still impose conditions for aid and debt relief that few people in

Africa want. One Tanzanian NGO discovered a leaked document which revealed 30 conditions imposed for one aid package, including the privatisation of electricity (Holtom 2007: 241–2). In such an environment, the scope for innovation by governments, let alone NGOs, is clearly limited. Finally, NGOs stand condemned for failing to practice what they preach by neglecting internal democracy. Kelsall suggested that NGOs in Tanzania brought little development or democracy (Kelsall in Barrow and Jennings 2001: 133–480), while Barr *et al.* questioned the extent to which Ugandan NGOs' formal accountability to members worked in practice. The publication of annual reports was often lax, and accounting information was of poor quality. 'Only a small number of NGOs circulated figures and reports that are sufficiently detailed, accurate and up-to-date to enable members to perform a real oversight role' (Barr *et al.* 2005: 674).

At the opposite extreme to the literature on the inadequacy of NGOs there are ample examples of NGOs proclaiming their belief in the transformation of society. They envisage equality, social justice and democratic participation at home, and a benign world order of fair trade. They advocate an end to the debt burden and to the destruction of the world's natural resources. Neither do they lack confidence in their own ability to contribute to such a transformation. The Tanzania Gender Networking Programme (TGNP) has a long record of taking a stand against foreign imposed free market policies and the international debt burden. It has spoken against 'the high income business class' enjoying 'a perpetual tax holiday' or evading taxes (*The Guardian*, Dar es Salaam, 5 June 2007: 5), and it has condemned the depletion of national resources caused by structural adjustment programmes (SAPs) (TGNP 2004: 2). Also in Tanzania, the objectives of HakiKazi Catalyst are:

[To] promote the rights of all the people to fully participate in social, technical, environmental and economic decisions that affect their lives. We support vulnerable people by facilitating a process that gives them an effective voice, 'the right to say' which enables them to work towards:

- Reducing poverty.
- Achieving sustainable livelihoods through social, civil and economic rights.
- Enjoying equality with others at community, national and international levels.

HakiKazi Catalyst also supports CSOs [civil society organisations] by providing social processing skills, training, advice and advocacy ...

We work to generate a common understanding of the implications of policy for livelihoods and local opportunities. This includes up-streaming community feedback into decision-making processes at local and national level.

We actively participate in civil society networks at local and national level. We also network with faith-based organisations, research institutions, academia and trade unions, as well as government and donor community (HakiKazi Catalyst 2004).

(The texts of the above and subsequent documents are reproduced in their original form, including minor grammatical blemishes.)

Another Tanzanian NGO also emphasised community participation to transform society.

HakiElimu seeks to broaden public participation and influence education policy making through a programme of research, analysis, advocacy and networking. We facilitate the involvement of wider set of people in national policy formulation and building alliances and developing joint actions with other CSOs (HakiElimu n/d).

In Uganda the Development Network of Indigenous Voluntary Organisations (Deniva) and the Kabarole Research Centre (KRC) both emphasise participation and social equality.

Deniva ... is a Ugandan Network of Non-Governmental and Community Based Organisations providing a platform for collective action and voice to voluntary local associations to strongly advocate for creation of more opportunities for people and NGO participation in the development of Uganda.

Deniva's specific objectives include:

Creating a platform of indigenous/local NGOs/CBOs [community based organisations] to influence poverty eradication and good governance policies and processes in favour of the poor and marginalised (Deniva n/d).

The KRC's integral approach to development is geared towards the transformation of the social, political and economic spheres of the people in the Rwenzori region and Uganda at large. It involves the grass root communities in identifying their needs, designing possible solutions, monitoring and assessing their progress. This trend of development promotes ownership, and therefore a more sustainable and cost effective approach in addressing the poverty situation in the Rwenzori region (KRC 2007: 1).

The conflicting perspectives on the nature of NGOs are not necessarily incompatible. One can be selective in the examples one cites, and one can either focus on what is typical, or on what is untypical but politically significant. The typical NGO in East Africa, if such an entity exists, is probably confined to a small locality, and concerned with immediate practical problems such as the needs of small farmers, AIDs victims, street children, peasants denied access to the land, or the victims of family violence. The typical NGO is unlikely to perceive its mission in the grand terms quoted above, but to pursue the art of the possible in a world where local, national and global elites, and market forces, impose severe constraints. Its aims are modest and, given these constraints, it may have plenty to be modest about. Its activities may provide a wealth of material for studies of the local distribution of power, and sometimes of links between this and the national political arena. The typical NGO may contain a minority of (sometimes more educated) members who have clear views on the injustices in the world around them, and their causes and remedies, but preaching on these matters is unlikely to be seen as relevant or effective. If one is looking at the typical NGO, or the majority of NGOs, there is much to support a sceptical view of their political relevance, even if one admires their dedication and such success as they achieve in helping their target groups.

Yet a more fruitful approach might be to move away from the 'typical' and to focus more on the extent to which a minority of NGOs have sought to achieve social and political transformation, and in the process possibly opening the door to a greater politicisation of the third sector as a whole. Can the grand objectives we have cited be translated into political action? Three overlapping strategies are often followed. First, NGOs try to make the relevant public aware of current issues, whether it is the effects of the budget on people's livelihoods, the misuse of resources in education or the likely consequences of a proposed international trade agreement. Secondly, NGOs conduct surveys to seek out people's views on these issues, which are then fed back to local and national political leaders. Thirdly, NGOs encourage the participation of a wider community to campaign for changes in policy, or for the more competent or honest implementation of existing policies. In discussing these strategies, it is difficult to distinguish between the activities of indigenous NGOs and international NGOs (INGOs). The latter obviously have more resources, yet may suffer the handicap of being treated by authority as less legitimate, or even of trying to foist alien demands on a sovereign government. But for all these differences, many INGOs with bases in Africa are largely autonomous and are staffed largely by Africans, while some of the more radical indigenous NGOs employ expatriates who can give an extra cutting edge to political debate, and especially to the need to challenge elite power.

Disseminating information is important in largely illiterate societies, where for years the main sources of information had been state officials, ruling party activists and state radio. HakiElimu disseminated information in 2005 on the discrepancy between official accounts of educational provision in Tanzania and what it saw as the reality of the misuse of resources (HakiElimu 2005: 2–3). HakiKazi has a regular practice of disseminating information to local communities in Tanzania 'in simple form', especially on the impact of national budgets (HakiKazi Catalyst 2004). In Uganda, Oxfam convened public meetings in Kampala to 'raise awareness' of inadequate help for the poor in public spending, and on the impact of the proposed economic partnership agreements (EPAs) with the EU on Uganda (Oxfam 2006: 9).

Surveys then facilitate a public response. The Policy Forum in Tanzania invited the population to offer its views on the causes of, and possible solutions to, poverty, and received over 30,000 replies, most of which emphasised policies on health, education and employment as solutions. Oxfam gathered responses from farmers in Uganda after distributing information on the likely effects of the EPAs (Oxfam 2006: 9). HakiKazi organised meetings with village residents on the 2005 budget which enabled residents to argue that resources were not being allocated fairly, and that single and widowed women, children, orphans, youth, elderly people and people with AIDs would have difficulty in accessing basic services (Mbilinyi and Rusimbi 2005: 627–30).

The final stage is to mobilise other NGOs and/or a sufficiently broad section of the community in the hope of influencing authority. Oxfam worked with other NGOs to urge the Ugandan Ministry of Trade to halt the implementation of a trade policy which had been developed with the 'assistance' of the EU, and which involved a free market approach that would, they argued, have damaging effects for farmers across the country (Oxfam 2006: 11). HakiElimu claimed to have won the support of virtually all CSO networks, including teachers and the press, in demanding that the government should acknowledge and rectify the weaknesses in education that had been revealed, including large class sizes, incompetent and drunken teachers, and the existence of schools without teachers. HakiElimu stimulated participation by getting some local groups to take over its role in monitoring and gaining access to information. This had the advantage not only of demonstrating the existence of wider public support, but of making it more difficult to close the campaign down as the numbers of centres of resistance grew (HakiElimu 2005: 36–7). In other cases broader participation from civil society had come about more spontaneously, but with NGOs able to use their campaigning skills and expertise to provide a degree of leadership. The successful campaigns to prevent encroachment on Mabira Forest and to prevent prawn farming in the Rufiji Delta took this form, as did the unsuccessful campaign against the Bujagali Falls Dam.

When it comes to global issues, it is more difficult to mobilise civil society than it is on issues where there is an immediately visible impact on people's lives, but it is still remarkable that a hard core of NGOs combine local campaigning with a critique of the global order and with pressure on MPs, governments and international bodies for a change of approach. The TGNP reported that President Mkapa had urged it and other NGOs to put more pressure on IFIs to make them recognise that their policies were making poor countries poorer (TGNP 2004: 2). The Tanzanian Association of NGOs (TANGO) has pressed international bodies on the question of fair trade, and has worked with Oxfam in fighting EPAs; and even a local NGO in Fort Portal has organised a 'stop EPAs campaign' targeting MPs, and working closely with Oxfam and other NGOs (Imanishimwe 2007: 15).

The results of this campaigning are generally less spectacular than the campaigns themselves, as is normally the way in pressure group politics. What difference did millions of anti-war protesters make to events in Iraq? It is seldom easy to persuade governments to change their policies, especially when they are governments facing little opposition challenge. Yet we have suggested that the political processes in Tanzania and Uganda today are very different from what they were a decade ago. There is a greater public willingness to question what is being done, and to question the version of events offered by politicians. To expect an African NGO to take on the World Bank or the EU and win may be unrealistic, but even these institutions are having to go through the motions of consultation and proclaiming concern for the needs of the poor. At a national level, scrutiny of governmental behaviour is becoming an accepted part of the political process. HakiElimu was exceptional with the skill with which it contrasted the government's optimistic version of what was happening in education with the reality on the ground, but more modest NGOs can still point out discrepancies between communities' local budgetary allocations and what they are actually receiving, or can show that policies allegedly designed to help the poor are actually doing no such thing. A survey in Uganda by the American NGO Civicus reported an increasing government willingness to consult Ugandan NGOs and civil society organisations (CSOs).

> CSOs have been given the opportunities to participate in national debates and programmes. Thus, Government welcomed their participation in PEAP [the Poverty Eradication Assessment Programme] ... and in a series of nationwide Participatory Poverty Assessments ... CSOs have recently engaged with the government Plan for Modernisation of Agriculture ... (Civicus 2006: 49).
>
> NGOs are increasingly involved in trilateral meetings with donors and government on major policy priorities. The voice of civil society is beginning to be heard more loudly on issues, including human rights, basic needs and people's marginalisation. Some networks and coalitions are proving to be effective in this respect, providing members with fora through which the collective consensus of organisations can be expressed to policy makers and others ... Taking a medium term perspective, there is some evidence that opportunities are growing for influencing government (*ibid*: 85).

In the end a variety of concessions, if only minor ones, are made in response to NGO pressure, or civil society pressure in general. Why should this be when we are taught that countries with Westminster style constitutions, as opposed to the American model with its checks and balances, are 'elective dictatorships', and that in the African context the 'elective' element is largely a formality? We shall look at the governments' perspectives in more detail in the next section, but we note two points here. Firstly, ruling politicians tend to get frightened of losing elections even when, to an outsider, the possibility seems remote. And even if the party survives defeat, the individual MP may not. It is therefore prudent to be seen to take some notice of public opinion, and to claim the credit for rectifying faults in policy and administration which NGOs have highlighted. Secondly, there is a democratic myth in both Tanzanian and Ugandan politics, however ill-defined, which implies showing some respect for public opinion. Government is not based on divine right, ideological wisdom, conquest or military prowess, though there is a residual element of the latter in Uganda, but on some notion of the need for public support. HakiElimu may have been a nuisance, but the government ultimately perceived a duty to talk to it and listen to its arguments. Destroying a large portion of Mabira Forest posed few practical problems for a government with a large majority, but the constant drip of public pressure and unfavourable publicity may have led to the conclusion that the wishes of the public should take precedence over those of one businessman.

This still leaves the question of how far public opinion should be equated with what an NGO demands, and why the government, or any other interested party, should recognise the legitimate right of an NGO to represent public opinion. There are certainly ample justifications (or excuses) for not doing so, which governments will be happy to wheel out when it suits them. The NGO comprises only a small group of people, and represent virtually no one else. It is a foreign-based organisation, or depends on foreign funds, and has no right to infringe the sovereignty of the government. It is a front for an opposition party, and lacks the courage to take on the government through the ballot box. Or, in extreme cases, NGOs should concentrate on service provision and have no business to indulge in politics. When an NGO or INGO challenges a deal between an African government and a foreign business, the chase may be joined by businesses, foreign governments and foreign journalists who support the right of global capital to bring the benefits of Western civilisation to Africa. *The Economist* (23 September 2004) criticised 'single issue fanatics in the West [who ensure that] fewer dams, roads and flood barriers are built in poor countries. More people stay poor, live in darkness and die younger' (quoted by Majot in Jordan and van Tuijl 2006: 223).

Yet it is clear that in practice African governments are in regular contact with a variety of NGOs. This is partly a matter of everyday necessity, rather than any philosophical commitment to democratic participation, as NGOs have the resources, expertise, and sometimes links with civil society, that governments lack. But there is also some acceptance of the view that a government which ignored NGOs would be acting in an arbitrary manner, ignoring one of the few means by which the voice of civil society can be heard. Any African government that is hesitant may be reminded, especially by foreign governments providing aid, of the currently fashionable notions of 'good governance' which include the participation, if not the 'empowerment', of civil society.

Majot's account of the National Association of Professional Environmentalists (NAPE) in Uganda provides a useful illustration of the conflicting views on the legitimate rights of an NGO to influence policy (Majot in Jordan and van Tuijl 2006: 211–28). NAPE was one of the most forceful opponents of the proposed Bujagali Falls Dam. It attracted the support of the International Rivers Network, an American NGO which had incurred the wrath of *The Economist* for being among the 'single issues fanatics in the West' that opposed many dams in poor countries. But challenges to the legitimate credentials of opponents of the dam did not stop at this foreign interloper. NAPE had only 25 members and, in the view of the Ugandan government and its supporters, had no business to stand in the way of an elected government. NAPE's defence was that it did not just represent 25 individuals. It was involved in a large environmental network of over a thousand organisations, it belonged to the NGO Forum (an umbrella organisation claiming to represent all NGOs in Uganda), and it served on various governmental and inter-governmental committees. The implication appeared to be that NAPE's legitimacy depended not on just the size of its membership, but on its extensive roots and branches. Its interaction with these other bodies, and the exchange of views and knowledge that this involved, presumably added to both NAPE's expertise and to the volume and variety of anti-dam groups that it could now claim to represent.

The battle against the dam was lost, but the study illustrates the weapons that an NGO can deploy to invoke its legitimacy. Governments wanting to get their own way may not be over concerned with philosophical arguments about who has the right to be heard or heeded, but they may need some rule of thumb as to who is to be treated as a legitimate participant, and who is an outsider at best or a subversive at worst. In the extreme case of Singapore, virtually all NGOs are regarded as beyond the pale, and tight regulations restrict the establishment of NGOs to apparently harmless 'non-political' bodies, on the assumption that only the elected government is qualified to judge the wisdom of any policy (Pinkney 2005: 134–5, 139–40). In the absence of any need for foreign aid, there are no donors to put the government right on the virtues of good governance. Tanzania and Uganda are clearly different. NGOs that overstep the mark and are perceived to be attacking the government as a whole, rather than attacking specific policies, may face temporary suspension, as with HakiElimu in 2005 and the Tanzanian women's group BAWATA in the 1990s. Groups suspected of promoting crime, terrorism, foreign subversion or personal enrichment will obviously not be permitted. But beyond these cases there has been a general acceptance of a place for NGOs in the political order. As in most countries, the prospect of success will depend heavily on the place in the pecking order of the groups they claim to represent. At one end of the chain, the Wildlife Conservation Society of Tanzania and the Ugandan Law Society have impeccable claims to be heard, as everyone in principle favours the rule of law and preserving flora and fauna. At the other, pastoralist groups and residents affected adversely by government deals with foreign mining companies, are more likely to find that their claims are given a low priority, but few groups are denied a voice altogether. For the most part NGOs, for all their differences in size, expertise and ideology, are accepted as a legitimate part of the political process, unless governments can persuade themselves that the NGOs have transgressed the written or unwritten rules of the game.

Governmental perspectives on NGOs

We move on from a focus directly on NGOs to a focus more on governments as actors in their own right, with their own policies, priorities and interests to defend in the face of growing NGO activity. We ask three overlapping questions. Firstly, what are the main ideals and priorities of these governments? Secondly, what have governments been doing that might bring them into conflict with NGOs? Thirdly, how have governments responded to the growth of NGO activity?

It is easy to portray African governments as amoral institutions presiding over neo-patrimonial systems within which ruling politicians lead a life of luxury, dispense patronage to friends, relatives and cronies, and leave the poor to struggle along as best they can. President Mobutu in the Congo (Zaire), Emperor Bokassa in the Central African Republic, a succession of military rulers in Nigeria, and even President Moi in Kenya and General Amin in Uganda, can be used to provide colourful illustrations of this model, but Tanzania and post-1986 Uganda have never been quite like that.

Ever since independence, Tanzania has had a long tradition of welfare provision for the masses and frugality for the rulers. The Arusha Declaration of 1967 laid down strict rules to prevent party and government officials from owning shares, holding company directorships, receiving more than one salary or becoming landlords (Cleary 1989: 16). The rules were relaxed by the 1990s, by which time the puritanical socialism of Nyerere had given way to free market capitalism, but there are still relatively few ostentatious displays of wealth, and we saw in Table 4.3 that the percentage of the GDP going to the poorest 20 per cent of the population (7.1) compared favourably with 5.7 in Uganda and 6.1 in Britain. Many ruling politicians insist that they still believe in Nyerere's socialist objectives, but that circumstances force them to follow a different route to the desired destination. Myths of egalitarianism and popular participation persist, even if they are not always matched by reality.

President Museveni began his career working with Southern African freedom fighters in Dar es Salaam, and some of the socialist ideology may have rubbed off on him. In his autobiography he emphasises his belief in participatory democracy, and by implication in an egalitarian order, even within the National Resistance Army (NRA). Soldiers did not obey orders passively, but had the opportunity to contribute their views on the actions to be taken (Museveni 1998: 176). As in Tanzania rulers insisted that basic beliefs in development, participation and equality remain intact, but that market forces are the only immediate means to the desired end.

An examination of what actually happens in Tanzanian and Ugandan politics raises questions of how far governments have moved from the initial ideals. Retaining power now requires winning votes in contested elections. The constraints of the global order prevent any significant choices between rival policies, so winning votes requires more direct offers of benefits to voters, as well as generous funding from wealthy backers, who themselves expect concrete benefits in return for their generosity. An elite of party and state officials, and indigenous and foreign businesses, becomes consolidated and is indeed indispensable to the whole political edifice. In Tanzania fundamental economic activities like mining, timber extraction and tourism become not simply engines of economic development, but means of consolidating elite power, often to the detriment of the rest of society. An NGO report in 2006 revealed that 85 to 90 per cent of Tanzania's timber was exported illegally (thus evading taxes), with the implication that politicians had been complicit in the process (TNRF 2006: 6). The 1999 Land Law encouraged individual rather than communal land ownership, to the benefit of existing landowners and to the detriment of pastoralists. Hunting rights were awarded to the Saudi Royal Family in the Loliondo and Yaida Valleys, with few concessions to peasants living in the areas. If many NGOs claim to have emerged to protect the interests of the poor, these developments suggest a likely clash of interests, to which we shall return.

In Uganda the natural wealth is less abundant, and there has not been such a long history of one party dominating the political scene. The political order is more fluid but, if anything, that makes the need to win or retain the allegiance of elite groups even more crucial. The process by which this is done is often more blatant than in Tanzania. The World Bank was critical of the way the President's brother acquired Uganda's state owned bank, and then arranged for substantial loans from it to companies which he owned (Watt *et al.* 1999: 49). There were few constraints on the looting of resources by soldiers during their occupation of the Congo, and we have seen that a large portion of Mabira Forest narrowly escaped destruction for the benefit of one businessman. The maintenance of the support of the army remains essential to the government, and the army exploits this dependence by putting its own interpretation on its constitutional position.

None of this is to argue that Tanzania and Uganda have departed from some elevated egalitarian, participatory social democracy. Power has always been distributed unequally and, in many ways elites were previously subject to less accountability and scrutiny than they are today. But today there is a combination of a more visible elite receiving visible favours from politicians, and a freer political environment of revelation, criticism, and sometimes formal scrutiny. This combination enables NGOs to lead the charge against what they see as social injustice, violations of constitutional democracy and the misuse of resources. How, then, are governments to respond to potential collisions between their own desire to protect their power bases, and the desire of NGOs to redress grievances and pursue a more just social order? If NGOs were given unlimited freedom, some of them would be likely to offer damning critiques of the way the country was being run, but beyond that there have been fears that if any group is free to call itself an NGO, there could be a general destabilisation. How could one be sure that a given NGO was not subverting the government, acting as a front for foreign governments or businesses, or extracting money for private gain? In Uganda there was the influence of practical experience as well as fears for the future. In 2000 the leader of a formally registered NGO, run by a religious sect, deliberately started a fire that killed over a hundred members of the sect, apparently as a form of religious sacrifice. In the north, NGOs had provided much of what basic administration there had been at the height of the war against the Lord's Resistance Army (LRA), and were often reluctant to hand the administration back to the public sphere once the war was over. In everyday politics the less subtle use of corruption and patronage, compared with Tanzania, left room for NGOs as unwelcome watchdogs if they were not at least partially muzzled. The government's main response to concerns such as these was the 2006 NGO Act.

The Act provided several means by which the government could deal with troublesome NGOs. Not only do they have to register, but they require permits in order to operate. Whether as a result of limited administrative capacity or deliberate foot dragging, the issue of a permit could become a long drawn out process, with the possibility of hints that it might be issued sooner if the NGO toned down some of the activities which displeased the government. The Act also introduced the principle of 'dual liability', which meant that staff could be held legally responsible for the activities of their NGOs, with the possibility of out-of-favour NGO leaders suffering personal liability (including financial liability) if a pretext could be found for taking them to court. The Act as a whole appears to be a powerful sledgehammer to crack any nut that gets in the government's way. A comparable Act was passed in Tanzania in 2002 which was more explicit in indicating that NGOs should conform to a view of the world held by the government. NGOs are required to harmonise their activities to conform to the national development plan, with the implication that criticisms or suggestions of alternatives to the plan could get the NGO into legal difficulties. The requirement 'to respect all traditions that are not against the law' again might suggest a need to conform to values or practices with which many would disagree, such as corporal or capital punishment, or even the values of a capitalist economy. There are also requirements, such as the need to submit audited accounts, which might seem sensible but which would put a strain on smaller NGOs run by less educated people (Kajege 2003: 98–9). In neither country has the legislation been invoked in a dramatic manner, but it is the tone and intention of it that is significant. NGOs are accepted as a legitimate part of the political landscape, but in the last resort it is the government, through its specific legislation, that has the right to set the boundaries as to what an NGO may do, rather than assuming that NGOs are collections of individuals who can act freely as long as their actions are within the general law of the land.

Beyond passing laws to provide an arsenal of weapons against troublesome NGOs as the ultimate deterrent, governments need more refined weapons to defend themselves against the steady advance of NGO activity. Yet at the same time they need to preserve the myth of democratic governance, and to avoid turning away donors who might sense any undue departure from the myth. In Tanzania interviews with NGO officers revealed such tactics as avoiding or postponing meetings, in the hope that NGOs would go away if they were ignored for long enough. In Uganda NGOs complained about nominal consultation being rendered ineffective when NGOs were given only a brief time to read complex policy documents.

In the longer term, there is the problem for governments of defending power bases which they regard as essential to their survival, but which many NGOs might see as centres of privilege, if not repositories of corruptly or violently acquired wealth. In Tanzania we noted the deals with mining and timber companies and with the Saudi Royal Family, and the continuing saga of the expensive (and possibly useless) air defence system bought from Britain. In Uganda the proposal for the Bujagali Falls Dam only succeeded at the second attempt, after revelations of a corrupt deal with a World Bank official had scotched the first attempt (Rice 2007: 21), while the question of the latitude to be given to the army and police continues to present a dilemma. Undue autonomy for state officials with guns would (and perhaps has) suggested a departure from the 'objective control' of armed force which many people regard as fundamental to constitutional democracy. The objective control model implies that armies enjoy internal autonomy but accept their ultimate subordination to an elected government (Luckham 1971: 8–34). Yet attempts to enforce the objective control model by reining in the police, and more especially the army, might antagonise an essential power base.

On most of these issues, the most vociferous NGOs, supported by sections of the media, are likely to be on the side of greater scrutiny, accountability and an assault on what they regard as the privileges enjoyed by elites, whether indigenous or foreign, at the expense of the rest of society. What has been the response of governments? In the last resort, the answer is probably the mundane one that they do what only governments can do. They wield executive power, whether in allocating hunting licences, allocating contracts, dispensing patronage or wielding armed force. They shut the door on parliamentary or other investigatory committees that come too close to discovering incriminating evidence, they use their overwhelming majorities in Parliament to enact legislation, they co-opt pliable NGO leaders who have become too effective and, particularly in the case of Uganda, they use actual or threatened army or police action to quieten NGOs or journalists. Many of these tactics are used by governments the world over, even in nominal liberal democracies, so these observations are not necessarily intended as criticisms of the governments of Tanzania and Uganda. The objective is rather to emphasise the limitations which NGOs ultimately face. They have made enormous progress in working towards greater openness, participation, scrutiny and accountability, but they are not some revolutionary force that can demand an end to a range of injustices and mal-practices. Stalin's rhetorical question 'How many divisions has the Pope?' could equally be asked of NGOs.

NGOs and external influence

If African governments can be a barrier to the aspirations of NGOs, will external forces be a help or a hindrance, and will their contribution make for a more democratic order? In their list of criteria for assessing the effectiveness of democracy, Beetham *et al.* included the questions (1) 'How free is the governance of the country from subordination to external agencies, economic, cultural or political?', and (2) 'How far are government relations with international organisations based on the principles of partnership and transparency?' (Beetham *et al.* 2002: 66). For our purposes we could add the question 'In what ways do NGOs contribute to or mitigate the subordination; and in what ways do they contribute to or inhibit the partnership and transparency?' Detailed answers would require elaborate case studies, but we can attempt a broad sketch here. We shall concentrate first on such formal institutions as foreign governments, businesses and IFIs, and then on INGOs and global civil society.

At first sight, any notion of relations with international organisations 'based on principles of partnership and transparency' are difficult to detect. African governments generally go into international negotiations from a position of weakness, lacking adequate manpower, expertise and access to the relevant information, compared with those on the other side of the negotiating table. The situation is often exacerbated by the fear on the part of African governments that failure to meet the demands of foreign governments or IFIs will mean biting the hand that feeds them in terms of aid, so that concessions are made which frequently go against the wishes of civil society, the interests of the poor and vulnerable, and even the weight of expert opinion. This was especially noticeable in nego-tiations with the EU over the economic partnership agreements (EPAs). The Ugandan government saw little alternative but to sign on the dotted line while NGOs, and especially Oxfam, urged the government to bide its time, and tried to make the population aware of what it might lose as a result of the agreements (Oxfam 2006: 11). In some cases NGOs are per-mitted to join the negotiating teams representing African governments, but this has not become a regularized process.

NGO attempts to influence deals between African governments and foreign businesses have hardly been any more successful. In 2002 the

Tanzanian Association of NGOs (TANGO) could not prevent the installation of the British Aerospace (BAE) air defence project in Tanzania (Tango 2002: 6–7). In 2003 the Lawyers' Environmental Action Team (LEAT) was unable to prevent a deal with a Canadian mining company which involved the eviction of thousands of Tanzanian miners and small traders (LEAT 2003: 1–3), and the Uganda National Association of Professional Environmentalists was unable to halt the building of the Bujagali Falls Dam. Deals such as these were frequently underwritten by the World Bank which, despite its lip service to consultation with NGOs in developing countries, has seldom stood in the way of global business.

When it comes to relations with INGOs and the wider global civil society, the picture is more complex. While some INGOs have been criticised for trying to impose Western values on Africa, such as putting the conservation of flora and fauna before the needs of African peasants (Sunseri 2005: 609–40), or even for being fronts for Western governments (Hearn 2000: 815–30), a large proportion are, by their nature, on the side of the underdog. Anyone wanting to exploit Africa rather than serve its citizens would presumably choose a career in business rather than the voluntary sector. Some INGOs, such as Amnesty International, Human Rights Watch and Transparency International provide a continuous process of scrutiny of African governments, often in collaboration with African NGOs. While it is virtually impossible to measure the effectiveness of such activity, it adds a deterrent to governments indulging in, or condoning, corruption, arbitrary imprisonment or human rights abuses generally. In interviews, NGO officers made much of the desire of their governments to conform to accepted international standards, or to maintain international respectability. Such matters range from the largely administrative, such as the standard of child welfare, to the more explicitly political, such as conducting fair elections or ensuring the public accountability of the police. While one can point to many cases where the standards are not observed, it is generally to the advantage of African governments to be seen to be observing them as far as their limited resources allow. Not only is there the fear of loss of aid, but there is also the desire to avoid damaging reputations that have been built up steadily since the more authoritarian days of the 1970s and 1980s. In the run up to the Commonwealth Heads of Government meeting in 2007, the Ugandan government was anxious to avoid anything that might damage the country's image in the eyes of the world. Even in areas that were not directly the government's responsibility, such as pay and conditions in the private sector, employers in Kampala were expected to avoid any scandals of bad practice. The case in 2003 of girls working in a garment factory being treated as virtual prisoners was not to be repeated.

Beyond the routine scrutiny by INGOs concerned with human rights, corruption or child welfare, there has also been INGO support for *ad hoc* campaigns. The US based International Rivers Network was prominent in the campaign against the Bujagali Dam, but more often INGOs find it prudent to provide background support to indigenous campaigns, in order to avoid the charge that it is mainly foreigners who are challenging an African government.

Yet the fact that an INGO wields influence from behind the lines rather than from the front line does not resolve the question of whether external influence over, or support for, African NGOs, is enhancing African democracy or undermining it. Beetham *et al.*'s concern about avoiding 'subordination to external agencies' implies that the will of indigenous governments ought to prevail. But what if these governments, even if not blatantly authoritarian, are pursuing policies that are illiberal, or seek to advance the interests of the privileged few at the expense of the many? Was it wrong for foreign NGOs, or for world opinion (in the guise of global civil society), to oppose President Moi's manipulation of elections in Kenya, or the recent manipulation in Zanzibar? Should Ugandans alone have been left to decide whether President Museveni should be permitted to stand for a third term, even if the referendum to decide the issue might be flawed? Is it anyone else's business if an African government decides to build a dam, even if the negotiations surrounding the decision (including those of the World Bank) lack some of the 'partnership and transparency' recommended by Beetham *et al.*? Do INGOs, possibly supported by Western governments, have a right to skew the priorities of the African NGOs they support, so that 'liberal' rights take on a greater importance than social and economic rights? And do the outcomes in practice suggest that external pressure has played a significant role in influencing the behaviour of African NGOs?

Let us remind ourselves first that the lines of political conflict do not necessarily put African governments and society on one side of the divide, and external actors on the other. One might, depending on one's ideological preferences, wish that African NGOs spoke up more for the social and economic rights of the masses, thundered against foreign exploitation and demanded a global order free from debt, dependency and trade relations imposed by the West. And one might wish that the masses in Africa stood up more robustly for their social and economic rights in the face of their governments' deals with foreign businesses. But in reality the differences between the aspirations of African NGOs and INGOs, or even African civil society and global civil society, are more a matter of degree than of ideological incompatibility. Those African NGOs that have horizons going beyond immediate service provision may have their own views on what an ideal world would look like, but they generally concentrate on pragmatic, practical attempts to reduce poverty, injustice and human rights abuses. INGOs, for their part, realise that they cannot transform IFIs or the policies of Western governments overnight, and adopt a similarly pragmatic stand, supporting any groups or activities that contribute to their ultimate objectives. In other words, they are pushing at a half open door, rather than trying to impose an alien culture.

This convergence might be seen by Marxists or dependency theorists as evidence that the West has subordinated Africa to the stage where Africa can only think in a language imposed by its neo-colonial masters. An alternative explanation would be that globalisation and the rise of global civil society have created a world in which new limitations on political action are recognised, and less than perfect solutions are devised within a consensus that embraces 'good governance', liberal democracy, sustainable development and debt relief, all with a mainly capitalist order. This consensus is reinforced by regular contacts between African NGOs and INGOs, whether through meetings and conferences, or via communications on the Internet. If Africans were told that they exhibited a false consciousness in subscribing to such a consensus, they might reply that the experience of arbitrary, authoritarian, corrupt, and often incompetent government, led them to a belief in the virtues of the converse concepts of democracy, human rights, transparency and the rule of law, at least as a starting point on the road to development. The notion that constitutional government and the rule of law are something better left to bourgeois governments in the West might be disputed in view of Africa's experience of brutal dictatorship, and of politicians unwilling to countenance opinions that differed from their own (see especially Akiba 2004). None of this is to argue against the desirability of African NGOs, INGOs or global civil society in general taking a more radical stance against the injustices within Africa and the global order, but simply to suggest that there are understandable reasons why their aspirations are often more limited.

This digression suggests that attempting to explain the impact of external influences on African NGOs is complicated by the fact that the impact of globalisation makes it difficult to separate the external from the internal. Ideas, interests and even individuals cannot easily be placed on one side or the other. Where does one place the Ugandan working for Oxfam or the expatriate campaigning for the land rights of Tanzanians? Is Human Rights Watch transmitting foreign values, or upholding the rights of Africans against their governments, when it draws attention to human rights abuses? While we have noted the view that some INGOs, possibly abetted by their governments, have pushed African NGOs in alien directions, whether in terms of administration or objectives, it is the common ground, rather than divergence, that is more striking. Many African NGOs speak a very similar language to their international counterparts. If the latter have influence on the behaviour of the former, it is often in reinforcing their beliefs, activities, and sometimes their successes, rather than diverting them along a different road.

Conclusion

To seek democracy without votes is to imply that 'democracy with votes' is either non-existent or inadequate. In the case of Tanzania and Uganda, and indeed the majority of African states since the 1980s, the process of holding competitive, multi-party elections at regular intervals is there for all to see. In a few cases, ruling parties have held on to power by fraudulent means. Malpractices have often altered the actual number of votes and seats won by each party, but generally not sufficiently to affect the final outcome. There is, as far as one can judge, an overwhelming public preference to retain the current rulers of Tanzania and Uganda, and it seems unlikely that the fairest elections ever devised would have unseated them. The problem for democracy is not so much the inadequacy of elections as the inadequacy of choices between competing parties. This can be explained partly by the absence of class structures, comparable with those in Europe, which enable parties to offer policies tailored to the interests of the social groups they represent, and partly by the current global order which leaves African governments with limited options. They have little control over their own economies, in the face of edicts from the IFIs and the conditions set by donors. While voting in elections provides an important safeguard against authoritarianism and the abuse of power, and to some extent enables constituencies to use their local MPs to press for more resources, it does little to translate the wishes of voters into action, or to ensure that ruling politicians are held accountable for their actions. The prospect of opposition parties 'turning the rascals out' are remote, and the prospect of an opposition victory making a significant difference to policy outcomes is equally remote. Political parties, in other words, perform little of their textbook role of aggregating interests, offering policy alternatives, or providing links between ordinary voters and the centre of power.

To expect NGOs to fill the vacuum left by the deficiencies of parties, and the absence of real electoral choice, would be unrealistic. NGOs do not seek to win power for themselves, and do not claim to have a blueprint of alternative policies, even though individual members may have their own ideas. If we go beyond the NGOs that confine their activities to service delivery or to serving small areas, most NGOs claim to have a 'vision' or a 'mission', but it is generally one related to particular interests or areas of policy, such as the rights of pastoralists or the development of education, rather than a set of priorities for the nation as a whole. NGOs will generally claim a representative role, sometimes in relation to their own (generally small) membership, such as Ugandan lawyers or Arusha beekeepers, but more often in relation to a section of society such as street children, pastoralists or the nation's wildlife, whose interests NGOs claim to know and to be able to advance. Not only do we have democracy without votes, but 'democracy without counting heads'. We saw that the claim to legitimacy of the professional environmentalists in Uganda was not the fact that the group had 25 members (a claim that no one would take seriously), but that its expertise and involvement in a variety of networks entitled it to be heard.

The relatively narrow concerns of NGOs, and their lack of mass power bases, does not suggest a promising starting point for providing an alternative avenue into democratic politics, and we noted the easy targets which NGOs have provided for their critics. They are, it is said, largely urban-based and ignorant of the real world of rural poverty, and their financial dependence on donors means that they are not free to express independent opinions or pursue independent campaigns. In other cases their independence is compromised by their dependence on government contracts, and any claim to be enhancing democracy is further undermined by the lack of internal democracy within NGOs. Many of these criticisms imply that NGOs have appeared, not as the voice emerging from a civil society which would otherwise have no voice, but as a response to the opportunities offered by donor funding and government contracts, which have provided many redundant public officials with new opportunities for employment. There is much truth in this, but it is only a part of the truth.

We have traced the way in which civil society emerged from the 1980s onwards, initially largely through self help groups and later through more formal NGO structures, as governments were unable or unwilling to provide a wide range of services. Service provision shaded into advocacy as NGO leaders began not merely to cater for the needs of their clients but to portray the needs of their clients as something requiring political action. Village communities, for example, did not just require social welfare, but an adequate share of the national budget, honestly administered, and ultimately a global order based on fair trade and debt cancellation. By the early twenty first century NGOs, or at least a significant minority of NGOs which set the pace for the rest, were giving a voice to local communities in a way that had not been attempted before. The common strategies were firstly to inform citizens of the nature of an issue, such as the allocation of the national budget or the likely effects on an international trade agreement; secondly to seek citizens' opinions, and then to present the arguments to politicians. As far as the input side of politics was concerned, a range of democratic channels had been opened up, not so much through votes or counting heads, but through indicating broad strands of opinion and public preferences. At the same time as articulating opinions in this way, NGOs began to play a growing role in scrutinising the activities of the government and state agencies, sometimes on their own, and sometimes through encouraging the wider community to participate. HakiElimu's confrontation with the Tanzanian government over education was not mainly about policy but about the failure to implement what the government had decided should happen. The achievements of NGOs in terms of promoting more effective scrutiny were to be found not just in their own work, but in the way in which more informal groups in civil society followed the NGOs' examples and put their own pressures on politicians and officials.

The promotion of greater democratic participation by NGOs would have come to little if governments had refused to recognise their legitimate right to lobby. On this, the government position in both Tanzania and Uganda was ambivalent. They had little objection to the rise of NGOs in principle, and they had little choice but to preserve the myth of a government resting on the principles of a democracy in which the voice of the people should be heard. To do otherwise would have been to antagonise foreign donors or to risk unrest if democratic channels were closed. In the case of Uganda, civil society had largely preceded the building of a formal constitutional edifice, and in Tanzania there had been a tradition of intra-party democracy even under one-party rule, which now needed to be channelled in other ways, so there was no obvious reason for governments to deny the right of groups in civil society to pursue a variety of causes.

Yet philosophical justifications for civil society participation did not always fit well with the practical requirements of government or the need to protect the interests that provided governments with their main power bases. In the absence of party competition based on distinctive social group or distinctive ideologies, ruling parties need to keep ahead of their challengers partly by using the resources of the state to win elections, and partly by seeking the support of wealthy individuals and corporate backers. These backers will, in turn, expect rewards for their generosity. The allocation of public resources required to satisfy these needs is likely to conflict with the allocation preferred by NGOs campaigning for poverty alleviation, help for the disadvantaged and social justice. This suggests that governments will need to try to stem the rising NGO tide if that tide threatens to question the wisdom or the propriety of deals with indigenous and foreign businesses, the allocation of hunting rights to foreigners at the expense of pastoralists, or policies that enrich party and state officials.

NGOs have won many battles through careful research and skilful campaigning, but we need to remind ourselves that they are not political parties in disguise, social movements with a mass following, or revolutionary cadres with the strength to overthrow the existing order. They can seek to persuade or embarrass governments, or remind them of the possibility of the loss of foreign aid if they stray too far from the democratic path, but in the end they have few sanctions if the government says 'no'. Governments, in contrast, enjoy the full weight of executive power, including the power to allocate resources, dispense patronage and negotiate deals with businesses; and they can use their overwhelming majorities in the legislature to enact legislation, including legislation to curb the power of NGOs. All this is also true of governments in the West, but we return to the point that African governments are seldom kept in check by credible opposition parties, and the prospect of losing elections remains a remote one. Democracy without votes, it would seem, reaches a ceiling unless it is reinforced with 'democracy with votes' where the votes really matter.

It is sometimes argued that the failure of multi-party 'democracy with votes' is the result of a zero-sum game in which the rise of NGOs and civil society implies weaker multi-party politics. Shaw asks whether civil society has been privileged to the detriment of formal multi-party politics. 'Civil society, especially legitimated or reinforced by global donors/media, can effectively squeeze out other democratic processes like elections' (Shaw in Mbabazi and Taylor 2005: 39). Yet it is not clear what more could be done to advance these other democratic processes.

Apart from economic constraints on any choice between rival party programmes, there also appears to be an aversion to the 'confrontational' style which party competition implies, or to head-on challenges to government policy. We noted the passive way in which Tanzanians accepted a complete reversal of socialist policies in the 1980s. In Uganda, despite the high level of political participation at the local level, the Civicus survey revealed that over 85 per cent of the population had never written a letter to a newspaper, signed a petition or attended a demonstration (Civicus 2006: 26). Logan *et al.* reported that 40 per cent of Ugandans would have preferred to retain a one-party state (Logan *et al.* 2003: 13). As long as African citizens shy away from more bruising challenges with their political masters, for whatever reason, there is little to fuel the more aggressive style which multi-party competition requires.

Finally we turn to the impact of external forces on the effectiveness of NGOs. We have seen that foreign governments, IFIs and businesses frequently work with African governments to the detriment of NGOs, in the imposition of free market policies, cuts in public spending, and the negotiation of projects which damage the natural environment. But African NGOs have also benefited from the support of like-minded INGOs, many of which are dedicated to human rights, the eradication of poverty and suffering, and the conservation of the environment. While globalisation has in many ways made economic exploitation easier, and reduced the policy choices available to African governments and their constituents, it has also helped to build a global civil society, to which we shall return in the next chapter. The concept implies a degree of consensus which transcends national frontiers. Partly as a result of experience of common problems, and partly as a result of regular communications, whether at meetings and conferences or through the Internet, African NGOs share many common values with INGOs such as Oxfam, Amnesty International, Human Rights Watch and Transparency International. INGOs such as these often prefer to remain in the background, for fear of giving the impression that NGO campaigns reflect the interests and wishes of foreigners, but they can provide invaluable expertise, manpower and financial support.

It may be objected that INGO involvement in African affairs is yet another facet of foreign domination, however well meaning, yet it is difficult to conceive of INGO-supported campaigns succeeding unless they have substantial indigenous support. The World Bank and foreign businesses may be able to shape decisions that are opposed by the broad consensus of African opinion; INGOs would have great difficulty in doing so. To take one random example, while INGOs worked with the grain of African opinion in opposing a prawn farming project, encroachments on forests and aid conditions that harmed the local economy, it is difficult to recall any INGO campaign against the cultivation of flowers in greenhouses for export. Powerful arguments could be deployed against such cultivation, including the diversion of water supplies from farmers and the alleged environmental damage done by airlifting the final product to Europe, but this cultivation generates employment for Africans, and foreign opponents of it might find few allies on the ground.

What, then, are the scope and limitations of democracy without votes? The whole concept assumes that there is more to democracy than mere majoritarianism. It would be a very limited democracy that allowed people to elect or remove their rulers, and to take a range of decisions via referenda, but which left no room for political discussion in homes, bars and market places, which in turn might be refined into political beliefs articulated by more formally organised groups. If the groups were not permitted to air their views in public, to recruit like-minded people, or to seek to persuade ruling politicians or administrators to listen to their views, we would be left with something closer to the Singaporean version of democracy, where only the elected politicians are deemed qualified to judge what is right. One might term such an arrangement 'votes without democracy'. It recalls Rousseau's observation in the eighteenth century that the British people were free once every seven years (on polling day).

Most democrats would presumably prefer a synthesis of the 'democracy without votes' implicit in a lively civil society with well organised NGOs, and 'democracy with votes' in a system of representative democracy, but we have suggested that the latter has not taken root easily in Africa, with limited party choices and governments exploiting the advantages of incumbency. The former, in contrast, has prospered as NGOs have become increasingly skilled in articulating the needs of their constituents and holding governments and administrators to account. If 'democracy with votes' is not working well, and if there is little evidence that it is likely to work any better in the foreseeable future, why not simply concentrate on strengthening NGOs and civil society? Here much depends on whether one sees Africa's position in the global order as fixed as far into the future as one can see, or whether one sees scope for a radical challenge to that order, possibly through the coming together of like minded groups from different parts of Africa or the developing world as a whole. Groups already exist such as the African Social Forum and Jubilee South which might offer a rhetorical challenge (Tandon in Bond 2003: 59–63; Jubilee South in Broad 2002: 275–81), but these are mainly voices in the wilderness. Some of the African NGOs we have examined, such as HakiKazi and TGNP, would seem to have the ideological baggage to be part of a broader global movement. It might even be the case, if one is not too squeamish about 'foreign interference', that liberal opinion in the West will gather momentum as anger grows at the contrast between wealth and poverty in the world, and that public opinion will push Western governments further in the direction of 'global justice'. Any of these outcomes might ultimately leave Africa with fewer debts, fewer trading arrangements which impose economic handicaps, and fewer conditions for aid which impose free market policies and expensive, unwanted white elephants. In such an environment, a wider range of policy choices would emerge, and 'democracy with votes' might begin to have some meaning.

Such speculation can, and probably will, be dismissed as fantasy, with its assumption that governments and interests that benefit from the existing order will willingly give up their privileges, though the same might have been said of the abolition of the slave trade or the dissolution of the British Empire. A third possibility is one of more gradual, incremental change, as has happened with debt relief and the modification of the Washington consensus. Such change might gradually shift political debate in Africa from making the administration more efficient to weighing the merits of alternative policies. A small example of this is the debate within NGOs as to how best to use the money saved through debt relief. If the trend is, or is likely to be, one of incremental change, a key question is then what 'democracy without votes' is likely to have achieved. Will it merely be a creditable monument to those who stimulated democratic and political accountability as best they could in the circumstances of globalisation and dependency? Or might it prove to be a point of departure for facilitating broader democratic choices?

6
NGOs and the Global Order: Theory and Practice

The growth in the number and activities of NGOs has not been confined within the boundaries of nation states. In 1993 only 48 NGOs had consultative status at the United Nations Economic and Social Council (ECOSOC). Now, according to Clark *et al.*, tens of thousands of NGOs participate 'in new ways' especially in 'world conference processes' (Clark *et al.* in Wilkinson 2005: 295). The creation of the structural adjustment programme review initiative (SAPRI) has led to hundreds of civil society organisations (CSOs) joining with the World Bank in reviewing the impact of its policies (Scholte 2004: 211–33). World membership of international NGOs (INGOs) rose from 148,501 in 1990 to 255,432 in 2000 (Anheier *et al.* 2001: 4–5), and the number and range of, and participation at, global NGO conferences rose rapidly. In 1972 fewer than 300 delegates attended the Stockholm Conference on the Environment. In 1992 1,400 attended the Rio Earth Summit (Clark *et al.* in Wilkinson 2005: 295) and 130,000 attended the World Social Forum at Mumbai in 2004 (Wainwright in Anheier *et al.* 2005: 94–115). It is now common for NGOs to hold 'parallel conferences' when inter-governmental organisations (IGOs) hold their conferences, with a view to monitoring and lobbying the official bodies (Clark *et al.* in Wilkinson 2005: 297). It is estimated that there are now over 5,000 world congresses of NGOs every year (Keane 2003: 5).

These figures might suggest that NGOs are now a major force in world politics, countering the power of individual governments, and of IGOs created by them. Supporters of this view cite such successes as debt relief, the defeat of the proposed Multilateral Agreement on Investment and the relaxation of patent rules to enable poor countries to distribute medicines to combat AIDS and malaria. Those taking a more sceptical view would point out that the gap between the rich and poor in the world is as wide as ever, that the rules of international trade, even when they are observed, are biased in favour of wealthy countries, and that lobbying and monitoring are no substitute for participating in the exercise of power. The fate of African economies depends heavily on the decisions of the International Monetary Fund (IMF) and the World Bank, and these decisions are taken in secret and under a system which gives Sub-Saharan Africa only 4.6 per cent of the vote at the IMF and 6 per cent at the World Bank (Glenn 2008: 217–38).

To assess the role and achievements of NGOs in the world order, we need to go beyond mere figures and to look at the foundations on which that order rests. In this chapter we begin by looking briefly at the way in which the world order has evolved in the past four decades, and especially at the growth in the importance of IGOs, and at the corresponding growth of NGOs to shadow them. To what extent have these developments led to a 'global' rather than an 'international' order in which national governments have become less effective and are increasingly bypassed? Insofar as such an order has emerged, does it provide more fertile ground for NGOs? While national governments can always belittle NGOs by saying 'We represent the people who elected us; whom do you represent?', IGOs have much less claim to any democratic mandate, and NGOs can claim to be reducing the democratic deficit by voicing the concerns of ordinary citizens who are on the receiving end of policies such as retrenchment, privatisation, the debt burden and trade rules which damage or destroy indigenous production. We shall then go on to examine the concept of 'global civil society', the extent to which it exists and the extent to which it provides a framework for NGOs to engage in a dialogue with authority at a global level in a comparable way with civil society dialogue with national governments. Having looked at the civil society side of the equation, we then go on to look at the nature of the actual global power structures. To what extent are they democratic or authoritarian, hierarchical or anarchic, and what bearing does this have on the opportunities for NGOs to influence events?

IGOs and the concept of globalisation

A principal source of academic debate on the nature of the world order before the 1990s was between 'realists' who saw world politics as a crude struggle for power between national governments, each pursuing its own narrow interests and subject to few rules or conventions, or to any mediating authority; and 'pluralists' who placed greater emphasis on the existence of harmony in the international order. Governments, according to pluralists, were constrained by supra-national authority above and inter-est groups below. Businesses, bureaucracies, groups and individual cit-izens needed a stable environment in which to flourish, rather than the international law of the jungle. Both realists and pluralist focused on the nation state and its government as the principal actors, which implied that NGOs and similar bodies had to work mainly within their own frontiers if they wished to influence events, rather than on the world stage.

The concept of globalisation emerged as it became increasing obvious that much political activity was bypassing or ignoring national fron-tiers, but the term meant different things to different observers. It has been used in at least three different ways: (1) a process in which coun-tries have become increasingly dependent on world trade (Hoogvelt 1997: 115); (2) a process by which external forces can increas-ingly impose economic, political and cultural controls on individual societies (Clapham 1996: 24); and (3) the uncontrollable crossing of national frontiers by a variety of forces, thus constraining the scope for action by national governments (Bobbitt 2003; Howard 2003: 17). It is the third of these conceptions of globalisation with which we are concerned. Dependence on world trade may as easily be a matter of choice as much as subordination. Industrialised countries such as Britain chose to import most of their food before 1914 in order to specialise in the production of manufactured goods and financial ser-vices; and the imposition of external pressures can as easily be by gov-ernments as by forces independent of governments. Much more relevant is the uncontrolled, and possibly uncontrollable, crossing of national frontiers by a variety of forces. Some of this is not new, but it has accelerated over the past four decades. Services and capital, in addi-tion to as goods, can now be moved at the click of a computer mouse or a decision taken in a remote boardroom, so that multi-national companies (MNCs) can move production from one part of the world to another, with sometimes disastrous results for the country from which production has been withdrawn. But national frontiers are also increas-ingly crossed by illegal migrants, mass media, fundamentalist religions, illicit weapons, drugs, terrorists, sexually transmitted diseases and fashions in clothing and music. There is room for debate on how far these processes have gone, and how far they have weakened the ability of governments to control their countries' or their own destiny, but most governments would acknowledge the greater constraints which they now face. Social democratic governments cannot easily impose progressive taxation without the fear of frightening away investors wanting a more generous tax regime. Traditionalist conservative governments cannot easily wish away 'permissive' morality when foreign-based newspapers and television companies can easily parade their wares. Neither can they easily halt what they see as the erosion of national culture when the economy is dependent on the employment of workers from very different cultures. Violent conflict in the Congo cannot easily be ended when there is a network of illegal traders, arms dealers and mercenaries exploiting local resources, and Ghana is unlikely to fulfil its dream of self-sufficiency in rice when the United States can dump its subsidised rice in Ghana with impunity.

Globalisation thus challenges both the realist and pluralist views of the world. If its underlying premises are correct, the realist belief in international political outcomes being determined by the crude exercise of power by national governments is undermined by the inability of governments to control much of what enters or leaves their countries. Equally, the pluralist notion that brute force can be replaced by consensus in world politics is undermined by increasingly limited governmental capacity. Governments and their citizens will not necessarily take kindly to such turns of events, even though they may bring benefits ranging from more material goods, through more varied diets, to easier communications and more varied entertainment. If individual governments cannot control events, they may seek to create, or participate in, supra-national bodies that will have greater power to do so. And if citizens find that knocking on the door of their own governments is ineffective, they too will attempt to work with like-minded groups in other countries to lobby the supra-national centres of power. This brings us on to the rise of international organisations and, more especially, global civil society.

As our concern is mainly with the voluntary rather than the state sector, we shall deal only briefly with the latter. The terminology is often confusing, and sometimes used inconsistently, but a number of groups can be identified. The term 'international organisation' (IO) is sufficiently vague to provide an umbrella to cover most bodies that work beyond national frontiers. It is generally taken to include inter-governmental organisations (IGOs), that is bodies created by national governments, and exercising power delegated by these governments, as well as bodies that include representatives of NGOs. The family of IGOs includes within it the international financial institutions (IFIs) such as the World Bank, the IMF and the World Trade Organisation (WTO). Beyond all these bodies with 'official' status, there is of course the world of NGOs operating on their own which seek to influence the official bodies and hold them to account.

IOs, like NGOs, have a long history going back well before the rise of globalisation. Many were much more administrative or technocratic than political, concerned with matters as diverse as health, postal services or safety standards on ships. Some, such as the IFIs, were created at the end of the Second World War with a view to promoting economic stability, as was the United Nations to try to secure a lasting peace. But globalisation required a shift in emphasis, with regulation directed not only at governments but increasingly at the second and third sectors. Businesses, if left unregulated, could create world financial crises, deplete the world's natural resources or change its climate irrevocably. Consumers, if left unprotected, might have their health damaged, whether by infected British beef imported into the EU, or by toys manufactured in China with toxic ingredients, imported into the United States. One might question the adequacy of the attempts at regulation, but hardly the quantity. Zurn records that the number of international agreements increased from 15,000 in 1960 to well over 55,000 by 1997 (Zurn 2004: 267). For NGOs, attempts to influence official decision-making required an increasing emphasis on the global level.

One could try to assess the success of global pressures by totting up the number of victories and defeats for NGOs, or for the democratic process as a whole. But it might be more constructive to consider how far a global order has been established which provides, or has the potential to provide, a means by which NGOs can perform a sustained role in representing, and campaigning effectively for, the mass of the poor and underprivileged citizens of the world. Is there a 'global civil society' which is beginning to enable NGOs to perform such a role, or merely an *ad hoc* collection of global structures, behaving in unpredictable ways, which only occasionally or by chance enable the have-nots to win consolation prizes? It is to these questions that we now turn.

Global civil society: myth, reality or a question of definition

At the optimistic end of the spectrum, Kaldor has no doubts about the existence and vitality of global civil society. It is a medium through which social contracts between individuals and the political and economic centres of power are negotiated and reproduced. With the end of the Cold War, governments and international institutions have become more responsive to peace and human rights groups (Kaldor 2003: 44, 88).

A system of global governance is in the process of being constituted through negotiations and bargains which involve ... various organisations as well as global civil society (Kaldor 2003: 110).

Anheier *et al.* examine this more in institutional terms. There has been a rapid growth since 1990 in the number of INGOs, and in looser grassroots groups, all making for greater social and political participation. 'Parallel summits' alongside the summits of official bodies, facilitate increased participation (Anheier *et al.* 2005: 3–22). Kaldor *et al.* spell this out further. Global civil society has been strengthened by both 'top-down' and 'bottom-up' processes. The former has involved sub-contracting work to NGOs such as Oxfam and Save the Children; and through businesses seeking civil society organisations (CSOs) as partners. The latter involves building up trust through networking, and monitoring and challenging power holders.

Warkentin asserts that all of us 'participate' in global civil society, and this increasingly shapes our environment. It influences our employment, our use of the Internet and our personal relationships (Warkentin 2001: 3). Held and Koenig-Archibugi are enthusiastic about the legitimacy and accountability of 'those who shape global policies' (Held and Koenig-Archibugi 2003: 129). They illustrate with reference to 'multi-stakeholder networks' such as the World Commission on Dams, the Roll Back Malaria Initiative and the Apparel Industrial Partnership – all networks of business, civil society organisations and national public agencies (*ibid*: 125–31).

The existence of a range of global institutions, networks and activities is not in dispute, but some writers question the validity of using the term 'civil society' at a global as well as a national level. Even within countries, many non-governmental bodies are notoriously uncivil, even though they wield power and influence, notably religious fundamentalists, groups spreading ethnic discord, drug barons and armed insurgents, but a case can still be made that more benign groups have done much to promote social cohesion and democracy. The absence of formal democratic structures in NGOs within countries might be overlooked if they are small enough to maintain informal links between members, leaders and officers, and possibly with the wider social groups they claim to champion. But at a global level some critics refuse to credit NGOs with being part of civil society if they are self-appointed, self-perpetuating groups of individuals, subject to weak scrutiny by any wider membership, and offering few opportunities for the membership to participate, no matter how worthy the objectives of the group or how knowledgeable its leaders may be (Scholte 2004: 230–1). Such bodies might be better described as part of an elite or an 'establishment' than a civil society. Such a society might also be taken to imply that there is a 'public opinion' beyond the NGOs and governmental bodies which jostle for power and influence, and that this public opinion can put its weight behind campaigners for popular causes. Yet at a global level, this is less likely to be the case. Media reporting within countries makes for some public awareness of how the actions of governments, parliaments or public officials are affecting ordinary citizens, but fewer column inches or television reports are devoted to decisions by the World Bank or the WTO that affect millions of lives (Nanz and Steffek 2004: 314–35).

Even if one does not see the global political process as a means by which the rich and powerful continue to exploit the poor, it might still be portrayed as fitting closer to a technocratic model than to a nascent democratic civil society. Indeed some writers question the logical poss-ibility of a global civil society existing if there is no 'global state'. Goodhart points out that supranational politics is qualitatively differ-ent from national politics, and not just different in terms of scale. It is multi-layered, and IGOs are organised functionally rather than ter-ritorially, with institutions overlapping and fragmented. There is, he argues, no global polity. There is no means of imposing sanctions on IGOs in the way that civil society within a nation can impose sanc-tions on state institutions (Goodhart 2005: 1–21). Laxer and Halperin (2003: 1–21) are similarly sceptical. They deny the existence of a global network of INGOs (*ibid*: 3–6), and argue that those that exist have no public accountability and are based mainly in the West. The authors detect an ideological campaign (though it is not clear by whom) to immobilise citizens by telling them that their states are ineffective. There is no need to seek democratic global participation when demo-cratic structures already exist within states (*ibid*: 9, 18).

These critiques leave us with two (at least implicit) assertions which require further examination. Firstly, from Laxer and Halperin, that pol-itics within nation states is largely a matter of business as usual; and secondly, from Goodhart, that if any global civil society ever came to exist, it would have to resemble national civil society to be worthy of the name. On the first point there is enough literature on the decline of public trust in, and in the effectiveness of, national political institutions, to raise doubts (see especially Bromley, Curtice and Seyd in Park *et al.* 2001: 204–6; Putnam, Pharr and Dalton in Pharr and Putnam 2002: 10–27; Dalton 2002: 36; Barber in Axtmann 2001: 295–311; Peeler 1998: 196–7; Scharpf in Pharr and Putnam 2000: 115–20).

Globalisation and the consequent ability of multi-national corporations to escape governmental control; changes in social structures as a result of de-industrialisation; consumerism, and the triumph of free market ideology, have all made it more difficult for governments to control events within their borders. And they have made it more difficult to persuade citizens that participation in politics is either a civic duty or a productive activity. In developing countries there was less governmental capacity or participation to begin with, but even here one could argue that increased poverty, conditionality, and external edicts to admit imports that devastate home production, have all devalued national politics, to say nothing of the self-inflicted wounds of authoritarian government. In these contexts, citizens might have doubts about Laxer and Halperin's call to utilise democratic structures within their own states in preference to global participation. The growth of global, or at least supranational bodies with political authority has not simply been the result of a conspiracy by national elites to retain power while passing responsibility to someone else. It reflects the inability to tackle a range of problems within the confines of a nation state, whether they be global warming, the conservation of fish stocks, hygiene standards in food production or the spread of malaria. One can of course argue about whether delegation to the supranational level has gone too far, or whether social and economic changes have been used as an excuse for privatisation and dismantling welfare services, often against the democratically expressed wishes of the people. Slogans uttered by political leaders such as 'There is no alternative' or 'what works is what's best' try to pre-empt the possibility of any ideological vision as a basis for action. But for all that, it seems unreasonable to judge the existence or adequacy of global civil society by standards of internal national political processes which no longer exist and which probably cannot be revived. National politics, for good or ill, has become less participatory, more elitist, more 'managerial' and narrower in scope. These realities might provide a better standard against which to measure the quality of global politics (see especially Benner *et al.* 2004: 206).

Even if we compare global politics with 'real' rather than 'ideal' national politics, there is still the danger of comparing structures rather than functions. If one believes that democracy only exists where an executive is answerable to an elected legislature, and where public officials are clearly subordinate to elected politicians, one is going to dismiss most global political processes, and perhaps even those in the EU, as 'undemocratic'. Alternatively democracy might be seen as attempting to ensure that public institutions serve a notional public interest, however difficult that may be to define. This might be done by subjecting these institutions to whatever forms of dialogue with people affected by their decisions (their 'constituents' or 'stakeholders'), or with their representatives, as seems appropriate in the circumstances. Grant and Keohane suggest that while accountability at global level cannot work in the same way as at national level, it can still be exercised along the axes of 'participation' and 'delegation'. Officers delegated with public tasks can be made accountable to their superiors, and both can be required to consult, or involve, their constituents. A mixture of seven mechanisms of accountability can be used: hierarchical, supervisory, fiscal, legal, market, peer and public reputational (Grant and Keohane 2005: 29–43). Some of these principles and mechanisms are common to the private sector as well as the public. But, taken together and applied in an ideal way, they might help to ensure that outcomes were pursued which reflected what stakeholders, or even the whole 'global community' wanted (or would want if they had sufficient knowledge), as opposed to serving the needs of the officials, or of private interests connected with them. In short, global civil society, like national civil society, may be conceptualised largely as providing an element of 'democracy without votes', as described in the previous chapter.

The real world is obviously more complicated. Many political structures at all levels can be captured by elites or privileged groups to serve their interests rather than any 'public good'. Any suggestion that the World Bank or the WTO serve the interests of the poor and underprivileged might meet with a hollow laugh. Yet critics of the concept of global civil society are often more concerned with demolishing the concept, without necessarily denying the existence of a growing range of interactions across national frontiers. Such interactions may not be as regularised as political activities within long-established nation states, but a wide range of them now involve not merely powerful politicians and technocrats, but NGOs which represent, or claim to represent, the wider communities affected by their decisions. Democracy does not, in most definitions, require that the majority of the population get their way all the time, or that the underprivileged enjoy parity with elites in terms of power, however desirable such a situation might be. It might be seen more as a process within which there are at least opportunities for the masses and the underprivileged to win political battles, and perhaps to replace their political masters. As such opportunities are turned into actual successes, decision-makers may have to modify their decisions increasingly in anticipation of the responses of their constituents.

The fighting of political battles in global politics has become increasingly the prerogative of NGOs. While defeats have almost certainly outnumbered victories, the existence of these NGOs has modified the ways in which many IGOs and global businesses function, as well as changing the nature of political outcomes, from the building of particular dams or destroying particular forests, to reducing the burden of African debt. Replacing the political masters is another matter, and here we have to acknowledge that global civil society is the weaker for not functioning within a 'global state'. This may be regrettable, but it also increases the importance of NGOs refining their techniques, and where possible their sanctions, in the absence of a 'global ballot box'.

The question of participation is also a difficult one. Warkentin asserts that 'all of us' participate in global civil society. Do we? Maasai peasants asserting their land rights by working through both indigenous and international NGOs might be said to do so (Shivji in Semboja *et al.* 2002: 101–18), but do child football stitchers in Pakistan, or their parents? Organs of global civil society may articulate their perceived interests, but this is one of many cases where ordinary people are subjects rather than participants. The case of poor peasants in Uganda is closer to the borderline. Groups such as those involved in SAPRI and the Uganda Debt Network 'represent' the poor in seeking to cushion the effects of debt and structural adjustment, and some members of these bodies will no doubt belong to, or be in close touch with, the poorest sections of society, but the average peasant's 'participation' in the process will at best be tenuous. Contrast this with the ability of citizens in more 'developed' countries to participate in global civil society. People in Britain have been able to join Anti-Apartheid, support Jubilee 2000, shop ethically or vote against politicians who supported the invasion of Iraq. They have also been able, if not always successfully, to press global businesses not to abandon production in Britain. NGOs such as Greenpeace and Friends of the Earth are criticised for encouraging passive, direct-debit membership, but even these groups have to create a sense of public commitment in order to raise the funds. A country with a high level of literacy, well developed communications, greater leisure time, generally well protected civil liberties and freedom to choose between competing parties, is likely to have an advantage over developing countries when it comes to participating in global politics. This might reinforce the arguments of those who see any global civil society that may exist as dominated by Western NGOs and values, with citizens of poor countries largely excluded on account of their poverty, lack of education and lack of organisation (see especially Albrow *et al.* 2008: 11; Fraser 2005: 317–40; Ishakanian in Albrow *et al.* 2008: 58–85; Keane in Anheier *et al.* 2001: 38; Laxer and Halperin 2003: 1–21).

The fact that participation and political influence are unevenly distributed in global politics does not, by itself, invalidate arguments about the existence of global civil society. Do we expect everyone to exercise anything like equal influence within national civil societies? Does the unemployed member of the underclass, or the low paid immigrant worker, in Britain exercise as much influence as the Archbishop of Canterbury or an officer of Oxfam? Within Africa we have noted the argument that NGOs are often dominated by urban elites, and that the rural masses are largely excluded from politics and civil society. Believers in the existence of civil society, as we saw in the previous two chapters, are not required to believe that it constitutes some utopia of civic virtue from which all the unpleasant elements are excluded, but merely that it provides a rough terrain through which at least some citizens enjoy greater influence than they would otherwise possess, often mediated through NGOs. We shall envisage global civil society in similar terms, even though the ways in which it operates will obviously be different. Against the background of a professed faith in the existence of a global civil society, however imperfect, our next task is to examine the nature of the global power structures which global civil society seeks to influence.

The nature of global power

There is a wide divergence of views as to how power is exercised in global politics. Some of the more enthusiastic believers in global civil society perceive something approaching a democratic order, within which many voices influence political outcomes, whereas others look at the domination of the world by the United States since the Cold War, and at the power of the IFIs, and conclude that might is right. Cutting across the democratic-authoritarian axis is an orderly-anarchic axis, with a polarisation of opinion between those who see relative order and stability, and those who see an inconclusive struggle for power in a game with few accepted rules. The possibilities are suggested in Table 6.1.

Table 6.1   Possible Power Structures in Global Politics

Power politics. Might is right. American hegemony, or domination by wealthy countries. Most NGOs are sidelined.	**Global democracy.** Relative equality of voice and influence. Effective global civil society exists. NGOs enjoy a legitimate and significant role.
Global governance. A variety of formal structures exist to ensure stability. Some NGOs may enjoy 'insider status'.	**Global pluralism.** There is competition between largely autonomous actors, both state and non-state. NGOs lobby from the outside.
Global technocracy. Decisions are based on technocratic imperatives to ensure the smooth running of institutions. Many NGOs are co-opted to provide expertise and legitimacy.	**Global anarchy.** Decisions are based on contested ideological and political premises, and are frequently resisted as illegitimate. NGO influence depends on potential sanctions rather than formal influence.

The relevance of each model to the democratic-authoritarian and orderly-anarchic axes is suggested in Figure 6.1. Global democracy and power politics obviously occupy opposite poles on the 'democratic-authoritarian' axis, with the other four models occupying intermediate positions, while global technocracy and global anarchy occupy the extreme positions on the 'orderly-anarchic' axis, with the remaining models in between.

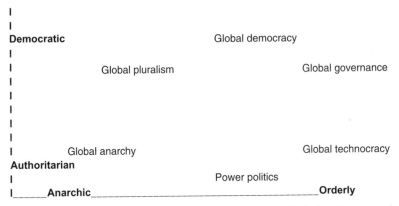

Figure 6.1   Models of Global Politics along Democratic-Authoritarian and Orderly-Anarchic Axes

The role of NGOs will depend on which of these models are closest to reality. We shall now go on to consider the basis of each model, and the extent to which each is illustrated by actual events and practices. We shall begin by describing each model uncritically, and then assess the relevance of each one.

The global order: six models

1.   Power politics

The power politics model assumes a world in which might is right, with power wielded by the strongest countries, and especially the United States. NGOs have little role in this order, except to act as service providers or contractors to the powerful governments. An obvious manifestation of this model is the behaviour of the US since 2001, with its ability to start a war of dubious legality and to ignore the authority of the United Nations and the Geneva Convention, but supporters of this model frequently argue that the actual behaviour is only a manifestation of a power structure that has existed since 1945. There may now be only one dominant power, so that the Russians can no longer invade Hungary as easily as the Americans invaded Iraq, but the imbalance of power between the strong and the weak has always been there. It is conceded that there was a brief interlude in the 1990s, when it was fashionable for the United States to believe in the virtues of civil society, both nationally and globally, especially when democracy promotion was high on the agenda. Then came the attack on the World Trade Centre in 2001, and the subsequent 'war on terror', and the pursuit of national security took on a higher priority. As civil liberties were encroached upon in Western countries in pursuit of that security, preaching the virtues of democracy abroad made less impact. As Anderson and Rieff put it (in Anheier *et al.* 2005: 35), the love affair between global civil society and IOs in the 1990s, each legitimising the other, had given way to an international system under the domination of the world's super power. Nation states are now more important. The global civil society-IO relationship had been only a minor affair with a minor mistress.

The American domination could be attributed partly to military might, but domination generally rests on more than the ability to kill people. Most of the formal institutions of world power reflect the pecking order of nation states in 1945, minus the Soviet Union. We have noted the way in which decisions at the IFIs involve counting money rather than counting heads in the countries represented. Monbiot suggests that the IMF is effectively run by the US, Japan, Germany, the

UK, France, Canada and Italy – the countries least likely to be affected by its policies (Monbiot 2005: 25. See also Glenn 2008: 217–38). Cammack also sees IFIs as fronts for advancing the interests of the powerful, though he is more interested in the advancement of 'global capitalism' than of any individual country. Despite lip service to moral crusades for the poor such as Tony Blair's Commission for Africa created in 2004, building global capitalism is more important than the common interests of humanity. Even the Commission for Africa requires that the actors in global politics should adapt to the needs of 'globally competitive capitalism' (Cammack 2006: 331–50).

In addition to military might and the manipulation of a global constitutional order largely established in the 1940s, power politics is said to be strengthened through the co-option of NGOs, in order to blunt any challenge from that source, and to give legitimacy to the decision-making process (Amoore and Langley 2004: 89–110; Fraser 2005: 317–40). This goes beyond the crude process of treating NGOs as appendages of the occupying power in Iraq, which we described in Chapter 3, to giving the impression that NGOs are willing participants in the implementation of IFI policies. Fraser argues that the poverty reduction strategy papers (PRSPs) have reinforced IFI domination over Africa by securing consent to 'liberal systems of political and economic management'. Even radical NGOs such as Oxfam participate in PRSP strategies in the hope of wielding some influence, but the reality is that IFIs confine their decisions to the free market mould. Mass-based groups such as trade unions, peasants and religious groups, which might challenge the free market orthodoxy, are excluded from any consultation (Fraser 2005: 317–40).

2. Global democracy

Global democracy in the sense of the existence of a world order sustained by democratic elections, and subject to institutionalised scrutiny, remains a very remote possibility. Indeed the authors we cite might deny that they believe in the existence of a global democracy, but they nonetheless see what they regard as democratic elements. These work partly in a confrontational way, with decision-makers making concessions in response to riots and demonstrations, partly in a consensual way as IGOs and NGOs seek common ground, and partly through the evolution of a global culture which constrains what political actors may do.

Just as national democracies have been forged not only through leisurely constitutional reforms but through the unrepresented masses taking to the streets and demanding a share of power, so the growth in the size and intensity of demonstrations outside conferences of world leaders is said to have made an impact. Desai and Said (in Anheier *et al.* 2001: 62–3, 75) suggest that demonstrations in Turkey and Argentina, and riots in Prague and Washington, influenced the pace of reform at the IMF and World Bank, while peaceful mass campaigns by bodies such as Jubilee 2000 in 68 countries hastened the cancellation of at least some Third World debts. The demonstrators possess few sanctions, yet Western governments and IFIs appear to have become more sensitive to global opinion, and especially to the demands of well-informed NGOs in the West which could attract substantial support. In addition to the quantity of support, it often helped if they could enlist bishops, pop singers or respected campaigners for the poor. Post-industrial society, infused with post-material values, appears to put greater pressure on decision makers who want to be seen to be acting virtuously. We noted Cammack's argument that serving the needs of global capitalism ultimately takes precedence over moral crusades, yet the crusaders may be nudging governments and IFIs to pay more attention to the plight of the poor in a way they would not previously have done. Political correctness requires at least some acknowledgment of the need for 'poverty eradication', rather than simply blaming the poor or their rulers for their own improvidence. Similarly with environmental problems, it would now take a very bold or foolhardy politician or administrator to deny the existence of climate change or the threats to endangered species. At a minimum, they would probably claim to share the concerns of campaigners on these issues.

The alleged need to seek the consent of global civil society, or sections of it, merges into the alleged desire to be seen to be acting virtuously rather than merely serving the interests of powerful governments and global capitalism. According to Zurn 'The results of international negotiations seem to depend increasingly on the consent of trans-nationalizing sectoral publics', and 'world politics are ... developing into a form of multilateralism borne by society and accountable to both national and transnationalizing publics' (Zurn 2004: 281, 283). Consent, in turn, merges into arguments about the existence of consensus. Fox and Brown claim that the World Bank is now more accountable, and contains more officials concerned with environmental and social problems. It now rejects 'the most harmful proposals' that would exacerbate these problems (Fox and Brown 1998: 528, 534). Political correctness apart, it seems plausible to argue that the failure of the free market fundamentalist policies to achieve their stated aims, in the initial Washington consensus, has created scope for a more flexible approach. The argument about consent and consensus is taken a stage further by Boli *et al.* who see the emergence and consolidation of a 'global culture', operating at an overarching level of social reality that takes the form of international organisations. INGOs are the prime arena in which world-cultural conceptions of values, principles, standards and norms are developed. Participation in INGOs is the exercise of rights and duties associated with world citizenship (Boli *et al.* in Boli and Thomas 1999: 73). If one is prepared to follow the arguments as far as this stage, one might begin to see global decision-makers as the dedicated servants of global civil society.

3. Global governance

'Governance' is a slippery concept, but it is usually taken to imply the existence of a range of inter-connected structures that operate in a relatively predictable way, according to generally accepted rules and conventions, in order to resolve a range of political and administrative problems (For a detailed description of the concept, see Hoffmann and Ba in Ba and Hoffmann 2005: 1–14). It is more elaborate than mere 'government', which places the emphasis on rule by and through recognisable formal institutions such as parliaments, cabinets and civil services. At the national level, especially in the West, much power has passed from these institutions to a range of quangos, and consultative and semi-autonomous bodies – a shift from government to governance. This reflects a process of governing that has become more complex. The range of decisions to be taken is more diverse, and the need to retain legitimacy by involving civil society has become more urgent. Many parallels can be drawn at a global level, though with the difference that there was never any 'global government' to precede 'global governance'. *Ad hoc* structures developed in a piecemeal way as the need arose. These dealt with everything from narrow issues, such as postal services and marine insurance, to broad ones such as maintaining world peace.

Governance does not necessarily imply democracy, because it is difficult for the wishes of any global population to be implemented when power is fragmented between a diversity of bodies. Any desire by a global consensus or a global majority to improve working conditions, for example, might receive sympathetic treatment from the International Labour Organisation (ILO), only to be negated by the free market policies of the World Bank. But neither is governance compatible with the power politics model, because it rests on co-operation between decision-making bodies and their client groups (or stakeholders). As in the global democracy model, it is assumed that authority will be more legitimate, and will be more likely to elicit public co-operation, if the relevant sections of global civil society are consulted. A few examples will suffice. While consultative relations between the United Nations Economic and Social Council (ECOSOC) and NGOs go back at least to the 1970s, it is said that NGOs since the 1990s have become more effective at monitoring and lobbying UN bodies. Their skills have been honed by the sharing of ideas and experience at the growing number of NGO international conferences (Hajnal in Kirton and Hajnal 2006: 279–81; Scholte 2004: 215–19). The World Bank, the WTO and other IGOs are said to consult civil society more, and SAPRI has enabled the governance process to extend down to the level of local NGOs, able to spell out the local effects of policies made in Washington (Chandler in Baker and Chandler 2005: 148–70; Alger 2002: 109). The NGO Working Group on the World Bank has been able to create strategic partnerships between NGOs, the World Bank and the UN, through bodies such as the Global Alliance for Forest Conservation and Sustainable Use, and the World Commission on Dams (Edwards 2000: 13–14). At the same time, NGOs at the global level, like those in Tanzania noted in the previous chapter, have taken the initiative in monitoring the extent to which their political masters are implementing their own policies successfully. NGOs have monitored progress in reaching UN goals on poverty eradication and gender equality; and human rights NGOs have monitored the compliance of governments with UN human rights conventions (Scholte 2004: 219). But these processes stop a long way short of democracy when we discover that NGOs are usually excluded from participation in the actual policy decisions. Decisions by the IFIs still rest with the representatives of a few wealthy countries meeting in secret, with NGOs often denied access to key documents (Edwards 2000: 14–15; Hoffmann and Ba in Ba and Hoffmann 2005: 249–57). There is also a democratic deficit, common also to national civil societies, resulting from a lack of any stakeholder control or scrutiny over the private sector, despite its enormous power in shaping the economies of many poor countries. While some NGO campaigns have achieved spectacular results in exposing deplorable working conditions, and in pressing individual businesses to behave more humanely, the context within which business as a whole is allowed to operate depends at best on voluntary agreements rather than any overall, enforceable framework subject to democratic accountability (Lipschutz 2005: 34–42).

4.   Global pluralism

Many observers see the global order, as portrayed in Figure 6.1, as closer to anarchy, or at least to an absence of orderly, predictable processes. Global pluralism provides a potential halfway house between democracy, where a modicum of order exists but where one can never be sure which civil society groups will force decision-makers out of their regular routines, and complete anarchy with the law of the jungle. The global pluralism model assumes the existence of a range of global decision-making authorities, as in the global governance model, but guards against belief in any invisible hand co-ordinating the work of the authorities, or ensuring that a common culture provides a consensus within which the authorities can work. Is there much common ground between the United Nations Development Programme (UNDP) with its social democratic tendencies and its concern for the plight of the poor, and the IMF with its faith in market forces? A rough parallel would be the proliferation of *ad hoc* bodies at the local level in nineteenth century Britain, each working within its narrow terms of reference to improve public health, relieve poverty, supply water or provide schools, but having difficulty in relating its activities to any broader public interest or policy objectives. Yet this global pluralism halfway house remains almost unoccupied by academics, who apparently prefer the extremes on the vertical axis of Figure 6.1 of global democracy or global anarchy, or the alternative on the horizontal axis of global governance. There may be good empirical reasons for steering clear of this unoccupied house, but the more adventurous explorers might wonder whether it does not provide an antidote to the overly neat and tidy global governance house, with its assumptions that order will somehow emerge from the proliferation of global governing bodies.

5.   Global technocracy

Following our parallel with nineteenth century Britain, much of the political/administrative process then was concerned with ensuring that the drains remained unblocked, that outbreaks of cholera were eliminated or that adequate cemeteries were provided, rather than with the grander political themes of free trade, the emancipation of the workers, the abolition of slavery or Irish home rule. In global politics today, it is also possible to take the view that the most urgent concerns are simply to ensure the smooth functioning of the world's infrastructure. Consumers should be able to buy goods that do not threaten their health or safety; AIDS and malaria should be combated; aircraft should be able to take off and land safely; patent laws should protect businesses from having their ideas stolen, and countries dependent on water supplies from distant sources should be protected from any diversion of supplies. Pianta describes a rise of supra-national power, hidden and unaccountable to the democratic process, exercised by specialised government officials and international technocrats. Power has been transferred increasingly to IGOs, and much decision-making is informal (Pianta in Anheier *et al.* 2001: 169–94). In a more convoluted way, Rosenau appears to see similar processes at work, leading to what he calls 'fragmegration' – a mixture of fragmentation and integration in response to technological changes. The result is that there are too many centres of authority for global civil society to be effective (Rosenau in Ba and Hoffmann 2005: 133, 138–9). Pianta's unaccountability to the democratic process, and Rosenau's diverse centres of power militating against global governance, thus mark the global technology model off from the previous models we have discussed. Some NGOs may be co-opted into the decision-making process because of their technical qualifications, such as expertise in health or conservation, but not because of any claim they may make to represent global civil society or elements within it. As long as the technocrat is king, or at least lord of the manor within his jurisdiction, NGO campaigns will come to little. They may win isolated battles against hydro-electric dams or encroachments on individual forests, but they will lose the war. Campaigns against dams or nuclear power will wither if the technocrat judges that the lights will go out without them. Opposition to genetically modified crops will fail because the technocrat rules that the alternative is starvation, and protests against the decimation of indigenous production in Africa will fall on deaf ears when the technocrat decides that the free market is the most effective way of ordering the global economy. While NGOs claiming to represent major sections of civil society will have little access to decisions, businesses will be less handicapped. Any discussion of the relationship between business interests and officials wielding power at IGOs would take us too far from our immediate concerns, but it would be remarkable if there was not a substantial movement of personnel between the two sectors, and a wide degree of shared values.

6.　Global anarchy

Some of the arguments here take us back to the power politics model. NGO influence, it is asserted, has been exaggerated and, insofar as it ever existed, it belonged to a brief interlude between the Cold War and the 'war on terror'. States, not NGOs or global civil society, are the real actors in world politics. According to Cohen, NGOs have lost their autonomy and capacity to influence big states, and sovereignty has reasserted itself since the 1990s. Global civil society is a myth, and NGOs cannot claim to represent society (Cohen 2003: 55–68, 133).

Where the global anarchy model parts company with the power politics model is in its rejection of the belief that the United States, possibly abetted by a few allies, dominates world politics. Cohen notes the way in which the US flexed its muscles in protecting its own pharmaceutical industry by delaying action against AIDs, tuberculosis and malaria. Such action would have threatened the patent rights of American firms. Yet Cohen sees this as a symptom of the way in which the world in general has become more selfish since the Cold War, with nations pursuing their own narrow interests, and failing to co-operate in dealing with transnational problems such as disease, violence, poverty, crime and inequality (Cohen 2003: 178–83). Here there are echoes of the 'realist' school of international relations, with nations pursuing their own interests, and subject to little mediation from global authority above or moderation from civil society below (Waltz 1979: 88–93, 105). The growing influence of India and China, and even the ability of Russia to intimidate its neighbours by threatening to cut off gas supplies, might be cited as additional evidence for the anarchic view. One can argue about whether what is happening today is new, or a reversion to the politics of the Cold War, or has gone on all the time, but the anarchic view is an antidote to the assumptions of respect for the authority of international institutions in the global governance model. The US continues to blockade Cuba illegally, to choose when to respect or ignore the Geneva Convention, and to avoid the clutches of the International Criminal Court. China is largely unimpeded in its support for the Sudanese government suppressing its citizens in large areas of the country, and Japan and Norway continue to hunt whales. Even in weaker countries, we have noted that for all the growth in the role of NGOs, national governments often see it as in their own interests (if not the interests of their constituents) to enter into agreements with stronger powers, whether in trade agreements with the EU or in purchasing an expensive air defence system from Britain.

The models and the real world

Is there any way of reconciling the widely different assumptions on which the models are based, or even refuting some of the models as too remote from reality to be relevant? It would be useful to begin with the global governance model because it is, in many ways, a hub around which the others revolve. One can hardly deny the existence of a variety of structures involved in the process of governance, but they can be viewed as the instruments used by the strong to exploit the weak (the power politics model); as institutions reflecting the wishes of global civil society (the global democracy model); as disparate groups ploughing their own separate furrows (the global pluralism model), as means of taking essential technical decisions, insulated from governments and public opinion alike (the global technocracy model), or as irrelevant bystanders, ignored in the struggle for national supremacy (the global anarchy model).

If the power politics model is taken to mean that the US government is now able to impose its will on other governments, in the absence of any counter balance from the Soviet Union, experience since 2003 suggests some severe limitations. Despite having a defence budget that accounts for over half the defence expenditure of the world, the US has hardly been able to subdue Iraq, and has made little impression on Iran or North Korea, the other members of President Bush's 'axis of evil'. Gunboat diplomacy seems less effective when the enemy is no longer a group of foreign powers but a range of armed groups, with no obvious base, which can make life increasingly uncomfortable for an occupying power. At the same time, public opinion within America appears to have lost any enthusiasm it had for imperial adventures. While crude force has severe limitations, a case could be made for the continuation of power politics in the economic sphere. With its dominant position in the IFIs and the Organisation of American States, the US is in a stronger position than most countries to shape the rules of world trade, or to ignore the rules when it cannot get its own way. Yet we have noted that insofar as economic domination is exercised through the medium of IFIs, the administrators of these bodies are increasingly people who reject the earlier versions of free market fundamentalism, who often have a genuine concern for the plight of the world's poor, and are more willing to talk to NGOs representing the poor. This does not mean that we have witnessed radical changes of policy, but there is at least a degree of flexibility on matters such as debt relief, privatisation and public service provision in Africa. Beyond these uncertain movements lie the imponderables of the consequences of the economic rise of Brazil, India and China, which may well be weakening American economic domination (Kennedy 2008: 7). If these countries gained a stronger foothold in the IFIs, this could push policies further in the direction of support for more interventionist economic policies.

For writers like Cammack the domination is exercised not so much by individual countries or governments as by 'global capitalism', using free market economics as its main weapon (Cammack 2006: 331–50). If this is true, NGOs have a more difficult fight on their hands, as they are confronting an invisible enemy, just as elusive as the enemy encountered by the Americans in the streets of Baghdad. Global capitalism may, in this view, find it expedient to put on a human face, but there will continue to be a global order in which poor people and poor countries remain at the mercy of forces they cannot control. The market, possibly policed by Western governments and IFIs, rather than votes or reasoned arguments, determines political outcomes. One could argue that it was ever thus, or that past attempts by African governments to plan their economies were not an attractive alternative, but we are still left with a highly unequal relationship. In colonial times, European rulers in many areas simply forbade Africans from entering areas of economic activity that competed with Europeans. Today free market forces and WTO rules frequently make for just as effective an exclusion. 'Power politics' might suggest too direct an exploitation of the weak by the strong, but the model is relevant to the extent that the weak face severe handicaps in articulating their demands.

As a footnote we might speculate on the significance of growing Chinese influence in Africa. It might at first sight suggest a revival of the opportunity for Africa to exploit the conflict between East and West, but it might also suggest a weakening of opportunities for NGO influence. Western powers, for all their faults, accept a pluralist order within which NGOs have a legitimate role, and this provides opportunities both for African NGOs to lobby Western governments or their embassies, or for Western governments to champion the cause of NGOs in the face of African governmental repression. In the conflict between HakiElimu and the Tanzanian government, the sympathy of most Western embassies was with HakiElimu. China, in contrast, has little tradition of pluralism or NGO autonomy. While Western governments in the past have been criticised for being indulgent towards African dictators like Moi and Mobutu, the Chinese government has shown virtually no inclination to relate aid to democracy or human rights, or to enter dialogue with NGOs concerned with these matters. The Sudan and Zimbabwe are obvious cases in point. The rise of China might give support to those who argue that national governments are now reasserting themselves at the expense of civil society.

The global democracy model, we noted, was based on the overlapping assumptions about direct public pressure, structures of consent and accountability, and the existence of a global culture which set limits to the behaviour of political actors. The influence of direct pressure is always difficult to assess, but it would be difficult to dismiss the combined effects of anarchists fighting the police in the streets of Seattle and Genoa, the thousands of peaceful protesters in Birmingham demanding an end to the debt burden, and the well organised NGOs lobbying and negotiating continuously with governments and IFIs. At the very least, the world's decision-makers have to acknowledge that there are alternative views to their own (largely free market) orthodoxy, and to express some concern over the plight of the poor and the environment. As regards consent and accountability, a charitable view would be that any democratic element in IFIs before the 1980s was close to zero, so that any developments from that base might be greeted with exaggerated enthusiasm. Zurn's notion of international negotiations depending 'increasingly on the consent of transnationalizing sectoral publics' and world politics involving increasing accountability to national and transnational publics (Zurn 2004: 282, 283) seems a trifle optimistic. A suspect detained by the police might 'consent' to answer questions after being given a caution, but the relationship between the authority and the consenter is hardly an equal one. Similarly, NGOs giving 'consent' to IFI decisions may have little alternative. Indeed the growing tendency to co-opt and consult NGOs puts some obligation on them to acknowledge the legitimacy of the current global order, whereas previously they had little to lose by railing against it. As for accountability, we return to the point that it is an elastic concept. IFIs, and possibly Western governments, may account for their actions in the sense of giving explanations for their decisions, and addressing these explanations specifically to stakeholders such as NGOs, but accountability does not necessarily imply that policies will be altered to meet the criticisms of stakeholders.

Is there a 'world culture', to which many international organisations and INGOs subscribe? If the belief in such a culture could be sustained, it would not merely mean that global civil society accepted the existence of global authority structures, but it might mean that civil society had a direct input into how the structures operated. Yet the arguments put forward by Boli *et al.* (in Boli and Thomas 1999: 56–7) leave many questions unanswered. Has their 'global culture' eliminated other cultures, or does it exist alongside them? Is it not possible to have a culture believing in peace, equality and fraternity, to which many NGOs and possibly some IGOs might subscribe, existing alongside cultures based on religious fundamentalism, or a belief in following the wisdom of bankers and financiers? Is it not possible that any culture which exists is one shaped by those who already wield power – hence the general rejection of social democratic alternatives to the free market? One might even argue that any culture built up around INGOs is a reaction against the dominant culture, and that what emerges is not so much a consensus as an attempt to build such bridges as are possible between the two sides.

To say that we do not live in a global democracy is to state the obvious, and few writers have argued otherwise. The disagreement is more between those who see increasingly important democratic elements within a basically non-democratic global order, and those who see business as usual. There are, as it were, agnostics and unbelievers but few, if any, believers who accept the 'global democracy' model as a literal truth. In procedural terms, there is something to be said for the view that more democratic openings have been created, with greater co-option, consultation, participation and accountability but, in terms of outcomes, the unbelievers have a stronger case. While one can reel off a list of victories for the 'have nots' against the might of the global order, these remain exceptions to the general rule. It is not just that elites get their own way more frequently than non-elites, which is common in many democracies, but that the whole system places such severe limitations on opportunities for non-elites, or their representatives, to influence events. Whether one thinks in terms of the interests of the major Western powers, of global capitalism, or of IGOs that have acquired interests and ideologies of their own, those who wield power have not, for the most part, yielded to the wishes or interests of the majority of the world's population.

The 'global pluralism' model, we noted, has attracted much less academic attention than its more colourful neighbours – global democracy and global anarchy. It does not seem appropriate here either to promote such a lost cause, or to seek to demolish it when it has so few friends anyway. It remains, nonetheless, a useful antidote to the assumptions in the global governance model that a complex set of global decision-making structures will necessarily imply coherent or coordinated policies. The same might be said of the growth of 'governance' within individual countries, where a proliferation of decision-making bodies can make for a fragmentation of interests and policies. The autonomous state school, for example, may improve its performance by expelling troublesome pupils, but the local social services department or police authority may see such a policy as adding to their problems. But in the national context there is 'government' as well as 'governance', and the central government can ultimately adjudicate, if it wishes, as to whose interests should prevail. At the global level there is governance without government, and a greater likelihood of incompatible policies being pursued without any superior authority to adjudicate. For NGOs there is then the problem that winning the confidence of some powerful IGOs, such as the ILO or the UNDP, may be negated because of the policies of the World Bank or the IMF.

The 'global technocracy' model raises familiar questions about the ability of technocrats to insulate themselves from both politicians above and public opinion below. There has always been two-way traffic. Formerly 'political' decisions, such as the fixing of interests rates, may be taken out of politics and given to autonomous bankers, while formerly technocratic decisions, such as the desirability of nuclear power, may become politicised as a result of public concerns about safety, pollution or the interests of workers in competing industries.

One can concede that large areas of decision-making are left to technocrats, possibly working in co-operation with NGOs possessing the relative expertise, where the wider world has little to gain from butting in. There are not many votes to be won in intervening in decisions on the design of aircraft seat belts or the means of processing marine insurance claims. But a major test of the existence of technocracy, in the narrow sense of technocrats wielding power, is the ease or otherwise with which determined governments or civil society actors can wrest power away from technocrats when circumstances demand this. Even an apparent supporter of the global technocracy model such as Pianta acknowledges that international organisations may respond to NGO pressure, whether by reforming their own rules and procedures, and making moderate concessions, or through a more radical re-designing of institutional tools, as with the creation of the International Criminal Court (Pianta in Anheier 2001: 192). The whole debate on what measures, if any, to take to combat climate change was once mainly the preserve of a narrow circle of technocrats. Now it is another case of political actors, and especially NGOs, invading the territory of the technocrats to demand political solutions. In other cases, what appear to be mainly technocratic decisions may turn out to be influenced in a largely unseen way by groups with a direct interest. One can speculate on the extent to which pressure on countries to grow genetically modified crops is based on purely technical considerations, or on the influence of Monsanto. In this, as in many other cases, there is likely to be an inter-penetration of personnel and values between IGOs and businesses which detracts from any notion of decisions being taken in a technocratic ivory tower. On the whole the global technocracy model does not stand up well to the competing pressures of governments, businesses and NGOs. Large areas of decision making are left to technocrats when no one else has anything to gain by intervening but, when vested interests or ideology are involved, other actors are quick to move in. The political process then moves closer to global pluralism, or even global democracy, if NGOs are able to exert some influence, or to power politics if governments or businesses predominate.

The 'global anarchy' model is attractive to those who take a nostalgic view of the recent past. Whereas in the late 1980s and 1990s powerful countries were helping those emerging from authoritarian rule to build democracy and civil society, this phase has been superseded by governments re-asserting their own interests in the face of security threats, economic uncertainty and disillusionment with the attempts at democracy promotion and help for the poor generally. Much of this thesis, of course, runs counter to arguments about the emergence of a post-Washington consensus which has moderated free market fundamentalism, and about IFIs now being run by benevolent officials promoting capitalism with a human face. One response to the global anarchy thesis is that it exaggerates the extent to which world politics has changed. There has always been a large element of the pursuit of national self interest, and this was not absent even in the heyday of democracy promotion and civil society building. Indeed such activities might be seen as attempts to ensure that the values of the Western powers prevailed in the former authoritarian states.

The thesis might be tested by asking what happens when governments pursue their own selfish interests in the way described by Cohen (Cohen 2003: 182). In relatively open political systems, civil societies often rein in governments, especially in an era when governments can less easily hide the consequences of their actions. As the American public became aware of the level of casualties among their own troops in Iraq, and of the excesses of the behaviour of some of their soldiers, the government could not easily continue relentlessly on the same course. This is in contrast to the way that governments behaved during the First World War when populations at home were less aware of the facts. Even in African countries where communications are more difficult and governments less tolerant of criticism, we have seen that the unbridled pursuit of self interest by politicians can be checked by alert NGOs, although the occupation of the Congo by Uganda might be seen as a throwback to global anarchy.

When more authoritarian governments pursue their own narrow interests, the nature of any checks is less clear, yet it seems excessive to describe the outcomes as anarchic. The Russians, for all their threats, have so far only briefly cut off gas supplies to their neighbours, and have maintained an uneasy peace with most of them. The Chinese have not been prevented from sustaining violent authoritarian regimes in Sudan and Zimbabwe, yet they are more sensitive to world criticism than were governments in the days of gunboat diplomacy. Governments in all parts of the world may pursue policies that meet with widespread international disapproval, but the question we might ask is not 'Why does this happen?' but 'Why does it not happen much more frequently?' This brings us back to the vague but important notion of observing 'international standards'. Governments would rather be loved than hated, especially in a period when global governance implies a continuous round of international conferences on matters great and small. If only from the point of view of self interest, a country might gain more benefits from such conferences if it is not seen as a pariah, isolated from the rest of the global community. Even if one accepts the arguments about selfishness and indifference to the suffering of others, there appears to be sufficient interdependence in the world to throw doubt on the global anarchy model. For NGOs, the dilemmas faced by governments in trying to reconcile crude self interest with international respectability, provides much fertile ground. There is always the chance that the most hopeless of lost causes can be transformed into an opportunity for influence if there is a shift in the balance of forces, or unexpected events. The disruption of the Chinese attempts to parade the Olympic Torch around the world in 2008 suddenly put China on the defensive over its activities in Tibet, just as the execution of Ken Saro-Wiwa in 1999 put the authoritarian government in Nigeria more under the international spotlight, and increased pressure on the military rulers to depart. Shifts in the balance of forces may not be sufficient to bring an immediate end to authoritarian rule in Zimbabwe, the civil war in the Sudan, or the American and Chinese occupations of Iraq and Tibet, but the policies within all these countries may be modified to minimise world disapproval.

Conclusion

The search for the role of NGOs in the global order has required us to negotiate a wide range of controversies. Many conflicting opinions can be simplified by incorporating them into theories and models, though this always runs the risk of misrepresentation if ideas are put into rigid pigeon holes. Our initial concern was to note the empirical evidence of a rapid rise in the number and activities of INGOs, and to speculate that this might suggest a comparable increase in NGO influence at a global level. This might in turn have suggested the emergence of a more democratic global order, in which the voices of the poor and underprivileged would be heard and acted upon. But much evidence and many opinions need to be collected along the way to obtain even a preliminary view of where NGOs fit into the world order.

Even the belief that an increasing amount of political decision-making and political conflict now takes place at a 'global', rather than an 'international', level does not enjoy unanimous support. We noted Laxer and Halperin's spirited defence of the ability of national governments to control events. But the broader consensus is that national frontiers are crossed increasingly by people, ideas, weapons and diseases in ways that governments find difficult to control, and that this leads to growing attempts at control by global bodies. NGOs then try to shadow these bodies to ensure that they respect the interests of the people the NGOs represent. This leads to the emergence of the concept of a global civil society, comparable with national civil societies in the sense that it constitutes an area of political activity between the ordinary citizen and decision-making bodies. Like globalisation itself, the concept of global civil society is hotly contested, whether on the grounds that globalisation has barely occurred, or that one cannot have a global civil society if there is no global state. We rejected the latter argument in the belief that it is the basic functions of civil society that matter, and that it can exist without being structured in the way that it is within nations. This does not necessarily mean, as some writers assert, that global civil society will consist exclusively of tolerant democrats with a social conscience, upholding the rights of the poor and oppressed. NGOs with such tendencies will have to take their place in global civil society alongside religious fundamentalists, tribalists, mercenaries and criminal gangs, and their wishes will not necessarily prevail against these groups. We also acknowledged that global civil society, like most civil societies within countries, is not a community of equals. Just as the wealthier and more educated citizens within countries wield disproportionate influence, so NGOs based in the West wield disproportionate influence globally, given their greater wealth, resources, trained personnel and access to authority.

Having argued for the existence of global civil society, operating in an attempt to influence and curb the power of IGOs, the next task was to inquire into the nature of the global political process, especially in terms of the extent to which it is democratic or authoritarian, orderly or anarchic. Six models were suggested to indicate different emphases on the nature of the distribution of power. The relevance of the 'global technocracy' and 'global anarchy' models can be dismissed relatively easily. Experience suggests that technocrats only wield power for as long as other actors allow them to. Once governments, businesses or NGOs decide that an issue is a political one, the focus of decision-making will shift away from technocrats. Global anarchy can also be dismissed because, however selfish and narrow minded national governments may be, there is too much interdependence, and too many mediating institutions, to allow the world to return to its pre-1914 state. With a few minor exceptions, most countries seek a degree of international respectability and aspire to observe international standards (though with a few occasional lapses). In a world of constant international conferences, where a range of decisions can enhance or damage an individual country's interests, it is safer not to be seen as a maverick, or to make too many enemies by disregarding the rules of the club.

If the global technocracy and global anarchy models are as shaky as we have suggested, this is to the advantage of NGOs. Once one moves away from the notion that technocrats will claim an exclusive right to take a decision because only they possess the relevant expertise, NGOs can move in and claim a superior right to judgement, whether on the basis of their own expertise or their moral certainty. And once one moves away from the notion that governments can do whatever they like to advance their own interests, and accepts that they are sensitive to the opinions of others, NGOs may be able to force even the most powerful government on to the defensive.

Of the other models, global governance emphasises the extent to which there is now an extensive routine decision-making process taking place beyond the reach of national governments. While this is undoubtedly true, the model in its most extreme form might suggest a degree of harmony, consensus and co-ordination that is far removed from reality. The global pluralism model allows for a looser process, in which different IGOs may be pursuing incompatible policies, and in which the authority of some of them is challenged by governments or NGOs.

This leaves us with the key question about the extent to which the global order is one of power politics or democracy. It is obviously a matter of degree. No one suggests that the US, Russia or China can get their own way through brute force as a matter of course, and no one suggests that the popular will can be enacted at a global level as smoothly as in a

Scandinavian social democracy, but the 'power politics' school would point to the American invasion of Iraq, and Chinese policy in the Sudan and Tibet, as examples of the ability of the strong to exploit the weak, regardless of the niceties of international opinions or laws. The 'global democracy' school, in contrast, points to the impact of mass demonstrations, the greater ability of NGOs to hold IGOs to account and to influence their decisions, and possibly to the emergence of a 'global culture' which forces political actors to work within an accepted consensus.

A major objection to the power politics argument is that imperial adventures in Iraq or Tibet are exceptions to the general rule. If military force alone mattered, there might have been invasions of Iran, Myanmar or large areas of Latin America, but global opinion, and perhaps internal public opinion, would not tolerate this. The democratic argument is also exposed to the objection of generalising from too small a number of particular examples. Global civil society, through the medium of NGOs, may win victories over debt relief or the Multilateral Agreement on Investment, but does that tell us much about the general run of decisions taken at the global level? By whom are they taken, how, and in whose interests? A crude answer would be: by non-elected bodies dominated by the Western powers, generally meeting in secret, without the effective participation of NGOs or representatives of poorer countries, and in the interests of wealthy countries and global capital. While power politics based on military force has its limits, power politics based on economic weight continues to achieve remarkable results.

None of this is to denigrate the advances that have been made by NGOs and global civil society in terms of demanding the right to be heard by IGOs and in holding them to account, or to ignore the genuine attempts that have been made by IMF and World Bank officials to respond to NGO opinion and to learn from past mistakes. But it still seems premature to speak of global democracy. To expect groups to press successfully for democracy when they do not, for the most part, possess votes, sanctions or large popular bases, is to expect the impossible. The main limitation on NGOs within Africa, we suggested in the previous chapter, was political. It is governments that have the power to allocate resources, dispense patronage, sign contracts, make deals with other governments, and use their majorities in parliament to enact legislation. Many of these powers, we suggested, were used to pursue policies which conflicted with the aspirations of NGOs. At the global level, a major limitation on NGOs is again the political/administrative structure, but in this case a structure that is not even subject to popular election. But beyond that structure (or structures) lie economic interests that are even more difficult to penetrate. Global civil society has never been asked whether it wants global capitalism, aid that is conditional on privatisation, free market policies that damage African economies, or investment decisions that benefit global businesses at the expense of indigenous businesses and residents.

To question the extent to which global democracy has advanced is not to suggest that NGOs have been unsuccessful, or that there is little to be gained from them continuing their work. On the contrary, it is to suggest that the relative absence of institutionalised democratic procedures, involving a more equal relationship between NGOs and decision-makers, means that every new issue requires a new battle to be waged from scratch. In these circumstances, the presence of NGO voices becomes ever more necessary to protect a range of interests that would otherwise go unheard.

7
International NGOs: Missionaries or Imperialists?

Two strands have run through much of the discussion in the previous chapters. On the one hand, there is the depiction of NGOs as idealistic groups, fighting for the needs of the poor, the disadvantaged and even the planet as a whole; and pursuing causes which politicians either neglect or wilfully obstruct. On the other, there is a global order in which decision-making frequently reflects the interests of Western governments and businesses, and possibly African politicians and elites who have struck deals with these interests, while the poor, the disadvantaged and the planet continue to suffer exploitation. Overlapping these worlds of civil society politics and power politics lie international NGOs (INGOs). In this chapter we consider some of the arguments about the ability or willingness of INGOs to seize the initiative and tilt the balance of power in favour of what they might regard as a more just social order; and consider the contrary argument about the extent to which INGOs are either reluctant or willing collaborators in consolidating the existing distribution of power.

Before examining the arguments we need to beware of some of the unresolved problems of definition. The distinction between an ordinary NGO and an INGO is not always clear. Should a small NGO with an office in London, which makes only occasional forays into Africa, be described as 'international'? The difference between such an NGO, and bodies like Oxfam and Amnesty International, which operate over most of the globe, might be regarded as one of degree, with difficulty in deciding where to draw the dividing line between 'national' and 'international'. Are INGOs synonymous with NGOs based in the West? A strict definition of the term would suggest not, but custom and practice suggests otherwise. While a few INGOs such as Jubilee South, which campaigns for the cancellation of all Third World debts, have built bases in the developing world, the vast majority of INGOs are based in Western

Europe and North America, and it seems easier to stick to custom and practice than semantic precision. A further problem is the loose use of terms such as 'NGO', 'agency' or simply 'donor' when discussing the impact of the West on African politics and society. The word 'donor' can obviously cover any individual or institution that provides help for Africa in money or in kind, but assertions such as 'donors follow the policies of Western governments' or 'donors impose unfair bureaucratic requirements on African NGOs' are not very helpful unless we know the status of the donor in relation to different power structures. All too often quasi-governmental agencies such as the Department for International Development (DFID) or the United States Agency for International Development (USAID) are lumped together with INGOs as 'donors', yet they are clearly quangos rather than INGOs. As such, it is unremarkable that they frequently follow the official governmental line. INGOs, with their 'non-governmental' status, are likely to enjoy greater autonomy, though we shall need to qualify this statement as we look at actual cases.

A further problem, though there appear to be no accepted definitions to overcome it, is the distinction between INGOs which are principally 'donors' dispensing funds to NGOs on the ground, and INGOs which are more directly involved in development or advocacy. The first category would include bodies such as the Ford Foundation, the Bill and Melinda Gates Foundation and possibly the Aga Khan Foundation, while the latter include bodies such as Oxfam, Amnesty International, Save the Children and the German stiftungen, whose presence is clearly visible in much of Africa. In the case of what we might call the 'donor INGOs', the very nature of their work makes it likely that they will set out stringent conditions for their aid, and thus lay themselves open to charges of paternalism, bureaucracy and imperialism, whereas what we might call the 'activist INGOs' may be more pragmatic, and more receptive to the demands of African civil society.

In seeking to establish the role of INGOs in global politics, we now go on to look at such questions as their varied ideologies, the bases of their legitimacy, and the extent of their autonomy or dependence on other institutions. This will lead us into a discussion of the ways in which INGOs seek to wield political influence, given their underlying strengths and weaknesses.

Imperialism, paternalism and emancipation: the diversity of ideologies

In the previous chapter we noted Boli and Thomas's view that INGOs had helped to build a 'global culture' within which there is a consensus on the nature and purpose of states and transnational corporations. INGOs are assumed to be a force for good in promoting development, individual fulfilment, security and justice, and INGO activity has often preceded and influenced the activities of states and international governmental organisations (IGOs) (Boli and Thomas 1999: 13–49). If one could be convinced of the existence of such a global culture, this would support the notion of INGOs as emancipators, eliminating the alternative of a 'neo-realist perspective' of a world based on the pursuit of self-interest (*ibid*: 15).

Yet the evidence for the existence of a benign global culture remains thin. At best, powerful governments and international financial institutions (IFIs) now claim to regard poverty eradication as a high priority, in a way that nineteenth century imperialists did not; and powerful businesses claim to believe in corporate social responsibility, which is taken to cover the existence of humane working conditions and respect for the natural environment. This would presumably have been alien to the East India Company and most nineteenth century mill owners. Actual practice, however, frequently diverges from proclaimed beliefs, whether the latter are based on genuine conviction or a desire for respectability. Where INGOs do seek to emancipate the people in the sense of relieving them of the burdens of repression, exploitation, poverty and disease, is this a reflection of a global culture in which common humanitarian values are being upheld, or is it a reaction against a global order in which the strong continue to exploit the weak?

In some cases there may be a sufficient humanitarian consensus (if not a 'global culture') to enable a group to raise funds, attract staff and gain access to the areas where it needs to work. Few people would question the objectives of the Red Cross or Save the Children. Yet in many other cases INGOs have emerged to challenge what they regard as an unjust world order, or at least to challenge particular manifestations of it. Far from working with the grain of global values, they are fighting to change existing values, especially those which emphasise the primacy of the free market and of Western institutions. Rugendyke (2007: 7–8) suggests that greater advocacy by INGOs is the result of experience of the current order. They realise the barriers to development such as unfair trade, debt, low commodity prices and uneven land distribution, and are often made more aware of these problems by the demands of their 'southern partners'. Much INGO work concentrates less on the major of issues of 'unfair trade' and debt, and more on one small area of global injustice, ranging from the recruitment of child soldiers through press censorship to the treatment of refugees. This narrow focus is generally justified on the basis of the 'stiletto heel principle' that it is most productive to strike hard at one small target. Whether the effect is emancipatory for society as a whole is open to question. Woollacott suggests that promoting developments such as a more independent press, sinking wells, organising weaving classes or helping refugees, may sometimes have the effect of stabilising a [possibility authoritarian] government and sometimes strengthening the opposition, but that the fate of regimes should not be the direct concern of INGOs (Woollacott 2005: 24). Even if the ultimate fate of regimes is too remote an issue for INGOs, DeMars criticises them for believing that their actions will create only the intended consequences and no others (DeMars 2005: 9–11). The humanitarian act of helping Hutu refugees from Rwanda has been blamed for the subsequent return of these refugees to their own country and the violence which they then inflicted on the Tutsis.

That many INGOs with emancipatory objectives exist is not in doubt. The problem is that there are many dimensions to emancipation beyond the formal one of establishing the political rights of universal suffrage and civil liberties. Politicians who pursued the goal of emancipation in nineteenth and twentieth century Europe at least had some control over the working of the social, economic and political processes they had set in train. As legislators and members of executives they could, within limits, adjust liberal reforms that had illiberal or destabilising effects. Thus the right to strike might be qualified by legislation to protect essential supplies, or freedom of expression might be limited by libel laws. Advancing the interests of the poor might stop short of prohibiting the rich from paying for private education or health care. INGOs, in contrast, generally have only limited control over the administration of the reforms for which they have campaigned, and still less over any co-ordination of policies which seek to reconcile the varied consequences of the reforms. If repatriating refugees to their homelands leads to genocide, or if greater press freedom leads to people responding violently to untruths about the misdeeds of their political opponents, it will not be INGOs that have to deal with the consequences. Attempts at emancipation by INGOs may thus leave much unfinished business.

Turning to the 'imperialist' view of INGOs, this takes us back to the 'neo-realist perspective' rejected by Boli and Thomas. At least three strands of the argument can be highlighted. Firstly, the strong will always exploit the weak by whatever means are available, and INGOs have been one useful means in recent years. Secondly, INGOs act largely independently of any political or economic exploiters, and are opportunists who build their own empires to expand jobs and perks for staff, with little regard for the impact on the societies within which they are working. Thirdly, INGOs are not so much the tools of powerful political and economic interests, as in our first strand, but are actors who take calculated decisions as to how far they will collaborate with these interests, whether from conviction or out of necessity.

On the first point, the argument has a pedigree stretching back to the criticism of the early missionaries acting as agents for political and cultural exploitation. Even if they did not knowingly seek to do this, the result was allegedly that where once the Africans owned all the land and the Europeans owned all the bibles, Africans now own all the bibles and the Europeans own all the land. Mlama re-tells the tale in modern dress with her assertion that NGOs in Tanzania were forming a new network of economic and spiritual exploitation of the people, promoting consumerism, corruption, promiscuity, violence, theft and hooliganism. Christian fundamentalist groups were diverting attention away from the need to attend to the daily struggle for sustenance in society, and the building of any national cohesion (Mlama in Semboja *et al.* 2002: 119–30). 'Spiritual exploitation', if it exists, can only be a slow and indirect process, and one can question how many of the consequences enumerated by Mlama were actually intended by the exploiters. Consumerism and corruption might have brought them concrete benefits, but did theft or hooliganism? 'Economic exploitation' is more immediate, and the argument is that INGOs may be a more effective medium than gunboats, and the use of INGOs may provide a more subtle means of winning hearts and minds than the blatant use of global businesses. Jacoby argues that 'blatant imperialism' may cost lives, votes or foreign markets, so that Western powers have pressed the NGO sector to bear more of the moral and ethical responsibility for international action (Jacoby 2005: 215–33). The (probably untypical) case of the US government using NGOs in Iraq as a means of showing the humanitarian face of occupation is often cited (Klein 2003: 16). People receiving medical and food aid from INGOs may, the argument runs, feel less hostility to the occupation.

The 'INGOs as autonomous exploiters' thesis is pursued by Osman. INGOs are often seen as neo-colonial, lacking respect for local culture, and bringing in too many of their own staff when local personnel could have been employed. A large proportion of aid is spent on administration, or pay and perks for the INGOs' own staff (Osman 2006: 1–3). Little evidence is cited, and it would be tempting to dismiss this as a caricature, but there has always been an element of opportunism in the running of NGOs, at both national and international levels. No doubt government agencies and businesses are guilty of similar sins, but there is an expectation of the 'voluntary sector' having higher standards of integrity and altruism, and an expectation that organisations asking for voluntary donations will use the money for good works rather than self-aggrandisement.

Thirdly we focus on INGOs as neither the tools of more powerful bodies nor as independent actors pursuing their own selfish ends, but as actors in an interdependent world who decide how to negotiate with other forces, bearing in mind what they regard as feasible, ethical and compatible with their main objectives. The assumption of 'imperialism' is still present, either because the INGOs can only gain a foothold by working with or under governments with imperial ambitions, or because the INGOs themselves wish to propagate beliefs that are (or were) largely alien to the recipient countries. In the former case we return to the example of Iraq, where INGOs may feel that helping the hungry, the sick or the wounded is so important that they have to accept being portrayed as an arm of the occupying force. This is an extreme case, but INGOs in many parts of the world face the dilemma of conforming to political objectives they dislike if they are to enjoy access to governments and governmental financial support.

In other cases the INGOs need little prompting from governments or businesses because they have their own strong conviction that their beliefs should be accepted in Africa. Right-wing Christian fundamentalist sects generally have little doubt that the beliefs they wish to spread are superior to anything in African culture, and this can have practical as well as theological implications. They may, for example, preach 'abstinence' in preference to contraception, disregarding the fact that many African women are not in a position to choose to 'abstain', and this can contribute to the spread of AIDs. In the economic sphere there are INGOs with a similar missionary zeal. While the religious sects preach sermons, the economic missionaries organise conferences and seminars to win the confidence of African elites, usually preaching the gospel of the free market. The Friedrich Naumann Stiftung, based in Germany, sets itself the task of 'partaking in the development of African activities in the field of the rule of law, human rights, liberal democracy *and market economics*' (Friedrich Naumann Stiftung 2003: 1. Emphasis added). Market economics, it seems, is elevated to an end in itself like democracy and human rights, rather than merely a means to higher ends which may be appropriate in certain circumstances. Again the implications may be practical as well as theological. If sufficient

INGOs and think tanks can win the confidence of sufficient African politicians, technocrats and academics, the path may be smoothed to the acceptance of a market economy integrated into the global capitalist order.

The 'paternalist' view of the role of INGOs rejects both the belief that they seek to empower the people and the belief that they seek to exploit them, whether politically, spiritually or economically. One aspect of paternalism is that of INGOs claiming to 'represent' the needs of Africa because Africans lack the means or the skill to articulate their own interests. Another is that INGOs possess superior expertise, so that their judgement on whether a dam should be built, or whether public spending should be reduced, should prevail irrespective of the wishes of African governments or citizens. Some of this may, of course, be a cover for the advancement of imperial ambitions, but it need not be. Indeed the paternalists may belong to the ideological left, wanting to protect the environment or endangered species while Africans are more concerned with where their next meal is coming from.

On claims to 'represent' Africa or the developing world generally, Edwards looks at the case of environmental NGOs in the US lobbying against the replenishment of funds for the International Development Agency, because of the social and environmental costs of its aid. In doing so, the INGOs found themselves in opposition to African NGOs which had more immediate material needs. Pressure by INGOs on the World Bank for tougher social and environmental conditionality, he argues, has increased its control over governments in developing countries, and therefore eroded the local democratic process (Edwards in Lewis 1999: 258–67). Dijkzeul suggests that INGOs are seen as floating above African society. They are satisfied with their work and their legitimacy, but are perceived rather differently by the indigenous population, which accepts their aid but may see them as pursuing their own interests (Dijkzeul in Richter *et al.* 2006: 241–59).

How can these conflicting views on the role of NGOs be reconciled? Authors can obviously be selective as to which NGOs they examine, depending on whether they wish to demonstrate the existence of emancipatory, imperialist or paternalist tendencies. All these elements clearly exist, and any individual INGO may adopt different roles in different circumstances. Some allegedly 'Western' values may be regarded as sacrosanct, so that an INGO may incur charges of 'imperialism' in pressing for democratisation, human rights or action against corruption. In other cases it may pursue its own convictions regarding specific matters such as homosexual rights or the banning of genetically modified crops, regardless of indigenous opinion, but it may still adhere to the general principle of empowering the people, so that they and their elected representatives can decide their own priorities. Yet the ability of INGOs to choose their role, and their attitude to African governments and society, is ultimately constrained by what is accepted as legitimate and what is feasible within the global order. It is to these matters that we turn in the next two sections.

Responsibility without power: the problems of legitimacy

Legitimacy is a commodity even more precious to NGOs than it is to the state or private sectors. Governments ultimately need the support and co-operation of the people, or at least their acquiescence, but they can survive in the short term by using their powers of coercion, taxing and spending. Their powers and functions are largely defined by law, so that their right to reform the educational system, close hospitals, deploy the police against rioters or deploy troops abroad, is not generally questioned. Businesses would prefer to have a respectable public image, and do not like threats of boycotts from consumers or regulation by the state, but they may continue to employ workers, attract investors and make profits even when they face public unpopularity or government censure. British public utilities such as gas, water and the railways after privatisation are a case in point.

INGOs, on the other hand, have little formal authority, and few people or institutions are compelled to have any dealings with them. While governments can draw their strength and legitimacy from the voters who elected them, and businesses have a power base among the shareholders who have an interest in their continued prosperity, INGOs do not normally have a comparable constituency to fall back on. Given these weaknesses, much INGO activity is based on asking 'May we?' rather than asserting 'We will'. Whether the 'May we?' question is answered in the affirmative depends heavily on whether the INGO and its proposed activities are regarded as legitimate.

This still leaves the questions of 'legitimacy in whose eyes?' and 'legitimacy to do what?' INGOs need to be accepted by African governments, which have the power to register or de-register them, and their work will be easier if they enjoy the confidence of African civil society and African NGOs, with whom they may have to work. Rugendyke suggests that 'the majority' of INGOs compromise their legitimacy by selecting issues for advocacy campaigns without consulting their 'southern partners' (Rugendyke 2007: 227), and Majot looks at the specific case of the International Rivers Network supporting opponents of the Bujagali Falls Dam in Uganda (Majot in Jordan and van Tuijl 2006: 212–14). This case raises several more general questions. Do INGOs have a right to interfere at all in national politics? Are they challenging the sovereignty of the state? Can their intervention be justified on the grounds that they are merely helping to articulate the interests of the majority of the local population, or of the poor who cannot easily speak for themselves, thus contributing to a more even contest between the government and its opponents? In the latter process, is the INGO bringing new knowledge or expertise to bear, which will contribute to a better informed decision? There is no constitutional rulebook to answer any of these questions. The different contestants will obviously select the arguments that suit their own cause, and in many cases the indigenous government will be oblivious to any argument that challenges its right to override INGO lobbying. In extreme cases, the governments of Myanmar and Zimbabwe have told INGOs that they have no business to uphold the claims of the victims of human rights abuses, or to provide relief for the starving, but in other cases the cogency of its argument may enable an INGO to justify its presence, or at least to prevent any drastic action to obstruct its work.

Beyond African governments and society, INGOs may need to establish an acceptable relationship with businesses, Western governments and IFIs. With businesses, much will depend on the perceived strength of the INGO, and of the cause it is promoting. Businesses may be able to dismiss the more eccentric causes without suffering any damage, but an INGO articulating an issue arousing public concern such as the exploitation of child labour, or the destruction of tropical forests, might carry greater weight (Keck and Sikkink 1998: 121–65). In relation to Western governments, few activities beyond promoting terrorism or public disorder would be regarded as wholly illegitimate, but we have noted arguments that there is growing pressure on INGOs seeking funds to keep in line with Western foreign policy, and to concentrate on development rather than advocacy (Tomlinson 2002: 277–8). With IFIs the relationship is a newer one, dating largely from the 1990s when it became less of a heresy to question the Washington consensus. INGOs now have greater access. IFIs, like businesses, now wish to be portrayed as friends of the poor and friends of the earth rather than as vehicles for capitalist exploitation. In that sense, it is their own legitimacy they are concerned with protecting, but this does not mean that INGOs are free to press for an alternative global order. This would be deemed illegitimate in view of their lack of democratic credentials

– what right has a small, unelected group of do-gooders to impose its own ideas? INGO legitimacy is narrowly circumscribed. They may be consulted, and their ability to demonstrate that they have researched the impact of IFI policies on African societies and economies may be respected, but they are not deemed to have a legitimate right to participate in the formulation of IFI policies.

From these empirical observations, can one develop any theoretical insights on the ability of INGOs to acquire legitimacy? Ossewaarde *et al.* suggest that there are four dimensions of legitimacy: (1) normative (the perceived value of what INGOs are doing); (2) regulatory (the willingness of INGOs to act within the law and the constitution); (3) cognitive (the value of the skills and knowledge they possess), and (4) output (the ability to demonstrate that their stated objectives have been achieved) (Ossewaarde *et al.* 2008: 42–55). Much of this would appear to be uncontentious, and might at first sight apply equally to governments and businesses. A government, for example, might gain normative legitimacy from the electorate by promising to establish a universal health service, but it would have to be careful to maintain regulatory legitimacy by not conscripting doctors or diverting money allocated to education into the health service. It would have to demonstrate its administrative ability to provide the necessary health facilities (cognitive legitimacy) and to demonstrate that its policies had ultimately produced a healthier population (output legitimacy). Similarly a business could gain or maintain its legitimacy by promising to invest in the construction of a new highway, employing competent staff, respecting the terms of its contract, and demonstrating the beneficial results in terms of increased profits and opening up the economy of the country concerned.

Yet the legitimacy of INGOs appears to be different from legitimacy in the state and private sectors in at least two respects. Firstly, as we have noted, INGOs lack any formal authority, in contrast to governments and businesses. Not only does this mean that they are more dependent on goodwill rather than exercising their statutory rights, but it also means that any hint of lack of integrity, incompetence or diversion of resources for dubious purposes is likely to lead to a degree of unpopularity. This in turn may make it more difficult to raise funds or to maintain the confidence of the other institutions with which they are working. One can imagine the outcry if Oxfam paid enormous redundancy benefits to directors who had been responsible for disastrous decisions, if the Aga Khan Foundation made its grants conditional on cutting essential public services, or if Save the Children employed staff under inhumane conditions. Governments and businesses have their own relatively secure power bases; INGOs have 'stakeholders' – a relatively ill-defined and fluid group who may withdraw their support whenever they choose.

Secondly there is the problem of reconciling the forms of legitimacy. This may also be difficult in the government and business sectors, but they generally possess the administrative and financial resources to pursue the desired targets and comply with the law. Cynics might add that they also possess the public relations resources to gloss over any failures in these respects. INGOs, Ossewaarde *et al.* suggest, require not just a mission but institutionalisation and organisation. Pressures for accountability and transparency by external stakeholders lead to a permanent struggle to reconcile mission with the requirements of regulative, cognitive and output legitimacy (Ossewaarde *et al.* 2008: 42). This may be partly a matter of 'opportunity cost'. The need to demonstrate that targets in improved literacy have been achieved takes resources away from the process of actually teaching illiterates. But there may also be a problem of the compatibility of the different types of legitimacy. We return to the diversity of stakeholders on whom the INGOs depend. The individual donor may wish to hear that more illiterates have become literate, that more lepers have been cured or that more Africans have access to drinking water, whereas the funding agency may want to know how the money spent has been accounted for or what qualifications the staff possess. Western governments may be interested in whether the outputs are being achieved in countries that have a strategic importance for Western foreign policy; and African citizens may want to know why the literacy campaign was conducted in village A but not in village B. We noted in Chapter 3 the body of literature bewailing the bureaucratisation of NGOs. Kelly quotes J-M Piedagnel of Medecins Sans Frontieres (MSF).

> He's particularly critical of the 'professionalisation and commercialisation' of the aid sector's fundraising. Where in our fundraising, he asks, are the values we supposedly stand for – values like transparency, honesty and humanity that he feels are lacking in the massive aid appeals that have become the stalwart of the international aid sector's response to a crisis situation … 'It's our responsibility to refocus [the] debate on violence and suffering on the countries and communities that need us most, and not let any government drive the agenda on where public attention should be' (Kelly 2006: 3).

This again suggests that the problem is not merely one of bureaucratisation as organisations become larger, which is common in many walks of life, but of acquiring greater legitimacy in the eyes of donors and governments, at the expense of the ideals and objectives on which an NGO is built.

Are there any other 'dimensions of legitimacy' in addition to the four set out by Ossewaarde et al? One could elaborate on non-partisanship, and add support and integrity. Boli suggests optimistically that the effectiveness of INGOs in influencing states depends on 'moral fervour and political non-partisanship', thus providing a 'voice of humanity' (Boli in Boli and Thomas 1999: 267–300). Whether governments are often swayed by moral fervour or voices of humanity is an open question, but it is important that INGOs do not have too explicit a political agenda or, if they do, that this agenda is dwarfed by a range of activities that are regarded as virtuous or useful. The German stiftungen are all offshoots of the main German political parties, but their work in Africa is largely concerned with promoting non-contentious forms of development, or with organising conferences on democracy and good governance without directly criticising the quality of governance in the host country. Oxfam does not disguise its criticism of the current global order, but its commitment and expertise in dealing with poverty enable it to remain in favour with individual donors, and with African and Western politicians.

Non-partisanship can be important in relation to governments and business. Warkentin speaks approvingly of the Rainforest Action Network working with the business community, and of businesses joining the network in its corporate social responsibility campaign, which demonstrates the 'inclusiveness' of its campaigns (Warkentin 2001: 57–8), but Vidal warns of INGOs becoming too close to governments and business. The three sectors make almost interchangeable statements, sit at the same tables, consult each other, shape each others' policies, and even swap staff. NGOs now spend more time branding themselves and writing policy papers, and less time campaigning, investigating and holding the powerful to account (Vidal 2007: 9). INGOs, it seems, have become more legitimate in the eyes of governments and business, but may lose some of the respect they once enjoyed from radical campaigners. Does this matter? As with political parties, donations from business may offset the loss of support from idealistic members, but the INGOs might eventually find themselves sidelined by newer groups if they become inhibited from standing up for their original beliefs.

'Support' can either be an asset or an Achilles heel. Boli claims that the legitimacy of INGOs is enhanced by their openness of membership and democratic structures (Boli in Boli and Thomas 1999: 267), but this can be a dangerous card to play. INGOs which imply that they are reincarnations of mass political parties, mobilising large swathes of public opinion, are not generally able to sustain such an assertion. They may be on safer ground if they emphasise their links with, and understanding of, the groups they serve (O'Brien in Lipschutz 2006: 423), rather than boasting of the (probably inadequate) size of their membership.

'Integrity' may be taken for granted as a source of legitimacy. We have suggested that it is particularly important for organisations that depend on voluntary support and co-operation, and are less able to win arguments with money, coercion or statutory power. Yet, as in cases of allegations of limited public support, INGOs have been forced on to the defensive. If they query the credentials of authoritarian politicians or of businesses exploiting their workers, and demand more accountability from both, they are likely to be asked to account for their own internal organisation. If they ask governments or businesses for funding, the probing may be still greater. Anheier and Hawkes (in Albrow *et al.* 2008: 124–43) describe the adoption of the INGO Accountability Charter by eleven large INGOs. The charter is concerned with the need for independent scrutiny of policies, conflicts of interest and disclosure, and the protection of whistleblowers.

The authors point out that grant-making INGOs, such as the Ford Foundation and the Bill and Melinda Gates Foundation, are among the freest in the world, independent of both market forces and the state, with few clear stakeholders and few participants in policy making. Various types of actual or desirable accountability are suggested, including the election of board members or their appointment by stakeholders, codes of conduct, monitoring and evaluation; and greater participation by the recipients of the INGOs' services. The very need to mention some of these practices might suggest the survival of a more casual attitude to democracy, participation and accountability. This might have mattered less in the past, as long as people and governments were satisfied that the INGOs 'did a lot of good' and could therefore be left alone, but they now face a more critical audience. Anheier and Hawkes do not say a lot about the reasons for the changed climate, but questions about fund raising activities are probably one factor. The drive to raise funds, at least partly motivated by professional fundraisers, often runs ahead of considerations of the feasibility of using the money to achieve the desired end; and the urge to spend the money quickly, sometimes in the face of competition from other INGOs, may again be at the expense of helping those for whom the money was being raised. In an era when citizens in the West receive an ever-growing number of 'begging letters', the need for an INGO to demonstrate that it has put its house in order becomes increasingly important.

The last point raises the general question of the extent to which different forms of legitimacy vary between different times, or even different places. Two or three decades ago there may have been more of a 'beggars can't be choosers' attitude to INGOs. African economies and societies needed help at a time when state capacity was at a low ebb and the current economic orthodoxy required the voluntary sector to step in. While the 'beggars' were not unduly concerned about questions of legitimacy, donors were glad to find institutions that would relieve Western governments of some of the need to provide aid. Today, we have noted that the combined effects of Western security concerns, the rise of new public management (NPM), competition for funds and the reassertion of authority by African governments have all led to a closer questioning of the extent of the role of INGOs. If one projected some of the more pessimistic (from an INGO point of view) observations about bureaucratisation and exploitation by Western governments, it might suggest that we are moving towards a world in which INGOs are becoming *de facto* agents of governments – quangos rather than NGOs – with little scope for flair, independent initiative or the ability to defend the poor. Yet the rise of groups such as the Jubilee Debt Campaign and the Coalition to Stop the Use of Child Soldiers, and the campaigns against land mines and unfair trade, all suggest that there are INGOs which are placing new issues on the global agenda in a way that few other groups could, and in some cases pressing governments and inter-governmental organisations (IGOs) into action as a result of the public support they have mobilised. If particular types of activity, behaviour or organisational structure lead to an INGO's legitimacy being challenged, it often has the flexibility to correct the weaknesses that made it vulnerable. Challenges to legitimacy are unlikely to go away, but neither are the initiatives by INGOs to open up new areas of debate.

Who controls whom? Autonomy and dependency

We face a paradox that while much of the literature on ideology sees INGOs as having an emancipatory mission, as does most of the literature produced by the INGOs themselves, the literature on the distribution of power argues overwhelmingly that INGOs are heavily dominated by Western governments and IFIs. INGOs, by implication, then impose Western priorities on Africa. When they do this via African NGOs, this makes these NGOs appear more alien and less legitimate.

How can one explain this paradox? It may be, as we suggested at the beginning of this chapter, that the term INGO is used imprecisely to include Western government agencies, which are really quangos and unsurprisingly work within their governments' policy guidelines. Secondly, the examples chosen can easily be selected to confirm one's prejudices: a study of Oxfam or Amnesty International would suggest an emancipatory mission, whereas the study of right-wing Christian fundamentalist sects might suggest Western domination. But a more serious answer might be that domination and emancipation are relative terms. Few people would question the proposition that we live in a world where power is distributed very unequally, and that those enjoying a disproportionate share of that power use it to impose their will on the weak. Conversely, few would question the proposition that those who possess a disproportionately small share can still, possibly with the help of others acting on their behalf, have some influence on events if they act with sufficient skill and determination. We all, in other words, live within the constraints of the existing distribution of global power, but the strong and the weak both have the capacity either to consolidate their grip on power, or to challenge particular aspects of that power. It is this ability to defend or expand the political resources one possesses, or to demand a greater share of resources for the have-nots, that is our concern here.

A small minority of writers are willing to believe that INGOs can accept a subordinate status but enjoy sufficient autonomy to bite the hand that feeds them. We have noted Warkentin's description of the ability of the Rainforest Action Network to work closely with business, yet advance its own interests in the process (Warkentin 2001: 57–8), and Rugendyke asserts that INGOs have little reason to fear that advocacy will lead to any loss of funds (Rugendyke 2007: 86). But the weight of academic and journalistic opinion supports the view that INGOs have become increasingly subordinate to Western governments and businesses, and are helping to implement alien economic and foreign policies in Africa (Abdelrahman 2004: 52–4; Ali 2006: 34; Duffield 2001: 10; Kelly 2006: 10; Vidal 2007: 9; Youngs 2004: 148–50). Vidal gives the example of the World Wildlife Fund partnering loggers, genetically modified soya companies and palm oil plantation owners in the belief that this will stop them from ravaging the environment. Other INGOs take money from banks, oil and automobile companies. These companies can now feel safe, 'and hold their chequebooks open' (Vidal 2007: 9).

There appear to be three main overlapping foci in the 'dependency' arguments: managerial, financial and ideological. The managerial focus stresses the growing discrimination by Western governments and IFIs in deciding which activities to support. With the growth of NPM, more rigorous scrutiny is exercised over precisely what INGOs are doing, and there is less scope for trusting the INGOs' own judgement. While some the scrutiny may be a bureaucratic end in itself, it may also be used as a form of ideological policing.

Aid conditions are said to reflect the priorities of the West rather than the needs of Africa, and the minority of INGOs that are committed to supporting the social movements of the poor, rather than the orthodoxy of the IFIs, find it difficult to work with formal development agencies (Wallace *et al.* 2007: 28, 162–3). INGOs wanting partnership agreements with the DFID must prove that they contribute to the British government's targets and priorities, and INGOs are implementing a 'Western agenda' (Agg 2006: 15–21). The managerial requirement for greater conformity is closely linked to the availability of financial carrots and sticks. Abdelrahman asserts that INGOs dependent on Western government funding almost always comply with their funders' foreign policies (Abdelrahman 2004: 53–4), and Morena notes that it is increasingly difficult for global justice NGOs to obtain funds unless they emphasise 'development' rather than campaigning, especially in the post-2001 political climate (Morena 2006: 33).

The ideological focus incorporates both the emphasis on free market policies and conformity with American and British foreign policy. INGOs are said to be used as vehicles for imposing the free market model on Africa, and in skewing aid to meet Western security requirements (Ayers 2006: 321–8; Kelly 2006: 3). Advocacy is frequently discouraged because it might pursue a different set of goals (Tomlinson 2002: 277–8). In the case of the German stiftungen, those that emphasise free market economics, like the Friedrich Naumann Stiftung, are encouraged (Ayers 2006: 332), while Western governments try to rein in those that place greater emphasis on social and economic rights (Youngs 2004: 148–50).

The arguments about Western domination, like those about INGOs being constrained by challenges to their legitimacy, seem attractive when empirical examples are related to the broader context of international politics since 2001, but a major problem is that the globalisation so praised by the Western powers can be a source of their own undoing. While the general ability of the strong to impose their will on the weak is not in dispute, such a situation is very different from a totalitarian order in which the weak are left powerless within a hierarchy where any initiative that displeases those at the top is easily crushed. Even the notion that that there is something unambiguous called 'Western foreign policy' or 'Western interests' is doubtful when one moves from the general to the particular. There is always the possibility that the aid agencies of Western governments will 'go native' in an ideological sense, and support such apparent heresies as greater state intervention or community participation. Indeed many of them have gone native in the ethnic sense of giving positions of responsibility to African personnel. Even if attempts are made to keep INGOs within the confines of an agreed foreign or economic policy, there is no guarantee that their actions will not have side effects that will conflict with the current orthodoxy. Encouraging African civil society to scrutinise state activities more closely, in the belief that the state sector is something to be treated with suspicion by adherents to the Washington consensus, may lead to a greater questioning of authority generally. This questioning might extend to aid conditions imposed by the World Bank, investment deals with Western governments, or the pollution and suffering created by foreign mining companies. The strong may continue to exploit the weak, but INGOs still have the ability, directly or indirectly to make life difficult for the strong, and to open up new fronts in the battle.

The routes to political influence

'Presidential power is the power to persuade'. So said an American academic on the power of the President of the United States. If the authority of the man frequently regarded as one of the most powerful figures on earth depends mainly on persuasion rather than giving orders, what hope is there for INGOs? They have little statutory authority, they generally lack mass power bases, they cannot claim a democratic mandate from any constituency, they possess no weapons, and they lack the money to buy political influence. For Western governments, they can be a source of embarrassment as they reveal the murkier aspects of foreign policy and inadequacy of foreign aid, and for African governments they may be seen as an alien force, trying to impose Western liberal and ecological values. For IFIs, they can be heretics, questioning the wisdom of free market ideology. For businesses, they can be a threat to sales and profits if they persuade consumers to boycott firms that maltreat workers, pollute the environment or drive peasants off the land.

Yet we have seen that INGOs have managed to acquire a degree of legitimacy in the eyes of all these potentially hostile institutions. They fill a gap in the global order that few others can fill. If the INGOs which concentrate on development, service provision or disaster relief disappeared tomorrow, it is difficult to imagine how political and economic order could be sustained in most of the world. The disorder arising would almost certainly spread to the 'developed' world, as global businesses no longer enjoyed any security in plying their trade, and mass migration out of the affected areas would create major social problems in the West.

While the economic and political necessity for 'service providing' INGOs might seem self-evident, governments, businesses and IFIs might still feel that they could do without self-righteous 'advocacy' INGOs making impossible demands and challenging well-established policies. Yet even here, INGOs might have a useful role in pointing out that the emperor has no clothes, or that his clothes are woefully inadequate, before the emperor causes himself any further embarrassment. If polices are not achieving their desired results, as evidenced by the persistence of poverty, sickness and instability, a timely warning from INGOs might be helpful. Many of the alternatives they advocated might be rejected, but at least a debate might be opened up and some of the more damaging policies might be modified.

Even for narrow reasons of self-interest, powerful global actors are therefore open to persuasion by INGOs. If we go on to assume that the actions of these actors are not guided solely by self-interest, but by the wish to be seen to be acting ethically, the scope for persuasion is still greater. Yet any persuasion needs to be pursued within the confines we have highlighted in this chapter. INGO activity has to be perceived as legitimate by the institutions the INGO is seeking to influence, both in terms of the objectives being pursued and the means by which they are being pursued. Demanding that rich countries give away their wealth is not likely to be regarded as legitimate; neither is a campaign of terror in pursuit of that objective, whereas more moderate demands articulated through official channels might achieve greater success. In addition to legitimacy there are questions of feasibility. We noted the existence of a highly unequal distribution of global power in the previous section, which means that INGOs generally need to navigate carefully through or round the powerful institutions rather than tackling them head on.

A common feature of INGO politics, and indeed of NGO politics generally, is an acceptance of the need to co-operate with others. This is in contrast to the policies of many political parties, liberation armies or even trade unions, where the assumption is frequently that 'we' alone know what is best, and 'we' alone will use whatever power we have (votes, guns or strikes) to achieve our desired goal. Winner takes all, or at least takes as much as he can. If compromise or co-operation with other groups is sometimes unavoidable, this is a necessary, temporary evil, and not something to be proud of. NGOs, in contrast, make a virtue of belonging to 'networks' and working with 'partners', and see the pursuit of consensus, rather than confrontation, as a virtue. But if the principles of co-operation and consensus are accepted, what are the means by which INGOs negotiate the treacherous waters of political influence, how does one explain their chosen routes, and what does this tell us about the place of INGOs in world politics?

Boli offers three useful models of INGO operation which, he suggests, reflect distinctive forms of authority (Boli in Boli and Thomas 1999: 267–300). Firstly there is autonomous INGO authority, where the organisation relies solely on its own members. An Esperanto group pursues its own activities without seeking to influence anyone else. The Federation of International Football Associations (FIFA) concentrates on organising football, and is more interested in its own governance than governance in the outside world. But if INGOs seek to influence others, they require collateral authority or penetrative authority. Collateral authority arises where INGOs wish to go beyond patrolling their own domain, and try to influence states and IGOs, though mainly from the outside. Thus the Red Cross laid the ground for the Geneva Convention, and development INGOs seek to influence IGOs' policies on aid. Penetrative authority involves INGOs being more closely involved with decision-makers, whether directly or via other organisations such as professional bodies. For example, human rights groups may have continuous role in interacting with individual states; or groups concerned with the protection of child labour may be in continuous dialogue with businesses.

Collateral authority is said to succeed because, firstly INGOs often possess the knowledge, expertise and technical competence that IGOs lack; secondly INGOs propagate a 'cultural framework' which provides them with a moral justification for the actions they are advocating; thirdly, INGOs possess a 'moral stature' which makes their voice legitimate. Finally, IGOs, like INGOs, possess a 'rational voluntaristic authority' in the sense that authority rests on 'freely exercised reason' as opposed to coercion. IGOs rely heavily on the voluntary compliance of member states, and this compliance is more likely to be forthcoming if demands are reinforced with the support of INGOs whose legitimacy is widely respected.

The effectiveness of penetrative authority is said to depend on the moral fervour and political non-partisanship of INGOs, which provide a 'voice of humanity'. In the case of both collateral and penetrative authority, the legitimacy of INGOs is said to be helped by the openness of their membership and their democratic structures, and by the qualifications, expertise and status of their members. Examples of INGO success in changing the policies of governments and businesses are said to include commitment to birth control, environmental protection and women's rights (Boli in Boli and Thomas 1999: 299).

These models provide some easy targets for sceptics, who might ask whether moral virtue, moral fervour, or rational arguments based on expert knowledge, generally triumph in the real world. Governments continue to abuse human rights and renege on polices to increase aid, businesses continue to exploit child labour and pollute the environment, and IFIs continue to adhere to economic dogmas that make the poor poorer. Yet most of these institutions at least proclaim a belief in democracy, sustainable development, poverty eradication and corporate social responsibility. This should, on paper, provide INGOs with an opportunity to persuade them to practice what they preach. While Boli's emphasis on legitimacy, morality and rational argument may seem over-idealistic, and his assertions about internal democracy in INGOs questionable, one still has to ask 'What other resources do INGOs possess?' The terrain is different from that of pressure group politics where threats of strikes, boycotts, financial sanctions, votes against the government, or even violence, may influence events. In contrast, INGOs can occasionally mobilise public opinion through mass demonstrations, as in the cases of world poverty and debt cancellation, but for the most part it is a matter of less spectacular attempts by the powerless to persuade the powerful, directly or indirectly, to change or modify their policies.

By what means do they do this? Table 7.1 is based on the results of questions put to eighteen INGOs based in London. While such a survey cannot claim to represent a worldwide pattern of INGO activities, the results raise interesting questions about the routes chosen in pursuit of INGO influence.

If we take the questions which elicited a positive answer from over half the respondents, the pattern is one of building links with African NGOs and IFIs, whereas less than half the respondents reported dealings with African governments, the British government or other Western governments. 82 per cent reported well-established contacts with African NGOs, 69 per cent provided material and financial support for African

Table 7.1   Questions to British and International NGOs

In dealing with African governments and African NGOs, which of the following best describes your relationships? (Figures in percentages).

	Frequently	Occasionally	Very rarely, not at all, or not applicable
1. We provide material and financial support for African NGOs	69	25	6
2. We express opinions on political matters in Africa (e.g. through press releases, publications, memoranda)	62	19	19
3. We pursue our objectives by working with or through African NGOs, but prefer not to be seen as directly involved in trying to influence African governments	54	18	28
4. We lobby African governments directly	31	19	50
5. We have well-established contacts with African NGOs	82	6	12
6. We communicate with African NGOs on an *ad hoc* basis	56	25	19
7. We have well-established contacts with African governments	41	27	32
8. We communicate with African governments on an *ad hoc* basis	46	27	27
9. We pursue issues with African governments, but only if we are approached by African NGOs	12	19	69
10. There are few African NGOs that share our objectives, so we work with other institutions	25	6	69
11. We are so closely integrated with African NGOs that attempts to influence African governments are based on a broad consensus between African NGOs and ourselves	36	0	64
12. We seek to influence events in Africa by working through the British government or other non-African governments	42	6	52

Table 7.1   **Questions to British and International NGOs** – *continued*

	Frequently	Occasionally	Very rarely, not at all, or not applicable
13. We seek to influence events in Africa by working through international organisations	63	12	25
14. We use informal channels to influence events in Africa	19	0	81
15. Please give details of any campaigns which have used permutations of the above channels	See text below		

NGOs, 63 per cent sought to influence events in Africa by working through international organisations, and 54 per cent pursued their objectives by working with or through African NGOs. 62 per cent expressed opinions on political matters in Africa through such means as press releases, publications and memoranda, though without trying to influence African governments directly. At the other end of the scale, only 42 per cent sought to influence events in Africa via the British or other Western governments, only 41 per cent had well-established contacts with African governments, and only 31 per cent lobbied African governments directly. A similar pattern emerged with the answers to the open-ended question on the contacts used in campaigns.

> We enable civil society to raise questions in parliament about mining contracts in country A.
> We support civil society organisations (CSOs) in challenging the proposed presidential third term in country B.
> We support technical assistance to CSOs in country C to challenge the government's economic policy.
> We support CSOs in analysing and monitoring national budgets in countries D, E, F, G and H.
> We support firms and small scale producers lobbying their national representatives at the WTO.
> We mobilise public opinion in Britain to put pressure on the British government over debt relief.
> We work in partnership with African NGOs to put pressure on their own governments. We also brief the UN Security Council.

We work with and through African NGOs. We only put pressure on African governments as a last resort.
We try to persuade businesses to live up to the standards they proclaim, and to respect the laws regarding the treatment of workers.
We work with civil society in Africa to monitor debt cancellation and the use of the funds thus released.

Most of this is far removed from the high drama of major INGOs pressing for more debt cancellation, or for an end to aid conditional on free market policies. It is also far removed from the more mundane but important activities of INGOs in negotiating with international bodies to secure changes in the rules or practices with regard to such matters as the provision of anti-malaria treatment, fish conservation or the rules on intellectual property rights. Yet the responses help to capture the ebb and flow of everyday INGO activity. In particular, they re-emphasise the picture of INGOs preferring to work with other non-elected, non-accountable bodies rather than dealing directly with governments.

This brings us back to the themes of legitimacy and power. INGOs appear to be wary of dealing directly with African governments if only because the fact of being foreign lays them open to charges of imperialism, or of interfering with the sovereign power of African states, whereas helping African NGOs to articulate their demands is more difficult to detect and can be disguised as a form of aid. The INGOs themselves often take the ideological view that it would be wrong for them to try to impose their views, when their correct role should be to help to empower Africans. There is also the practical question of power. African governments may not appear to wield enormous power, but INGO pressure can do little to prevent a determined government from signing a deal with a foreign government or business, no matter how harmful the apparent effects on the indigenous population. And in the last resort, troublesome INGOs can be de-registered.

Working with and through African NGOs has produced mixed results. It did not prevent the construction of the Bujagali Falls Dam, but it was important in the rejection of the proposal for the prawn farming project in the Rufiji Delta, and has probably strengthened the ability of Maasai pastoralists to defend their rights. The Royal Society for the Protection of Birds (RSPB) is currently supporting the Wildlife Conservation Society of Tanzania in its opposition to the construction of a soda ash factory on the shores of Lake Natron, which would threaten the lives of half a million flamingos (Rice 2007: 16). This will provide an interesting contest between the powers of business and conservation.

As regards lobbying Western governments, the relatively low profile of INGOs could be explained partly by the nature of their work. Much of it has grown out of 'aid' in the narrower sense, and the examples of campaigning we have given might be seen as complementing that aid by ensuring that African governments and global businesses do not destroy the benefits through corruption, incompetence or infringing the rights of the poor. Pressure on Western governments tends to be reserved for the bigger issues such as adhering to the Millennium Development Goals (MDGs) on development and poverty eradication, or debt relief and arresting climate change. Even here there is an element of gesture politics rather than real engagement with governments. An INGO may wish to embellish its annual report by recording that it has urged the British government to cancel more debts or to take a tougher line on climate change, but only a minority of well-established INGOs are likely to have direct access to the government. In terms of power, they bring few sanctions to bear, and in terms of legitimacy they may have difficulty in demonstrating that they represent a substantial section of public opinion. Exceptions such as the Jubilee Debt Campaign may hit the headlines as thousands of people join in demonstrations in support of INGO demands, but the focus of most INGO activities is too narrow to attract such support. For the most part, INGOs occupy a relatively lowly position in the pecking order at the door of Western governments.

The figure of 63 per cent of INGOs seeking to influence international organisations, including the IMF, the WTO and the World Bank, as against only 42 per cent seeking to influence Western governments, might suggest a perverse desire to take on the biggest giants, but it chimes in with Boli's argument that these non-elected bodies, unlike governments, share the INGOs' insecure purchase on legitimacy, and may be able to generate more of it if they are seen to be less aloof from groups representing the people on the receiving end of their policies. Who has gained more from this interaction is a matter for debate. The international organisations may now be able to claim a stronger mandate for their policies after having consulted more widely, but without having had to change the policies radically. On the other hand, INGOs could claim that the need for these organisations to listen to the voices of the poor and its representatives has an important long-term effect on their thinking.

Conclusion

The global environment within which INGOs operate is not easy to characterise. Is there a 'global culture' which embodies a set of benign values, or is there a set of conflicting cultures, many of which put self-interest before any common good? Is the unequal distribution of global power so great that INGOs can do little more than provide limited relief and comfort for the victims of exploitation, or does the absence of any monolithic world authority mean that there are few ways of preventing INGOs from going about their proclaimed business?

The discussion in this chapter leads to a rejection of the 'global culture' thesis in favour of the conception of a more hostile environment, and a rejection of the fatalistic view on the consequences of global inequality in favour of a belief in the scope for INGOs to carve out a role of their own. There appears to be no hierarchical authority to stop them – only institutions that wield limited power in limited spheres. There may be a law of the jungle in the sense that those who stand directly in the path of the bigger beasts are not likely to survive, but the jungle can still accommodate a diversity of life. Indeed the bigger beasts might find it difficult to survive without the presence of the smaller ones, and such dependence provides opportunities for the latter. We saw, for example, that the implementation of World Bank policies might be more difficult if it did not take into account the warnings of INGOs on the hardship and unrest which unmodified free market policies might cause.

In previous chapters we noted that there is global governance but no global government. The system (if such a term can be used) depends ultimately on a range of (often vague) unwritten understandings as to who has the right to do what, and in what circumstances. In this chapter we have emphasised the importance of three main variables: ideology, legitimacy and power. We acknowledged that some INGOs have been used by Western governments in pursuit of their foreign policies, that some are determined to propagate economic, religious or cultural beliefs rooted in the West, irrespective of the beliefs of the people in the recipient countries; and that some INGOs are largely concerned with creating job opportunities for their own staff. But for the majority there is 'missionary' spirit in the sense of wishing to improve the lot of the people of Africa and of encouraging Africans to take the initiative in asserting their rights. This then raises questions of what legitimacy is going to be accorded to INGOs when they pursue objectives that can affect the balance of political power within Africa, and can possibly challenge the policies being followed by Western governments and IFIs. Here a delicate path has to be trodden. African governments may question the right of foreigners to interfere in their affairs, and Western governments may question the wisdom of funding bodies that may be hostile to what INGOs regard as neo-colonial policies. Yet INGOs cannot easily be wished away. Bodies that promote develop-ment, and provide relief for suffering, take the burden off African and Western governments alike, and are therefore accorded a degree of tol-erance; but legitimacy is still something that has to be earned on the basis of what INGOs do, rather than something inherent in the polit-ical structure. We noted that the whole question of legitimacy was a more important one for INGOs than for governments and businesses, because INGOs have fewer resources to fall back on. They have to demon-strate qualities that are not always easily compatible, including the pursuit of desirable objectives, respect for indigenous law and culture, competent management and accountability to their stakeholders. In reconciling these goals, there is always the danger that the quest for legitimacy in the eyes of Western governments and donors will blunt the pursuit of the 'mission' that initially motivated them.

In looking at power, INGOs at first sight have severe handicaps in dealing with other institutions that have legal authority, guns, money or mass power bases. In some respects the handicaps have become greater as Western security concerns have increased and African states have regained some of their authority after the nadir of the 1980s. Yet as rapidly as one INGO may become subordinated to the interests of ano-ther institution, others may rise to challenge perceived injustices in other areas, whether over the debt burden, land mines or the exploitation of child soldiers. Despite all the handicaps of lack of formal authority or means to enforce it, INGOs frequently claim the moral high ground. That claim is equally frequently challenged, yet governments, IFIs and busi-nesses do not like the embarrassment of pursuing activities that are seen to be immoral, especially when they see a rising tide of public opinion against them. The apparently weak are able to exert some influence on the strong.

In view of INGOs' lack of formal power, the processes by which their influence is exerted is all-important. Governments can easily ask what right a body with no visible base of support has to demand policy changes. But if the emphasis is on working with and through African NGOs and civil society, rather than governments, this can produce significant, if unspectacular results. At the same time, INGOs have a remarkable degree of rapport with IFIs, despite the ideological gulf between them. The IFIs share with INGOs the liability of being unelected and unaccountable, and are often more unloved. They have therefore salvaged some legitimacy for themselves by being seen to co-operate with groups advocating more popular policies. Who has benefited more from closer INGO-IFI relations is an open question, but policies made in Washington that have serious implications for the people of African are at least subject to greater scrutiny than in the early years of the Washington consensus.

On balance, the argument is that the missionary element in INGO activity outweighs the imperialist. INGOs have not transformed a world order in which the unequal distribution of power and wealth is as great as it has ever been. Just as NGOs within countries cannot be regarded as a substitute for the political parties and mass movements of yesteryear, so we should not expect INGOs to challenge global capitalism or US domination effectively. But there appear to be an infinite number of unmet needs and injustices that can be pursued, given sufficient commitment, expertise and resources. Much of the strength of INGOs lies in their ability to push public authorities into accepting the necessity to address these needs and injustices. And in at least some cases the argument is accepted, often against all expectations.

8
The Winning and the Taking Part: The Global Game of NGO Influence

NGOs have claimed several trophies in the game of global politics in recent years. The World Development Movement claimed to have halted the General Agreement on Trade in Services in 2002, which would have opened the door to extensive privatisation of public utilities in Africa (Timms 2005: 8–10). Oxfam, it is said, influenced World Bank policies on debt relief, fair trade, the position of mining companies in East Timor and the African Union's response to the EU's proposed economic partnership agreements (Anderson in Rugendyke 2007: 84). In Tanzania, HakiKazi reported that 40 per cent of the resources previously used to repay debts were, as a result of its efforts, now being used for education, health and water; and in Ethiopia a campaign by Oxfam enabled coffee growers to obtain intellectual property rights on their brands of coffee, after initial resistance by Starbucks (*The Guardian*, Dar es Salaam, 3 July 2007: ii). Pressure from the Jubilee Debt Campaign and others had by 2008 secured more than $88bn of debt cancellation in the world's poorest countries (Jubilee Debt Campaign 2008: 1). The proposed multilateral agreement on investment (MAI), which would have restricted the right of African governments to control the activities of foreign businesses within their frontiers, was scuppered in 1998 as a result of pressure from a diverse range of NGOs (*Tanzanian Affairs*, May–August 1998: 10–12).

Most individual NGOs would willingly admit that most of these achievements were not the result of the efforts of any one group alone, yet without the presence of NGOs few of these achievements would have been possible. All the examples cited here date from the late 1990s and beyond, and it would be difficult to record comparable successes from earlier decades. Not only are more NGOs joining in the game of global politics, but many of them now have a greater expectation of winning, and not merely taking part.

Why should this be, and what are the main types of issue on which NGOs have increasingly campaigned? How have they organised themselves to provide a more effective force? How far does the type of organisation vary according to the issues being contested? This chapter explores some of these questions by looking at the context within which NGO activity is taking place. We look first at the global political order within which particular issues and interests become more salient. Then we examine the ability of NGOs to co-operate across national borders with each other and with other sympathetic institutions. Finally we take a more 'micro' look at NGO activity, in terms of the different strategies used in relation to different types of issue. In passing, and in deference to the analogies with the Olympic tradition, we also look at some of the NGOs which have little expectation of winning, but for which taking part may nonetheless be important in itself.

The global context (1): the changing agenda

Global politics in the first decade of the twenty-first century have been substantially different from global politics in the previous two decades, although observers disagree as to the nature of the changes. Some emphasise the shadow of the 'war on terror', which has not been conducive to NGO activity. In this view, NGOs have at worst been enlisted as non-combatants in that war, serving the interests of the US and its allies by providing relief in the war-affected areas, and helping to give the invaders and occupiers a more humanitarian face (Ali 2006: 34; Klein 2003: 16). At best, NGOs have avoided partisanship in the war, but have had their wings clipped as financial support has depended on concentrating on development rather than advocacy, and preferably development in countries of strategic importance to the West (Tomlinson 2002: 273–82). A second school, which we have met frequently in previous chapters, is less concerned with war than with the new managerialism which blunts radicalism, idealism and innovation, as NGOs grapple with complex grant applications and performance targets, so that activity is driven more by the prospects of financial support than by the desire to promote development, self-sufficiency, participation or social justice. Taken to its logical conclusion, this view might imply that NGOs are becoming more like quangos – agents of governments or powerful donors rather than autonomous innovators.

An alternative view pushes American-led wars and managerialism into the background. For most of the world, terrorism and managerialism are remote from everyday life, even if local conflicts are not. More pressing is the fact that problems of poverty, sickness and illiteracy have persisted, or even worsened, since the end of the Cold War, in spite of (or perhaps because of) a variety of initiatives in the West. The World Trade Organisation (WTO) continues to allow, or is unable to prevent, protectionism and subsidies to agriculture in the West, while prohibiting such practices in Africa, thus leaving African producers unable to gain a foothold in Western markets, and often unable to maintain their share of their own markets in the face of Western dumping. Both structural adjustment and debt relief are dependent on conforming to the requirements of creditors who demand 'Do as I say, don't do as I do'. African governments are frequently required to retrench public services and privatise public utilities, often to the benefit of Western investors and to the detriment of African citizens who are now required to pay for drinking water, hospital treatment and even the use of communal latrines. Or if they are unable to pay, they become part of the statistics covering disease and high mortality rates.

This analysis implies that the global order has undergone a qualitative, and not merely a quantitative, change since the Cold War, with Africa more dependent on the West not just as a result of the vagaries of world trade, but as a result of deliberate policies. The Western policies might, in turn, be attributed partly to the alleged rise of American hegemony since the Cold War, which has facilitated greater economic exploitation, but they might also reflect the rise of a more aggressive form of capitalism which is 'global' rather than being confined to any one country, and which national governments cannot or will not control. Indeed India and China have joined in with the same relish as Western countries. (None of this is to belittle the contribution of incompetent and corrupt African governments and elites to poverty in their own countries, but our concern in this chapter is with NGO action to influence events at a global rather than a national level).

While what we might call the 'Western security model' and the 'managerial model' emphasise the weakening of NGOs in the face of Western pressure, the 'global poverty model' frequently suggests a renaissance of NGOs in the face of hardship and perceived injustice. This occurs at both the African level, as we saw in the chapters on Tanzania and Uganda, and in the West where many NGOs are not merely asking citizens for donations to help the poor as act of charity, but are campaigning for policies that would tackle the causes of poverty. Rugendyke describes 'new' forms of personal responsibility being encouraged by NGOs, including signing petitions on debt, lobbying politicians, buying fair trade goods, funding advocacy campaigns, joining demonstrations and wearing wristbands. This, she says, is in contrast to earlier practices such as promoting immunisation and increased educational supplies, or urging donors to sponsor a goat, a child or a well. In a decade there has been a 'major shift' in NGO practice. INGOs that once concentrated on development projects have now become advocates lobbying global actors (Rugendyke 2007: 231–2). The contrast between past and present seems somewhat overdrawn. Many NGOs do continue to promote the material development of Africa, which is essential irrespective of what politicians do, and some continue to sponsor goats, but the general point is well made. NGOs increasingly see their task not just as helping the poor and the sick in the manner of a Victorian charity, but are urging Western powers and international financial institutions (IFIs) to reverse the policies that have caused much of the poverty and sickness. Rugendyke cites the examples of the successes of Jubilee 2000 and the fair trade movement, with advocacy gaining a momentum as a result of experience. There is a growing realisation of the barriers to development such as unfair trade, debt, low commodity prices and uneven land distribution, and this realisation is helped by INGO links with 'southern partners' (Rugendyke 2007: 237–8). These partners have themselves placed a greater emphasis on campaigning rather than charity, as we saw in the examples of Haki-Kazi, the Tanzania Gender Networking Programme (TGNP) and the Tanzania Natural Resources Forum. None of this necessarily contradicts the forebodings of the proponents of the Western security model or the managerial model, who place emphasis on the growing subordination of NGOs, but it is a case of one door closing and another opening. While some NGOs are helping the needy in Iraq on terms largely dictated by the US government, others are advocating radical changes in the global order.

If there has been a trend towards NGOs openly advocating major policy changes, how far have changes in the global political environment been conducive to the success of their endeavours? At the level of ideological debate, there appears to be less rigidity than in the early 1990s when the unmodified Washington consensus held sway. It has been conceded by Western governments and IFIs that African states have a positive role to play in development and are not merely an encumbrance, and that poverty eradication should become a major priority. It is acknowledged that the debt crisis is attributable at least partly to creditors having lent carelessly to corrupt and authoritarian rulers, and not merely to the improvidence of Africans. In this environment there are fewer taboos against providing public services or interfering with market forces, and there is more scope for NGOs and decision-makers to negotiate policy changes at the margin, or to 'split the difference'. All African debts cannot be cancelled overnight, but the principle has been conceded that at least some debts should be cancelled because they were incurred by immoral means, or simply because the debt burden in a given country causes unbearable suffering. Similarly, once it is conceded that governments can sometimes have a role in promoting development, different NGO demands can be considered on their merits instead of being ruled out as ideologically incorrect.

The global political environment has also been more propitious as a result of the spread of democracy, some of which was either the result of Western pressure or of contagion between countries. While formal democratisation, in the sense of permitting multi-party elections and civil liberties, largely pre-dated the period we are considering, the past decade has seen a growth of democratic behaviour as well as democratic institutions, with NGOs and civil society asserting themselves more boldly and governments, whether out of conviction or necessity, showing greater tolerance of autonomous activity. The activities of bodies such as HakiElimu, TGNP and the Uganda Debt Network are only possible in relatively open political systems, and the ability of these national NGOs to flourish then facilitates the building of links with global groups, which are themselves strengthened as a result. Knowledge of the condition of the poor, or of human rights, at a local level can be fed into INGOs which can then use their superior resources to campaign for change. Sikkink suggests that there can be a 'spiral effect' as action at a global level then opens out greater space for political activism in countries making the transition from authoritarianism to democracy (Sikkink in Della Porta and Tarrow 2005: 151–73).

Beyond ideology and democratisation are more practical questions of how to handle the agenda that has emerged. Former orthodoxies have been challenged, NGOs have begun to articulate new demands, and governments and IFIs have shown a greater willingness to compromise, or at least to make concessions. This is a different world from the pre-1990s where the Washington consensus was regarded as either the ultimate in economic wisdom or as something as largely unchallengeable by civil society. This rise of NGOs to challenge the global order, like the earlier rise of the working class in national politics, required new devices for resolving conflict, or at least new means of heading off challenges that might undermine the *status quo*. Global governance, which we examined in Chapter 6, already existed as a flexible device for bridging the gap between international decision-makers and ordinary citizens; as experts, interest groups and businesses could be drawn in to make the decision-makers less remote. Without any radical changes in the formal institutions of governance, NGOs have also been drawn in as additional intermediaries between the decision-maker and the citizen.

In relation to the public sector, we noted in the previous chapter the greater willingness of IFIs to consult NGOs in order to give a greater appearance of legitimacy in their decisions. It could be claimed that civil society was no longer ignored when controversial decisions were taken. While the emphasis was on consultation rather than participation, and few dramatic changes of policy could be detected, the presence of NGOs may at least have deterred the adoption of the sort of harsh measures that had been adopted previously, often based on ignorance of how African economies really worked. To describe NGOs as 'winners' would be a gross exaggeration, but the new order might at least prevent runaway victories for their adversaries. In relation to the private sector, global governance shades into the narrower questions of decisions on wages and working conditions, but even in an era of free market economics one cannot treat business activity as 'outside politics'. Indeed it is often the wide latitude given to business by governments that has led to NGOs trying to fill the vacuum by demanding that global businesses act more responsibly and accountably, in view of their impact on civil society.

Three broad explanations of the ability of NGOs to assert a degree of influence over business have been advanced in the literature: structural, administrative and moral. At the structural level, Edwards argues that the modification of the Washington consensus has placed a greater emphasis on the need for a stronger institutional infrastructure. Once the point has been conceded that what is good for business is not necessarily good for national economies as a whole or for civil society, the question then arises as to who is best able to impose a degree of regulation. Governments and inter-governmental organisations (IGOs) are often ruled out not only for ideological reasons, but because it is believed that NGOs can do the job more competently. As one narrows the focus, structural considerations blur into administrative considerations. Edwards gives the example of the growth of voluntary regulations, negotiated with NGOs, to deal with global warming when a 'legally binding regime' proved impossible. Similarly with the case of child labour in India and Pakistan, NGOs provided a practical means of monitoring and enforcing global agreements (Edwards 2000: 10–14; Husselbee in Eade and Lighteringen 2001: 127–44).

The moral explanation brings us back to questions of legitimacy. Businesses, like IFIs, are fearful for their reputations and their profits if they are seen as indifferent to the plight of the people in the countries where they operate, and may be haunted by histories of pollution, carelessness with dangerous chemicals and the employment of child labour. There is therefore much emphasis on corporate social responsibility and seeking consensus with NGOs. Glowing accounts have been written of partnerships with NGOs that have enhanced the reputations of businesses and enabled them to tap into the knowledge of NGOs. Sayer notes that 45 per cent of the top US companies produce regular sustainability reports, and that 'civil regulation by NGOs is enforced through incentives to the companies to gain social, economic and reputational capital', thus reducing the risk of boycotts, direct action or ethical disinvestment, leading to falling sales or share prices (Sayer in Rugendyke 2007: 128–9).

The tone of much of this seems unduly optimistic. Businesses may prefer voluntary regulation by NGOs to statutory regulation by governments not simply for ideological reasons, but because they feel that the former is less effective. Corporate social responsibility and proclamations of ethical behaviour may be applauded, but one wonders how easily a public relations exercise can give impression of moral virtue when many of the raw capitalist practices are still hiding below the surface. But, as with NGO relations with IFIs, the ability to get a foot in the door, and to set out desired standards and to monitor progress, are all important in their own way. Again one may not find major radical innovations, but the mere presence of NGOs may help to prevent backsliding into a more exploitative role.

The global context (2): the response of NGOs

Global changes since the mid-1990s have, we have suggested, stimulated greater NGO advocacy, and to some extent forced global decision-makers on to the defensive. This in turn has led them to work more closely with NGOs, and thus created new openings for NGO influence. But the description so far treats NGOs largely as dependent variables, rather than innovators. Has the changing global context also led to innovations by NGOs to enable them to cope more effectively with the new order? Here we consider arguments about the more professional approaches of NGOs, attempts by national NGOs to build *ad hoc* links with the outside world, and then attempts to transform such links into more regular, institutionalised communications.

The more 'professional' attitude of NGOs to their work is difficult to quantify, yet it is remarked on by African politicians, European and American diplomats and academics alike. More traditional pressure groups might once have spent years advancing the moral arguments for fluoride-free water, noise abatement or an end to vivisection, without making much impression on politicians or the general public. Now NGOs produce facts, figures and examples to advance their cause, distribute newsletters to show their supporters the progress they are making, and are often able to brief politicians more effectively than the politicians' own official advisers. We saw in Chapters 4 and 5 how HakiElimu was able to produce its own assessment of the state of education in Tanzania which made the official version look woefully inadequate, thus making the government look more fallible, and how Oxfam was able to gather information from civil society to warn the Ugandan government against signing an economic partnership agreement (EPA) with the EU. Once NGOs acquire a reputation for knowledge, expertise and an ability to mobilise public opinion, politicians and officials will find it difficult to ignore them.

How did this emergence of professionalism come about? New technology is part of the explanation. The computer and the Internet are great levellers, available as much to NGOs as to the most powerful governments and businesses. An NGO can now communicate with both the humblest village and the mightiest politician, and can seek allies abroad at the press of a button. Immediate supporters and potential supporters can be kept informed of the objectives and activities through a printed or electronic newsletter, with neat illustrations to convey simple facts and arguments. The defeat of the MAI, largely as a result of email communications alerting a range of activists, was exceptional in terms of the scale of the operation and the size of the giant that was slain, but the processes themselves are an everyday part of an NGO's armoury. Another explanation might be that NGOs have been fortunate in recruiting talent which might at other times have gone elsewhere. In Africa many public servants threatened with redundancy, in the face of retrenchment, became prominent in NGOs, and in the West the decline of political parties had the effect of driving many activists into NGOs. Skills such as fund raising, press relations, or even establishing basic administrative structures, have been honed. Beyond that, learning from experience probably played an important part, as successful campaigns provided a model for further successes, and the vulnerability of political decision-makers and businesses became exposed. If an NGO could quote chapter and verse on the extent of arbitrary imprisonment or torture in a given country, or the extent of failure of a Western government to fulfil its promise to cancel African debts, the onus was increasingly on politicians to respond to the NGO's agenda.

There is, of course, a danger of exaggeration. NGOs may claim the credit for decisions which politicians would have taken anyway, or which were more the result of the quieter activities of administrators, techno-crats or diplomats. Major NGO activities such as the World Social Forum may attract much public attention, and the immediate impression may be that governments will respond to their demands, only for the long-term effects to be insignificant. Cohen sums up this more sceptical view with his assessment that a few major NGOs have made a sig-nificant impact, often through exploiting the expertise that the state lacks, but that NGO influence generally is *ad hoc*, unpredictable and irregular (Cohen 2003: 57).

Ad hoc links with the outside world can be traced back to the days of authoritarian rule in the 1970s and 1980s when churches, trade unions or professional groups in Africa might seek help from their opposite numbers in the West to cope with government attacks on their members or their integrity. But for many NGOs it has often been the twilight zone of semi-authoritarian rule that has facilitated new oppor-tunities. Semi-authoritarianism comes in many forms, but a common feature is that governments are able to rig elections to ensure their own survival, and to suppress civil liberties when they feel under threat, yet they permit a relatively pluralist order within which NGOs and other groups are allowed substantial freedom to go about their business.

Within a semi-authoritarian order Keck and Sikkink have advanced the 'boomerang' thesis of NGO influence. The political system is not sufficiently open for NGOs to influence their own governments directly, but they can appeal to global bodies or foreign governments, which may in turn come back to put pressure on the indigenous government. Keck and Sikkink give examples of NGOs in Brazil and Malaysia demand-ing action against the exploitation of forests in their countries. They appealed to Western governments and to the foreign banks involved in the exploitation, and these achieved some success in ensuring greater discrimination in the making of loans, and international agreements on environmental standards. In the case of Brazil the government was pressed into exercising more rigorous control over the use of forests (Keck and Sikkink 1998: 1–38, 121–65). Similar examples have been found in Bolivia and Kenya. In Bolivia NGOs were not consulted over their government's anti-poverty strategy, and they pressed INGOs to raise the matter with their own governments, which then put pressure on the Bolivian government and the World Bank to engage local NGOs more fully (Wood in Deacon 2000: 45–61). In Kenya, human rights activists took up injustices with Africa Watch, which passed them on to Amnesty International, which urged Western governments to demand changes in the behaviour of the Kenyan government (Goodin in Held and Koenig-Archibugi 2003: 83).

Seeking allies in the outside world is not without its problems, however, especially if the African government treats subsequent attempts at Western intervention as a revival of imperialism. DeMars suggests that the outcome may be closer to a 'bungee cord effect' than a boomerang effect, with greater repression as a result of appeals to the West. He cites the example of the Egyptian police following up the murder of two Christians by arresting and torturing other Christians, fearing that the arrest of the Muslim murderers would foment religious conflict. Protests by Egyptian human rights organisations led to an inflammatory article in the British *Sunday Telegraph*, which in turn led to the Egyptian government reacting by imprisoning the leading human rights campaigners. Human rights NGOs were thus weakened rather than benefiting from foreign support (DeMars 2005: 30–1).

When is the boomerang more likely to come into operation than the bungee cord? DeMars's example might suggest that African NGOs need to be careful in their choice of allies, and that a body such as Amnesty International might have been a wiser choice than a conservative British newspaper, but a fine line may need to be drawn between appealing to the better nature of a potentially friendly African government and antagonising a hostile one. Gentle British pressure, in response to demands from African civil society, probably contributed to the holding of free elections in Kenya in the 1990s, and possibly to the Ugandan government reining in its army after assaults on sections of the civilian population. But appeals from Zimbabwean NGOs to Western institutions appear to have led to greater repression as the government has become more paranoid about foreign imperialism. It may be the 'semi' in Keck and Sikkink's semi-authoritarianism that requires emphasis. Countries that are, or were, ruled by semi-authoritarian governments, such as Brazil, Bolivia, Kenya, Malaysia and Uganda may be amenable to Western pressure, especially if there is a formal commitment to complete the transition to democracy, and if Western aid depends partly on evidence of fulfilling that commitment. More blatantly authoritarian governments, such as those in Egypt, Myanmar and Zimbabwe, are less likely to be moved, and might react more positively to persuasion from less critical neighbours than to what they see as sanctimonious condemnation from their former colonial masters. In these countries, NGOs' time has not yet come, and they may have to restrict their actions largely to development and welfare rather than advocacy.

Attempts to use the 'boomerang' have achieved significant results, but over the longer term African NGOs may want a more regular, institutionalised relationship with outside institutions. This is particularly important in view of the changed global order we have described where, on the one hand a more rampant global capitalism brings additional threats to African economies and societies and, on the other, Western governments, international organisations and businesses are now more willing to listen and negotiate. Della Porta and Tarrow describe a process of 'externalisation' in which movements are active super-nationally. National NGOs and INGOs stimulate alliances with nationally weak social movements; human rights NGOs help a weak United Nations bureaucracy to acquire more specialised knowledge, and development NGOs offer high quality, low cost human resources. But the most dramatic change, they assert, is towards 'transnational collective action', with co-ordinated campaigns by networks of activists against international institutions. This change has developed out of environmental, cognitive and relational changes. The environmental changes include the ending of the Cold War, which had previously blocked many forms of action, and the development of electronic communications, cheaper travel and the growing power of INGOs. Cognitive change emerges from the influence of previously successful campaigns, which go on to fuel subsequent campaigns. The authors cite the examples of the rise of indigenous movements in Latin America and, less plausibly, attacks on McDonald's restaurants in France. Relational change involves national actors coming together in transnational coalitions, as in the case of human rights organisations lobbying the United Nations, and opponents of the current World Trade Organisation (WTO) regime protesting in Seattle in 1999 (Della Porta and Tarrow 2005: 6–10).

Gaventa follows similar themes at a more empirical level. Vertical alliances combining the local, national and international have contributed to greater debt relief in Uganda, with Jubilee 2000 working with Ugandan NGOs. Not only has Uganda as a whole benefited, but the process has given the poor, and NGOs representing the poor, greater leverage over the Ugandan government which now practices greater budgetary transparency and is more responsive to the needs of the poor. The Ugandan Participatory Assessment Process involved Oxfam, other NGOs and the Ministry of Finance. This helped to ensure that debt relief helped the poor. Active education and mobilisation at local levels helped to strengthen awareness and to voice the priorities of the poor (Gaventa in Edwards and Gaventa 2001: 281).

These accounts may be optimistic about the achievements of NGOs, though they capture the general flavour of recent developments. One can question whether the protesters at Seattle achieved any permanent gains, and whether smashing a McDonald's restaurant achieved much beyond a sense of personal satisfaction and a feeling that an alien force had been cut down to size. In the case of Ugandan debt, a more sceptical observer might have said more about the limitations imposed by extensive corruption and patronage. But none of this detracts from the fact there are now more significant links between NGOs at national and global levels. Our task now is to look at the mechanics   of this in more detail.

Horses for courses, and fighting on broad and narrow fronts

We now look at different types of NGO, and NGO coalition, in relation to the search for victory over the perceived forces of injustice. In particular we look at the extent to which conventional NGOs are being outflanked by less structured, more militant groups, at the links built up with states, businesses and IFIs, and at the different strategies required for 'broad' and 'narrow' campaigns. Finally we draw attention to the fact that there are large numbers of losers as well as winners in this search for victory, and ask if there are any explanations as to why apparently well organised groups are defeated when others succeed.

The global changes which have opened the door to a greater intensity of NGO activity have also facilitated a greater diversity of NGOs and similar movements. In the early years of democratisation in Africa, governments had a clear view of what constituted an NGO, and groups that failed to conform to the requirements were denied registration. For some this did not matter because they were simply serving immediate local needs, and could not give offence to any politician, but a group that wanted to indulge in advocacy and political campaigning would soon be disbanded if it failed to register. The law may have changed little since the early days, but many NGOs have gradually branched out into becoming what are frequently called 'social movements', campaigning for the rights of underprivileged groups or for 'global justice'. The TGNP in Tanzania is frequently cited as an example, where a group nominally concerned with women's rights now expresses clear views on social inequality at home and the inequities of the current global order abroad. With the rise of a greater diversity of INGOs based in the West, many of them driven by growing public anger over continued poverty, the debt burden and environmental destruction, there are opportunities for African NGOs to build links with like-minded partners. In the process this may put them in touch with like-minded groups in other parts of Africa or the developing world generally. This can facilitate the emergence of militant bodies such as the African Social Forum and Jubilee South.

The rise of less structured, more militant groups is charted by Bennett and Reitan. Bennett draws a contrast between NGO advocacy networks and global justice movements. The latter are more diverse and flexible, with continuous protest rather than strategic campaigns (Bennett in Della Porta and Tarrow 2005: 214–15). Reitan plots the trend away from formally organised NGOs, especially INGOs, towards Third World indigenous groups that are directly affected by exploitation. Local action often leads to a realisation of the need to 'go global' when results are not achieved at local or national levels, and new allies are embraced. The trend is away from centralised NGO advocacy models of limited, policy-oriented campaigns aimed at governments, towards hybrid models between 'NGO advocacy and direct action and justice networks'. The latter are characterised by a polycentric structure of mass activism and multi-issue, diversely-targeted campaigns proliferating via the Internet. NGOs are no longer the sole initiators of action, and are sometimes shut out by more radical groups such as Jubilee South. Groups such as these have often emerged out of the World Social Forum, indicating again a move away from NGOs based in the West (Reitan 2007: 100–1). Neither author produces a lot evidence or examples to support their arguments, so this is an area for further research to clarify. One could also quibble over their narrow definitions of what an NGO is. 'Global justice movements' and 'justice networks' and protest groups are surely just as 'non-governmental' as Oxfam or the Red Cross, even if the former groups do not formally register their existence with any government. It might therefore be more helpful to think of the emergence of different types of NGO, rather than claiming to have spotted a different animal altogether.

The growing links between NGOs and states, businesses and IFIs is well documented. They reflect both the desire of businesses and IFIs for greater legitimacy, which we discussed in the previous chapter, and the greater professionalism of NGOs which has given them the confidence (whether justified or not) to calculate what sort of bargain they can drive. While there is nothing novel about NGOs working with bodies that may appear to be their natural adversaries, many of the links have had a sharper focus in recent years. Grant *et al.* describe the 'mixed actor coalitions' of state and non-state groups around such issues as trade in conflict diamonds, 'venal oil production', the banning of land mines, and illicit trade in small arms. In the case of diamonds, co-operation between NGOs, representatives of the diamond industry and the United Nations (UN) led to a UN resolution in 2000 which tightened certification standards on diamonds to ensure that they were the result of legitimate production rather than being traded by warlords (Grant *et al.* in Cohen and McBride 2003: 134). The ambiguous relationship with apparent adversaries emerges again in Kaldor's description of the successful campaign for cheaper drugs for HIV/AIDs victims. She describes it as a global campaign *'against, or in co-operation with,* states, international organisations and pharmaceutical companies' (Kaldor 2003: 95. Emphasis added).

Thomas describes NGO attempts to work with the World Bank, one of the biggest adversaries of all. An extremely vocal and efficient transnational alliance of NGOs canvassed for debt cancellation via Jubilee 2000, with civil society groups showing the impact of IFI policies on the poor in Africa with the destruction of the health infrastructure, user fees for medicine and water, and the spread of AIDs with increased poverty. This led to the World Bank agreeing to involve NGOs in establishing the Structural Adjustment Programme Review Initiative (SAPRI) to assess the impact of structural adjustment. While the immediate results were disappointing, with the World Bank and SAPRI issuing separate reports, there were long-term benefits with a shift in the post-Washington consensus, greater emphasis on poverty reduction and a greater emphasis on partnership between nominal adversaries (Thomas in Taylor and Williams 2004: 179–99. See also Fox and Brown 1998: 497, 528–39). All these cases take us back to the theme of pushing further at doors that had been partially opened by changes in the nature of global politics. The results were mixed, and there was the ever-present danger of NGOs being used to give greater respectability to governments, businesses or IFIs without gaining much in return, but the fact that it was often the latter bodies that sought out NGOs might suggest that NGOs could bargain from a position of strength.

The distinction between 'broad' and 'narrow' campaigns is a rough one, but one test would be whether the issue being pursued is one that can bring thousands of protesters into the streets, or whether it is more likely to be the concern of specialists. Concern over Third World debt, and the trading advantages enjoyed by wealthy countries at the expense of the poor, can bring tens of thousands of peaceful protesters into the streets of Birmingham, and similar numbers of less peaceful demonstrators into the streets of Seattle, whereas few large public rallies have been held in support of the needs of child soldiers or the desirability of more ethical behaviour by businesses. Successful campaigns depend on finding the right horses for the right courses. The Jubilee Debt Campaign has been able to keep up the pressure on the British government in the knowledge that it enjoys the support of a large section of British public opinion. Its main requirement is not so much technical knowledge, though it needs to be well briefed on the specific hardships caused by the debt burden, but to keep up the pressure on the government to honour its commitments, which were themselves made largely in response to popular pressure. The campaign against the MAI was a different type of broad campaign, with extensive use of the Internet in a range of countries. While the heart of the argument, which appealed especially to liberal opinion in the West, was that businesses should not be able to dictate policy to elected governments, it was also necessary to attract popular support in Africa by showing how specific local interests would be harmed by the agreement. There was a real threat to the livelihoods of African workers, and to the prospects for investment in Africa that would benefit African communities, and not merely a theoretical assault by global capitalism on the poor.

In contrast to these campaigns to mobilise the maximum number of citizens, Benjamin describes the work of Global Witness in campaigning against the illicit exploitation of natural resources. Few people will take to streets to demand an embargo on the import of timber felled by Liberian warlords, yet here was an NGO which succeeded by conducting thorough investigations on the ground and could then confront governments with the facts. Global Witness was deliberately kept slim, with no membership base or fund raising, but its expertise in tracking illicit trade earned it respect. Not only did it help to persuade the UN Security Council to impose sanctions to prevent importation of Liberian timber, but it helped to end the illicit timber trade in Cambodia, and contributed to the prevention of trade in 'conflict diamonds' (Benjamin 2007: 17). While the broad campaigns of groups such as the Jubilee Debt Campaign, Amnesty International and Human Rights Watch hit the headlines, more narrowly focused campaigns continue to proliferate. Obvious examples include the Coalition to Stop the Use of Child Soldiers, the Ethical Trading Initiative and Reporters without Borders, which deals with freedom of the press and the protection of journalists from intimidation. In all these cases, the skill lies in defining the problem clearly, defining the targets for lobbying and confronting the relevant institutions with facts which they would prefer not to hear.

What of the losers in the game of global politics? Some expect to be 'taking part' rather than 'winning' from the outset because they are pursuing causes whose time has not come, and may never come. The African Social Forum and Jubilee South are demanding changes in the conduct of world trade that are not likely to be conceded in the foreseeable future by the governments and global businesses that benefit from the existing order. Many of the groups that attend gatherings such as the World Social Forum make a virtue of not contaminating themselves by talking to any of the power-wielding institutions. These are perfectly respectable positions to take, and the views of groups on the fringe may in time percolate through to the mainstream, but the satisfaction gained by members of these groups presumably comes from having presented their case in public, while foregoing the satisfaction that more moderate groups gain from pointing to the political changes that they have engineered.

In other cases the losers do not necessarily set out with an expectation that they will lose. The Bank Information Center (BiC) shadows the work of the World Bank in the hope of pointing it in the direction of social justice and economic sustainability. It presented a well-briefed case against the construction of the Bujagali Falls Dam, drawing attention to the effects on the water levels of Lake Victoria and the River Nile, and the consequent loss of generating power, and the inadequate consideration of any alternatives, but to no avail (BiC 2006). Armstrong notes the patchy results achieved by the Ethical Trading Initiative, with little impact on trade unionism, low minimum wages, and little protection for casual or migrant workers (Armstrong 2006: 6), and Fox and Brown point to similarly patchy results in lobbying the World Bank (Fox and Brown 1998: 497).

As in many walks of life, the effort put in, the skills deployed, and the volume of public support generated, do not guarantee success. In the case of the World Bank, Fox and Brown suggest that important variables are the position of national states, local government, divisions within local communities, national and international private sector interests and policy currents within the World Bank. There is also the question of whether an issue arouses people's anger, especially in the case of dams, mines and the destruction of forests (Fox and Brown 1998: 497–9). Beyond these considerations, one needs to bear in mind again both the strengths and weaknesses of NGOs as distinctive institutions. On the positive side, they have been able to mobilise public opinion in a way that few other institutions could, over issues such as poverty, debt and fair trade, and they have achieved notable successes. In other cases small groups of dedicated individuals have taken up hitherto neglected causes, and through diligent research, skilled presentation of the facts and a careful selection of the relevant targets, they have pressed powerful public and private bodies to change their ways. On the negative side, NGOs are ultimately dependent on persuasion, with few tougher sanctions available to them. Unlike many other political actors, they do not possess weapons such as votes, guns or legal or financial power. Armstrong's description of the limitations to the influence of the Ethical Trading Initiative illustrates the situation. Problems such as inadequate wages, and the exploitation of casual and migrant workers, could be tackled by businesses re-allocating resources or by states passing laws. NGOs can only try to persuade, and persuasion is a fickle weapon. It may work if an NGO can build up a large enough head of steam of public support, present sufficiently convincing arguments or find a sympathetic ear at an institution being lobbied, but the other side may possess many more powerful weapons in its armoury and have no difficulty in winning the day.

Conclusion

This chapter has tried to juggle with several variables, and many of these variables change over time or are in a state of flux. The international political order has changed, with the 'war on terror' and the rise and fall of alleged US hegemony. The global economic order has changed less obviously, yet years of Western policies based on free market assumptions have done little to achieve their proclaimed objectives of poverty eradication, economic development or improved health or education, and in many cases the situation has deteriorated. Yet, paradoxically, Western powers have encouraged democratisation in Africa, which has opened up new opportunities for NGO influence both within Africa and in building links with like-minded groups outside. These groups include campaigners who are increasingly angry over the impact of Western policies in Africa, especially over discriminatory trade policies, the debt burden, and the pressures for retrenchment and privatisation. Thus economic liberalisation has probably worsened Africa's plight, but political liberalisation has provided it with opportunities to fight back.

The economic and political changes we have described have contributed to a changed NGO agenda as the conviction has spread that the Washington consensus was worsening Africa's plight. While Western governments and IFIs could hardly be said to share this conviction, they were now less confident in their free market orthodoxy, and more amenable to criticism. At the same time, what we may term a new political correctness, for want of a better term, emerged. It included support for such concepts as poverty eradication, economic sustainability, participation and partnership. The reasons for the emergence of such fashions are never easy to explain, but they may have reflected a loss of confidence in the previous policies, a need to placate a growing volume of public concern amongst voters in the West about global justice, a fear of what would happen in Africa if there was not a change of course, and in some cases a change of personnel in key positions.

It was then left to NGOs to seize the opportunities created both by greater political pluralism and a greater willingness by Western institutions to consult them, and by the dire conditions which stimulated public protest in both Africa and the West. Links between Africa and the outside world were forged, so that external support could add weight to local protest. This could lead to spectacular campaigns such as those against the debt burden and the MAI, but also to a more structured day-to-day relationship between NGOs and Western governments, businesses and IFIs. The spectacular campaigns have usually been over issues that arouse strong public feelings, with NGOs able to press their case by using not only reasoned, well-researched arguments but also by taking advantage of the weight of public opinion. In other cases a more low profile approach has been used where an issue does not arouse widespread public indignation, but where a dedicated group of people are still determined to right a perceived injustice, whether over child soldiers, over trade with warlords in natural resources which is sustaining their brutal rule, or over the employment of labour in inhumane sweatshops.

Many NGOs, individually or collectively, have achieved remarkable successes, but there have been many losers as well as winners. Some of the losers realise that they are pursuing what are, for the immediate future, lost causes, but others lose even when they present moderate, well-researched arguments. No one has yet written an instruction manual on how to guarantee NGO success. NGOs certainly enjoy assets in comparison with other institutions, such as traditional pressure groups, political parties and trade unions. For the most part they exhibit flexibility, they avoid narrow political dogma and they are willing to take a pragmatic view on working with their adversaries. They may often lack mass support, but neither are they burdened with a mass membership that may cramp the style of the leadership. Yet if we are trying to explain why there are so many losers as well as winners, we return to the point that the main asset of most NGOs is their power of persuasion in presenting a case that is either broadly in tune with public opinion, or at least not antagonistic to it. Persuasion may sometimes succeed for a variety of reasons. Decision-making institutions may simply be persuaded by the force of the arguments and a new awareness of the facts. Institutions carrying out unpopular policies or actions, whether it is businesses employing child labour, or the World Bank forcing poor Africans to pay for hospital treatment or drinking water, may want to rescue their reputations or seek a degree of legitimacy. In other cases a debate that goes beyond NGOs and global decision-makers, eventually sees one side win the argument, whether over the impracticability or immorality of maintaining the debt burden, or of allowing Western pharmaceutical companies to withhold essential, affordable drugs from AIDS victims.

But persuasion can only go so far. States, IFIs and businesses, backed by the powers of law-making, legal authority, money or coercion continue to dominate the global order, and if they say 'no' there is little that NGOs can do. Returning to the Olympic analogy, those who take part without winning may emerge with some glory, but in the final analysis the amateurs are no match for the professionals.

9
Conclusion

This study has raised a range of questions, explicitly or implicitly, many of which are difficult or impossible to answer. Why do NGOs exist at all? To what extent are they a distinctive type of institution and, if they are, what is it that marks them off from other institutions? What can they do better than other institutions, and subject to what limitations? What is the political context within which they operate at both national and global levels? How are they affected by different degrees of authoritarianism and pluralism, and by the shift from government to governance? How far has globalisation created new opportunities for co-operation between NGOs at different levels? Has globalisation reduced democratic control over powerful institutions, and how far have NGOs been able to reduce any subsequent democratic deficit? What are the main resources which NGOs possess for wielding political influence, and what strategies can they follow to maximise their influence?

While the growth of NGOs has been largely the result of political and social change, one could ask what further changes NGOs have subsequently set in train. In what ways have they affected the outcomes of who gets what, how and when? Then, returning to the initial question, one could ask not only why NGOs exist, but about what the forces giving rise to their existence tells about the nature of modern politics and society. Are NGOs inextricably bound up with post-industrial society in the West and unconsolidated democracy in Africa? With the rise of NGOs, do we now need to conceive of democracy in a different way after a century or more of representative democracy, mediated by political parties, pressure groups and mass movements? Similarly in world politics, one could ask whether NGOs help to sustain a system that is suspended between super power domination and global democracy.

The emergence of NGOs

The origins of NGOs have been traced by some writers back to the emergence of such nineteenth century bodies as the Anti-Slavery Society and the Red Cross, but these bodies were small islands of voluntary activity in a sea of traditional political institutions. For most of the nineteenth and twentieth centuries there were charities which made only occasional incursions into politics, and there were pressure groups which sometimes offered services to those adversely affected by the forces against which the group was campaigning. Thus the Red Cross might press the government to provide urgent medical supplies, and the Royal Society for the Prevention of Cruelty to Animals (RSPCA) might campaign for changes in the law regarding the treatment of animals, while also administering animal welfare. But charity and advocacy were generally kept separate, and it was not until the later years of the twentieth century that there emerged a network of NGOs in the generally accepted sense of the term.

The emergence of NGOs had very different origins in Africa from those in Europe, yet developments north and south of the Sahara have had a profound effect on the political process at national and global levels. In Africa, NGOs emerged in large numbers from the early 1980s onwards as growing poverty, and the collapse of state welfare provision, forced citizens to co-operate to meet their basic needs. Many of the early groups were small, local and rudimentary in organisation, yet they marked a departure from both the passive acceptance of aid from above, and from the more traditional self-help provided by ethnic organisations. With the weakening of authoritarian governments as they became less able to deliver benefits to their constituents, a parallel but overlapping type of NGO activity emerged to demand basic human rights and eventually democratic elections. With opposition parties generally prohibited, NGOs were able to play a prominent role by claiming that they merely wanted democratic choice rather than an overthrow of the government.

Meanwhile in the West the rigidity of the class-based mass politics of the industrial era was giving way to a post-industrial politics in which political parties were losing their capacity to shape and implement distinctive policies, and losing their ability to retain many of their members and activists. NGOs (even if they did not describe themselves as such) offered an alternative by campaigning for specific cause that transcended the old class and ideological barriers. As in Africa, there was also a largely unconnected parallel development, as governments were anxious to shed expensive and administratively cumbersome public services, and to encourage the 'voluntary sector' to step in. This sector included not only old fashioned charities but also more militant groups which saw themselves as campaigners for the underprivileged.

The next link in the chain was to transcend national frontiers, and again there were forces at work which had little in common with each other. It was the accepted orthodoxy in the West by the late 1980s that African states were incapable of delivering many public services and that, as in the West itself, the voluntary sector should have a greater role. Aid was generally conditional on accepting this orthodoxy, so NGOs soon proliferated. At the same time, liberal opinion in the West was becoming increasingly concerned about growing inequality between rich and poor nations, apparently worsened by the policies of Western governments and international financial institutions (IFIs) such as the imposition of free market economics, trade agreements that stunted development in Africa, and the reluctance to cancel a growing debt burden. Asking for charitable donations to help starving children in Africa was increasingly complemented by pressure on governments and IFIs, by bodies such as Christian Aid, Oxfam and Jubilee 2000, to remove the causes of starvation. The Western NGOs spearheading the campaigns for 'global justice' were able to build links with NGOs such as the Tanzania Gender Networking Programme (TGNP), HakiElimu, HakiKazi and the Uganda Debt Network which were exploiting the opportunities created by greater democratisation in their own countries. These groups were pressing their own governments to take action to deal with poverty and inadequate social provision, and to demand a tougher line in negotiations with Western institutions. While globalisation had added to many of Africa's hardships by leaving its markets unprotected, it had also facilitated easier communications between like-minded groups in Africa and the West to fight for what they saw as a more just global order.

The distinctiveness of NGOs

Such descriptions still leave us with a hazy notion of what an NGO actually is, and what its distinctive features are. There is the vague generalisation that NGOs belong to the 'voluntary sector' which marks them off from both governments and private enterprise, but in practice even this distinction is blurred as some NGOs work as agents for governments and some governmental decision-making incorporates voluntary bodies that are nominally outside government. In relation to the private sector, NGOs may help to formulate voluntary agreements to regulate the behaviour of businesses on matters such as fair trade, minimum wages and the employment of child labour – spheres of activity which might once have been regarded as the prerogative of the state. More important than semantic questions of where the voluntary sector begins and ends is the practical question of how NGOs go about their business, and how far this business is conducted in a way that is distinctive from the state and private sectors, where the ballot box and the profit motive may be the ultimate arbiters of decision-making.

We step into the controversial area outlined in Chapter 3. We noted the contrast between the 'virtuous model' of NGOs as altruistic bodies pursuing causes that no one else would pursue, under the auspices of idealistic staff sacrificing better paid careers elsewhere; and the 'functional model' of NGOs created for opportunistic reasons by (often unemployed) people seeking grants and employment, and losing their virtue in order to conform to the political, administrative and economic dictates of Western donors. NGO activity, like most human activity at various times, involves supping with the Devil. Large numbers of NGOs have to seek to bargain, compromise and, where necessary, tone down their stated objectives. This may upset some purists, but NGOs may still survive with much of their idealism intact, and with the capacity to fulfil much of their proclaimed mission. If that means acknowledging the names of some less than wholesome sponsors in their annual reports, they may echo the words of General Booth when the Salvation Army began collecting money in public houses – 'Give me dirty money and I'll make it clean'. One has only to look at the range of activities carried out by NGOs to answer any charge that they are merely plugging gaps in public service provision, or are opportunistic bodies for people wanting to attract funds, who would otherwise be in the dole queue or on the fringe of the criminal world. The latter groups clearly exist, but are hardly a criterion for judging the overall activities of NGOs.

An alternative line of attack is that NGOs are distinctive, but this distinctiveness may be characterised by a pigheadedness that is dysfunctional to the political process and to social cohesion. With its tunnel vision, it is alleged, an NGO will pursue a specific cause without regard to the side effects of any success it achieves. Aid for refugees may help them to return to subvert their governments, successful campaigns to release political prisoners may lead to greater violence, and pressures to end press censorship may lead to greater distortion of the truth or to incitement to violence or hatred. Such allegations are difficult to deny, though one wonders whether similar charges might not be made against sectarian or ethnic political parties, or even heads of state who disregard human suffering in pursuing their specific cause – that of holding on to power at all costs.

A more fruitful search for NGO 'distinctiveness' might be to ask about the nature of their resources or power bases. On the face of it, the voluntary sector is at a disadvantage compared with the public and private sectors. NGOs cannot raise taxes, pass laws or threaten to execute or imprison those who disagree with them. Unlike businesses, they cannot blackmail governments, citizens or employees by threatening to take their investment elsewhere if they do not get their own way. Unlike governments, they do not enjoy a large constituency of voters who acknowledge their legitimacy in return for the public services they provide. Unlike businesses, they do not enjoy a large constituency of shareholders who acknowledge their legitimacy in return for the profits they distribute. Yet NGOs do enjoy the advantage of having relatively few enemies, even if they have fewer self-interested supporters. Unlike the institutions in the public and private sectors, they do not have to face public opprobrium by raising taxes, cutting services, exploiting or dismissing workers, or polluting the environment. For the most part, NGOs are more like Father Christmas than Scrooge. They are generally seen to be honest and altruistic, rather than existing to promote narrow, selfish interests. When they are promoting relatively narrow causes, such as the welfare of child soldiers or the prohibition of trade in 'blood diamonds', they will have few enemies beyond the small groups benefiting from the *status quo*. And when they promote causes which capture the public imagination, such as debt relief or fair trade, they may be able to mobilise public opinion in such a way as to make governments listen. Despite all the handicaps we have enumerated, NGOs possess a power of persuasion that helps to explain many of their successes. This power may rest on the ability to present reasoned arguments which their adversaries find it difficult to refute, or on leaving governments, IFIs or businesses with a choice between continuing with unpopular (and possibly unethical) policies which undermine their support and possibly their legitimacy, or making concessions to NGO demands. Even at a more mundane, day-to-day level, NGOs may be given the benefit of the doubt when it comes to proposing or taking any course of action, in the belief that they are acting out of noble motives.

Yet the whole basis of NGO activity goes against much of the grain of public understanding of politics, which makes assumptions about the power of votes, money, law-making, coercion and patronage. Unless they are run by millionaires such as the Aga Khan or Bill Gates, NGOs have to ask for money; they cannot demand it. They can only ask African states for the privilege of registration, rather than demand it. They can urge the World Bank to modify its policies that are causing hardship in Africa, but they possess no electoral or financial sanctions to reinforce their demands. The fact that NGOs have succeeded at all in fighting political battles might suggest not only that the power of persuasion is an underrated asset, but that the powers of governments, businesses and IFIs are over-estimated. They, too, are often insecure despite all the apparent weapons at their disposal. Western governments in the post-industrial era rely on shaky electoral bases, and dare not alienate too many sections of public opinion. African governments were seldom strong to begin with, and recognise the danger of alienating either service providers or advocacy NGOs demanding greater respect for human rights. IFIs which apparently have the power of life and death over whole nations by deciding how to dispense funds, and subject to what conditions, turn out to possess a precarious legitimacy. Unlike governments, IFIs cannot even claim a popular mandate for their actions, most of which would almost certainly be rejected emphatically in any hypothetical worldwide referendum. To retain any legitimacy, they must at least be seen to be consulting NGOs. Businesses appear to be more powerful than ever in a world of free market orthodoxy, but power without responsibility carries its own dangers. As governments increasingly abdicate their responsibility to control investment, wages, working conditions or even collecting taxes, NGOs step into the vacuum. They demand action not on the bases of imposing laws, but in the name of ethics and morality. Why should businesses listen? A cynical answer would be that the appearance of ethical behaviour is ultimately good for the balance sheet, as investors and consumers turn their backs on unethical firms. But it may also be the case that, like a child given unlimited freedom to misbehave, many businesses would prefer power *with* responsibility so that they and their competitors are working within accepted 'rules', or at least conventions, that bear some relation to accepted standards in society. There may still be a wide gap between what businesses regard as 'corporate social responsibility' and what advocacy NGOs regard as civilised behaviour but, as in the case of dealing with governments and IFIs, NGOs enjoy a degree of leverage out of proportion to their often meagre resources. If we return to the question 'What is distinctive about NGOs?', one could turn the question round by asking which other institutions have the ability to influence decision-makers in the ways we have described, whether the decision-maker is a major Western government, an IFI, a global corporation or even a relatively lowly African civil servant seeking a 'development partner'.

Political opportunities and constraints

The focus has so far been largely on 'why' rather than 'how'. Policy outcomes occur not simply because different institutions possess different degrees of 'power' but because political systems are structured in particular ways. To quote an old textbook example, you cannot become Pope by shooting all the other bishops, and you cannot become President of the Soviet Union by praying. What works in Uganda may not work in Brussels, at the World Bank or in the boardroom of General Motors. Processes such as democratisation in Africa, the growth of new public management (NPM) in the West, and the evolution of global governance, all help to determine what NGOs are able to do and how they do it. So too do changes in political attitudes and behaviour, such as the rise of post-material values on the one hand and free market fundamentalism on the other, or the apparent rise of a more participant culture in Africa. The chapters on Tanzania and Uganda illustrated the ways in which political processes could differ between two apparently similar countries, though they also illustrated the ubiquitous presence of such factors as poverty, dependency and neo-patrimonialism which are common to most of Africa. On the differing political processes, we noted that extensive public participation preceded the emergence of a stable semi-democracy in Uganda, while participation emerged within the stifling constraints of a single party in Tanzania, and was rejuvenated in a more pluralist system as civil society gradually found its voice. In Uganda, the current political system emerged out of an insurgency movement which still claims a moral superiority over those who are not committed to its 'revolution', whereas in Tanzania the legitimacy of opposition is less of an issue even though the opposition's ability to wield influence is constrained severely by a highly organised ruling party. All of these variations have a bearing on what NGOs can do, and how. The Ugandan government still has a suspicion of NGOs acting as a front for opposition parties, whereas in Tanzania the problem for NGOs is less one of harassment by the state and more of a well organised system that is able to maintain the privileges of ruling politicians and the elites that sustain them, often to the detriment of NGOs demanding greater equality, openness and social justice. In Uganda, the constraints on NGOs and civil society in general are often coercive in the last resort, whereas in Tanzania they are more bureaucratic. But in both countries, and indeed in most of Tropical Africa, the general rise of multi-party democracy and pluralism has facilitated a rise in the effectiveness of NGOs, which in turn have imparted greater confidence and new skills in civil society as a whole.

While there may be a broad consensus on the nature and significance of political change in Tanzania and Uganda over the past two decades, the nature of change in the global order is much more contested. We examined six possible models in Chapter 6, covering such variables as naked power and democracy, and global technocracy and anarchy. In much of the literature, 'global governance' provides a broad umbrella to describe what is going on, in the sense that there are diverse centres of decision-making rather than a relatively co-ordinated, hierarchical structure that exists in nation states, or at least existed until recently. What the free market-oriented World Bank does is only loosely connected to what the more social democratic United Nations Development Programme (UNDP) does, and both are remote from organisations performing more technocratic functions such as control over postal services or marine insurance. Yet this consensus on the existence of global governance does not prevent widely conflicting views on the extent to which the US can flex its military muscles to make NGOs do its bidding, or the extent to which global capital can largely escape any sort of political control, or can indeed be a source of such control. Some academic authors point to the growing ability of NGOs to hold governments, IFIs and businesses to account, others to the survival of a world in which only marginal changes have occurred in levels of poverty, sickness and ignorance. This study has tended towards the conclusion that the military might of the US and other Western powers has not been a major constraint on NGOs, but that the power of global capital, and its ability to influence global decision-makers and individual governments, remains an ever-present reality. But rather than dwell on this unequal distribution of resources, we preferred to focus on what NGOs are able to do within an imperfect world.

Even if one accepts the thesis that global capitalism is the dominant force, there is no global politburo, no global secret police, and no global ruling party with a cell in every street and every village to enforce conformity. In the absence of any such hierarchy, NGOs are able to take on specific centres of power such as the World Bank or the EU without having to challenge the whole global order. The ability of

NGOs to mount such challenges assumes the existence of certain 'rules of engagement', however vaguely defined. We rejected the cosy notion of the existence of a 'global culture' in which most global political actors subscribed to a range of civilised values, in favour of a belief that there are many cultures, some of which provide a benign environment for NGOs, and many of which do not. Any NGO influence depends less on the existence of a consensus on how the world should be ruled, and more on the ability to exploit the weaknesses of other institutions. We suggested that the key variables included ideology, legitimacy and power. The ideology implicit in the behaviour of most advocacy NGOs is generally remote from that of the free market ideology of the major global decision-makers and Western governments. It might be slightly closer to that of African governments, but many of these have persuaded themselves that they have little alternative but to acknowledge the dominant orthodoxy. In addition to external pressure, African governments need to serve the interests of the elites that sustain them in power. There is thus a wide gulf between ideologies, or least political expedients, that imply serving the interests of global capital and African elites, and the (at least implicit) ideology of NGOs which seek to serve the interests of the poor and the underprivileged, and to seek a political order based on 'global justice'. It might be objected that this is an aspiration rather than an ideology, but it implies a social democratic belief in a more equitable distribution of wealth and a liberal belief in human rights and civil liberties.

How, then is any dialogue possible between NGOs and their adversaries? To a large extent it depends on each side claiming (or pretending) to believe in some of the tenets of the ideology of the other. With the emergence of the post-Washington consensus, the World Bank and Western governments claim, to varying degrees, to believe in poverty eradication, the facilitation of development by the state and the empowerment of the citizenry. NGOs, for their part, generally disclaim any belief in centralised planning, nationalisation, the dismantling of existing global institutions or the de-linking of Africa from the global order, although many of these beliefs were part of the left-wing ideological armoury until the 1980s. While some of the more extreme ideological weapons may be kept in hiding by both sides, perhaps in the hope that they can one day be wheeled out again if circumstances change, dialogue between NGOs and their adversaries depends on acceptance of a vaguely defined middle ground where neither side is asking the other to abandon its basic principles.

Legitimacy is an important asset to NGOs, when they generally lack constitutional, financial or coercive assets. They need to demonstrate the legitimacy of their actual objectives, and their willingness to pursue them within the prevailing legal and constitutional norms. They need to demonstrate managerial competence and to account for their actions to diverse stakeholders, from governments wanting to know what NGOs are doing to advance the nation's foreign policy, to individual donors wanting to know how many children have been saved from starvation. It is not always easy to gain legitimacy in all these diverse spheres. Pleasing donors and producing immaculate balance sheets, for example, may be at the expense of the achievement of the actual 'mission' of helping people on the ground. The charge is frequently made that seeking to please governmental or business donors means compromising ideals that are remote from those of governments or businesses. Some NGOs may thus be reduced to the status of obedient quangos, yet one only needs to look around to see that many are able to take the money and still pursue radical causes.

In the case of power, the power of persuasion has to be wielded with all the skill and subtlety available in the absence of most other powers. Some of this persuasion will be based on an acknowledgment of the NGO's superior knowledge or skills. 'Only we understand country X sufficiently to be able to disburse food aid there' or 'only we possess the medical knowledge to deal with the epidemic in country Y'. But to a large extent it is a matter of claiming the moral high ground and, if possible, claiming that public opinion occupies the same ground. Governments, IFIs and businesses may be a few miles away from this ground, yet their own legitimacy may be brought into question if they are seen to be too close to the immoral low ground. This is especially true in the case of IFIs, which can claim no electoral mandate for their actions, and these actions are often seen as blatant attempts to preserve an unjust order. If they can give at least an appearance of co-operating with, or making concessions to NGOs, their image will be greatly improved. Similarly with businesses parading their corporate social responsibility. Governments are often a tougher nut to crack, since they can demonstrate that they represent a much larger constituency than the NGOs. But if many of the most articulate constituents turn out to be on the side of the NGOs, as in the case of debt relief or fair trade, then governments too may be amenable to NGO influence.

For influence to triumph in the face of power, there is still the question of devising the necessary strategies. Which institutions are feasible or desirable for NGOs to lobby, negotiate or co-operate with? Much of the literature and evidence collected in this study suggests the need for a subtle, step-by-step approach. Spectacular mass campaigns to influence

Western governments are the exception, as are INGO attempts to influence African governments, which might then make accusations of foreign interference or imperialism. Within African politics, it is generally the indigenous NGOs that are in closest contact with their governments, but their success will often be helped by the financial, moral and administrative support of INGOs. Many battles to conserve the natural environment have been won in this way. When the traffic is in the other direction, indigenous and international NGOs may again be complementary to each other, with indigenous groups producing the evidence on the ground of poverty, sickness or pollution, which can then feed into the global campaigns of Oxfam or the Jubilee Debt Campaign. Even then, the force of moral argument will not normally be sufficient without an extensive network of contacts, both between different NGOs and between NGOs and decision-making bodies. And the effectiveness of these contacts in turn depends on NGOs having the skill to recognise what sort of demands are realistic, and in what ways the arguments should be couched. The context within which these games are played does not remain static, so that a modification of the Washington consensus may open some new doors, while the declaration of a 'war on terror' may close others. For all their skill in networking, NGOs do not enjoy influence at the top table as of right, in contrast to the position of pressure groups in mid-twentieth century political processes in Britain, when it was asserted that the Church of England would not stand for any liberalisation of the divorce laws, that farmers would not allow any reductions in agricultural subsidies, or that the coal miners would not tolerate moves towards European integration. NGOs have to begin each battle anew rather than being a constant power behind the throne. The achievements of the winners are easy to record, but no one is guaranteed victory. As long as NGOs lack the sanctions of traditional pressure groups, and depend heavily on persuasion, governments, IFIs and businesses will continue to overrule them if they are sufficiently determined to do so.

NGOs and the nature of contemporary politics

Finally we turn to the question of what the rise of NGOs tells us about the nature of politics and society today. NGOs are a product of social, economic and political change in both Africa and the West, and in the wider world, but they have gained a momentum which, one could argue, is transforming the political order still further. One can produce mundane, and sometimes meaningless, examples to illustrate how society has changed. Does it matter, as some authors insist, that The Royal Society for the Protection of Birds (RSPB) now has a larger membership than any political party in Britain? Probably not, beyond telling us that a large section of the population enjoys sufficient affluence and leisure to indulge in a worthy hobby such as bird watching, while many political issues are seen as remote or irrelevant to people's lives. Does it matter if a local branch of Make Poverty History attracts a larger attendance than the average local party executive committee? Or if it can be demonstrated that leading NGOs in Tanzania are a much bigger thorn in the flesh of the government than any opposition party? Probably, because this is indicative of a different attitude to political priorities and political strategies.

It brings us back to the concept of 'democracy without votes', which can manifest itself in HakiElimu's ability to throw the Tanzanian government into a panic by revealing the inadequacy of the nation's educational system, or in an unelected Oxfam going into battle with an unelected World Bank, to try to modify the policies which the latter has imposed on elected African governments. That NGOs are often a more effective vehicle than representative democracy for resolving a range of grievances is hardly in dispute. Equally, it is difficult to dispute the argument that no other institution could have opened up the democratic process in Africa in the way that NGOs have done, given the social, economic and political context of the past two decades. It is also indisputable that a taxi is often a better vehicle for getting from one place to another than a bus. But if taxis proliferated to such an extent that the bus services were driven out of business, would the overall transport needs of the community be served better? Taxis are useful in an emergency, but people might prefer a reliable range of bus routes running to reliable timetables. Are NGOs the taxis of modern politics, driving out trusted representative institutions such as political parties and parliaments?

We may note the lament of some traditionalists for the decline of clear-cut adversary politics, in which the oppressed spoke of class solidarity rather than talking about sensitising civil society or finding development partners, but the possibility, let alone the desirability, of reconstructing anything resembling mid-twentieth century politics seems remote. If all NGOs were dissolved tomorrow, some activists might find their way back into political parties and attempt to rejuvenate them. But the majority probably would not, given the widespread perception, possibly grounded in reality, of parties moving increasingly close to each other ideologically, and asserting that little can be done to change society in the face of the power of global capital. When NGOs are constantly pushing back notions of what can be achieved in a hostile world, it takes a dedicated activist to prefer the humdrum round of delivering leaflets and attending party meetings to elect people to posts from which they wield little power. Activists in Africa might find parties an even less attractive alternative to NGOs, as opposition parties despair of gaining power, and ruling parties exist mainly to sustain the nations' rulers and their courtiers.

We asked earlier in this chapter whether we now need to conceive of democracy in a different way from the representative democracy of yesteryear, mediated by political parties, mass movements and pressure groups; and we asked whether one now requires a different understanding of the nature of politics if it can be shown that persuasion can frequently triumph over the apparently stronger suits of votes, money, law-making, coercion and patronage. In the first case the answer is probably 'yes', at least as far as the West is concerned. Although civil society is in many ways thinner than it was 50 years ago, it is often the *ad hoc* campaigns concerned with debt relief, fair trade, animal rights or conservation that create an impression. Whether the campaigning bodies call themselves 'NGOs' or not, they exhibit the NGO characteristics of generally lacking a mass base, and relying on the leadership of articulate people, skilled in the arts of persuasion. In contrast, the professional, labour and religious groups which once had deep roots in society, as well as mass-based parties, now carry much less weight. In Africa, representative democracy never gained such a foothold in the first place, and the rise of democracy and NGOs has gone hand in hand. As to the power of money, law-making, coercion and patronage, no sane person would claim that they have gone away, but what is significant is that people wielding such weapons can sometimes be bested by NGOs in a way that would have been exceptional a generation ago. As politicians and political institutions have fallen in public esteem and have shakier bases of support, NGOs are better able to exploit the less monolithic political structures that now prevail. As government gives way to governance, decisions are less likely to be imposed from on high, and NGOs can penetrate the various nooks and crannies of a less centralised structure. Reasoned persuasion, based on extensive expertise and detailed research, does not always win the day, but it is now a more integral part of the political process. In Africa we noted the conflicting pulls of ruling politicians and elites, and of NGOs. NGOs for the most part seek a more egalitarian, libertarian and participatory social order, whereas the imperatives of staying in power frequently pull governments in the opposite direction of using patronage, corruption and favours for businesses. If one does not require a new understanding of the political order, one should at least be alert to the fact that the pull of NGOs, using their skills of persuasion, exists as a parallel political process, even if it is not the dominant process.

At the global level, persuasion has always been a major element. Not only are there no global parliaments, armies or police forces to impose decisions from above, but a range of institutions are constantly having to negotiate with each other, and with national governments. For NGOs, the task of reaching up to this level is formidable, but the institutions they are seeking to influence share with NGOs the common handicap of lacking any mass base or popular mandate. If international organisations pride themselves on wisdom based on extensive expertise, NGOs may still be able to match them blow for blow. More important still, NGOs are frequently advocating policies which are in tune with opinion in civil society, whereas IFIs are defending policies which are seen to be impoverishing Africa. To retain a degree of credibility and legitimacy, the IFIs at least need to be seen to be consulting NGOs, in a process that has become increasingly institutionalised in recent years.

Weaving these threads together, is there any discernible end product? Those who had hoped for the empowerment of ordinary citizens or, for a 'just' global order in which international institutions serve the needs of the poor and underprivileged, will be disappointed. African politics are still generally characterised by neo-patrimonialism at home and dependency abroad. IFIs and Western governments may express a genuine belief in the need to help the poor, but they will not countenance the establishment of a global order that would make such 'help' less necessary. Yet the rise of NGOs has contributed to significant changes. Businesses no longer assert that their sole duty is to their shareholders. NGO pressure has encouraged them to preach, if not always to practice, corporate social responsibility, and to accept greater monitoring of the impact of business on sweated labour, the employment of children and the natural environment. African governments, and the foreign donors supporting them, preach the virtues of 'a vibrant civil society'. This does not always receive priority when politicians, seeking to retain their power and wealth, enter into contracts with indigenous and foreign businesses, or with individual millionaires. But African politicians and administrators now have individual NGOs and civil society as a whole looking over their shoulders, and may find themselves on the wrong side of NGO campaigns, often supported indirectly by INGOs. IFI officials, and inter-governmental organisations generally, may not yet be shaking in their shoes at the prospect of an NGO crusade to dismantle the power structures that maintain Africa in a state of debt and dependency, but the door has been pushed open for NGOs to demand a right to be consulted and for IFIs to be required to offer some justification for their policies. To return to the Olympic metaphor of winning and taking part, NGOs have won many more trophies in the past decade than would previously have been conceivable. Many, probably most, of the biggest trophies have still eluded them, but the enormous increase in the numbers 'taking part' may yet yield further prizes.

Bibliography

Abdelrahman, M.M. (2004) *Civil Society Exposed: The Politics of NGOs in Egypt*, London: Tauris.

Agg, C. (2006) 'Winners or Losers? NGOs in the Current Aid Paradigm', *Development*, 49 (2), 15–21.

Akiba, O. (ed.) (2004) *Constitutionalism and Society in Africa*, Ashgate, Aldershot.

Albrow, M., Anheier, H., Glasius, M., Price, M.E. and Kaldor, M. (eds) (2008) *Global Civil Society 2007/8*, London, Sage.

Alger, C.F. (2002) 'The Emerging Roles of NGOs in the UN System: From Article 71 to a People's Millennium Assembly', *Global Governance*, 93–117.

Ali, T. (2006) 'Bought with Western Cash', *The Guardian*, Manchester, 7 April, 34.

Amoore, L. and Langley, P. (2004) 'Ambiguities of Global Civil Society', *Review of International Studies*, 30, 89–110.

Amoore, L. (ed.) (2005) *The Global Resistance Reader*, London, Routledge.

Anderson, I. (2007)'Global Action: International NGOs and Advocacy' in B. Rugendyke (ed.) *NGOs as Advocates for Development in a Globalising World*, London, Routledge, pp. 71–95.

Anderson, K. and Rieff, D. (2005) 'Global Civil Society: A Sceptical View' in H. Anheier, M. Glasius and M. Kaldor (eds) *Global Civil Society 2004/5*, London, Sage, pp. 26–39.

Anheier, H., Glasius, M. and Kaldor, M. (eds) (2001) *Global Civil Society*, Oxford, Oxford University Press.

Anheier, H., Glasius, M. and Kaldor, M. (eds) (2005) *Global Civil Society 2004/5*, London, Sage.

Armstrong, M. (2006) 'Ethical Traders Work Overtime to Help' *The Guardian*, Manchester, 6 November, 6.

Avirgan, T. (1997) *SAPRI/SIPRIN: Emerging Worldwide Movement*, Washington, Development Group for Alternative Policies *blhttp://www.igc.org.dga.

Axtmann, R. (ed.) (2001) *Balancing Democracy*, London, Continuum.

Ayers, A.J. (2006) 'Demystifying Democratisation: The Global Constitution of (neo)Liberal Polities in Africa', *Third World Quarterly*, 22 (7), 321–38.

Azarya, V. and Chazan, N. (1987) 'Disengagement from the State in Africa: Reflections on the Experience of Ghana and Guinea', *Comparative Studies in Society and History*, 29 (1), 106–31.

Ba, A.D. and Hoffmann M.J. (eds) (2005) *Contending Perspectives on Global Governance*, London, Routledge.

Baker, G. and Chandler, D. (eds) (2005) *Global Civil Society*, London, Routledge.

Bank Information Center (BiC) (2006) *About the Bank Information Center*, http://www.bicusa.org//en/Page.About.aspx

Barber, B. (2001) 'Challenges to Democracy in an Age of Globalisation' in R. Axtmann (ed.) *Balancing Democracy*, London, Continuum, pp. 295–311.

Barkan, J.D. (1994) *Beyond Capitalism and Socialism in Kenya and Tanzania*, London, Lynne Rienner.

Barr, A., Fafchamps, M. and Owens, T. (2005) 'The Governance of Non-Governmental Organisations in Uganda', *World Development*, 33 (4), 647–79.

Barrow, O. and Jennings, M. (eds) (2001) *The Charitable Impulse: NGOs and Development in East and North East Africa*, Oxford, James Currey.

Bazaara, N. (2005) 'The Ability of Civil Society Groups to Influence the Debate on the Role of the Market in Rural Asset Building in East Africa' in K.B. Ghimire (ed.) *Civil Society and the Market Question: Dynamics of Rural Development and Popular Mobilization*, Basingstoke, Palgrave, pp. 132–61.

Beetham, D., Bracking, S., Kearton, I. and Weir, S. (2002) *International IDEA Handbook on Democracy Assessment*, London, Kluwer International.

Benjamin, A. (2007) 'Rough Diamonds', *The Guardian*, Manchester, Society Guardian supplement, 31 January, 9.

Benner, T., Reinicke, W.H. and Witte, J.M. (2004) 'Multisector Networks in Global Governance: Towards a Pluralistic System of Accountability', *Government and Opposition*, 39 (2), 191–210.

Bennett, W.L. (2005) 'Social Movements Beyond Borders: Understanding Two Eras of Transnational Activism' in D. Della Porta and S. Tarrow (eds) *Transnational Protest and Global Activism*, Oxford, Rowman and Littlefield, pp. 203–26.

Berman, M. (2001) 'Waiting for the Barbarians', *The Guardian*, Manchester, Saturday Review, 6 October, 2.

Berrigan, T. (2008) The New Military Frontier: Africa, *Just Commentary*, Kuala Lumpur, 8 (3), March: 7–8.

Bobbitt, P. (2003) *The Shield of Achilles*, Allen Lane, London.

Boli, J. (1999) 'Conclusion: World Authority Structures and Legitimations' in J. Boli and G.M. Thomas (eds.) *Constructing World Culture: International NGOs since 1875*, Stanford, California, Stanford University Press, pp. 267–300.

Boli, J., Loya, T.A. and Loftin, T. (1999) 'National Participation in the World Polity Organisation', in J. Boli and G.M. Thomas (eds) *Constructing World Culture: International NGOs since 1875*, Stanford, California, Stanford University Press, 50–77.

Boli, J. and Thomas, G.M. (eds.) (1999) *Constructing World Culture: International NGOs since 1875*, Stanford, California, Stanford University Press.

Bond, P. (ed.) (2003) *Fanon's Warning: A Civil Society Reader on the New Partnership for Africa's Development*, Trenton, New Jersey, Africa World Press.

Bornstein, L. (2006) 'Systems of Accountability, Webs of Deceit? Monitoring and Evaluation in South African NGOs', *Development*, 49 (2), 52–61.

Broad, R. and Cavanagh, J. (2002) 'The Death of the Washington Consensus' in R. Broad (ed.) *Global Backlash: Citizen Initiative for a Just World Economy*, Oxford, Rowman and Littlefield, pp. 56–9.

Broad, R. (ed.) (2002) *Global Backlash: Citizen Initiatives for a Just World Economy*, Oxford, Rowman and Littlefield.

Broad, R. and Landi, M. (1996) 'Whither the North-South Gap?, *Third World Quarterly*, 17 (1).

Bromley, C., Curtice, J. and Seyd, P. (2001) 'Political Engagement, Trust and Constitutional Reform' in A. Park, J. Curtice, K. Thompson, L. Jarvis and C. Bromley *British Social Attitudes: The Eighteenth Report*, London, Sage, pp. 199–225.

Brune, S. Betz, J. and Kuhne, W. (eds) (1994) *Africa and Europe: Relations of Two Continents in Transition*, Munster, Germany, German Overseas Institute.

Bujra, A. and Adejumobi, S. (eds) (2002) *Leadership, Civil Society and Democrat-isation in Africa*, Addis Ababa, Development, Policy and Management Forum.

Butler, D.E. (1955) *The British General Election of 1955*, Basingstoke, Macmillan.

Cameron, G. (2001) 'Taking Stock of Pastoralist NGOs in Tanzania', *Review of African Political Economy*, 28 (87), 55–72.

Cammack, P. (2006) 'Global Governance, State Agency and Competitiveness: The Political Economy of the Commission for Africa', *British Journal of Politics and International Relations*, 8 (3), 331–50.

Chachage, C.S.L. (2002) 'Leadership in the Civil Society in Tanzania: A Case Study of the Tanzania Gender Networking Programme (TGNP) and the Asso-ciation of Journalists and Media Workers (AJM) in A. Bujra and S. Adejumobi (eds) *Leadership, Civil Society and Democratisation in Africa*, Addis Ababa, Development, Policy and Management Forum, pp. 129–83.

Chale, F. (2005) 'With SAPs: None is Spared', *Gender Platform*, 10 (2), in Tanzania Gender Networking Programme (TGNP): 6–15.

Chandhoke, N. (2003) 'Global Civil Society: A Text without a Context' in M. Kaldor, H. Anheier and M. Glasius (eds.) *Global Civil Society*, Oxford, Oxford University Press, pp. 411–12.

Chandler, D. (2005) 'Constructing Global Civil Society' in G. Baker and D. Chandler (eds) *Global Civil Society*, London, Routledge, pp. 148–70.

Chazan, N. (1991) 'Political Transformation in Ghana under the PNDC' in D. Rothchild (ed.) *Ghana: The Political Economy of Recovery*, London, Lynne Rienner, pp. 21–47.

Chazan, N. (1988) 'Ghana: Problems of Governance and the Emergence of Civil Society' in L. Diamond, J.J. Linz and S.M. Lipset (eds) *Democracy in Developing Countries, Vol. II: Africa*, London, Adamantine Press, pp. 93–139.

Chew, S.C. and Denemark, R. (eds) (1996) *The Underdevelopment of Development*, Thousand Oaks, CA, Sage.

Civicus (2006) *Civil Society in Uganda: At the Crossroads?*, Kampala, Deniva.

Clapham, C. (1996) *Africa and the International System*, Cambridge, Cambridge University Press.

Clark, A.M., Friedman, E.J. and Hochstetler, K. (2005) 'The Social Limits of Global Civil Society: A Comparison of NGO Participation in UN World Con-ferences on the Environment, Human Rights and Women' in R. Wilkinson (ed.) *The Global Governance Reader*, Abingdon, Routledge, pp. 292–321.

Cleary, S. (1989) *Tanzania: Surviving Against the Odds*, Catholic Fund for Overseas Development.

Cohen, M.G. and McBride, S. (eds) (2003) *Global Turbulence: Social Activists and State Responses to Globalisation*, Aldershot, Ashgate.

Cohen, S. (2003) *The Resilience of the State*, London, Hurst.

Collingwood, V. (2006) 'Non-Governmental Organisations, Power and Legitimacy in International Society', *Review of International Studies*, 32, 439–54.

Comaroff, J.L. and Comaroff, J. (eds) (1999) *Civil Society and Political Imagination in Africa*, London, University of Chicago Press.

Community Development Research Network (2005) *Southern Voices for Change in the International Aid Architecture: Listening and Learning from the Voices of Civil Society*, Kampala, Community Development Research Network.

Costello, M.J. (1996) 'Administration Triumphs over Politics: The Transformation of the Tanzanian State', *African Studies Review*, 39 (1), 123–48.

Cox, R.W. (2005) Civil Society at the Turn of the Millennium' in L. Amoore (ed.) *The Global Resistance Reader*, London, Routledge, pp. 103–23.

Dalton, R. (2002) *Citizen Politics*, London, Chatham House.

Deacon, B. (ed.) (2000) *Civil Society, NGOs and Global Governance*, Sheffield, Globalisation and Social Policy Programme Occasional Paper Number 7/200.

Della Porta, D. and Tarrow, S. (eds) (2005) *Transnational Protest and Global Activism*, Oxford, Rowman and Littlefield.

DeMars, W.E. (2005) *NGOs and Transnational Networks*, London, Pluto Press.

Deniva (n/d) *Networking for Poverty Eradication and Good Governance*, Kampala, Deniva.

Desai, M. and Said, Y. (2001) 'The New Anti-Capitalist Movement: Money and Global Civil Society' in H. Anheier, M. Glasius and M. Kaldor (eds) *Global Civil Society*, Oxford, Oxford University Press, pp. 51–78.

Development Studies Association (n/d) *Africa after 2005*, Bideford, Development Studies Association.

Diamond, L., Linz, J.J. and Lipset, S. M. (eds) *Democracy in Developing Countries, Vol. II: Africa,* London, Adamantine Press.

Dicklitch, S. and Lwanga, D. (2003) 'The Politics of Being Anti-Political: Human Rights Organisations and the Creation of a Positive Human Rights Culture in Uganda', *Human Rights Quarterly*, 25, 482–509.

Dijkzeul, D. (2006) 'Transnational Human Action in Eastern DRC: State Building and Citizenship' in I.K. Richter, S. Berking and R. Muller-Schmid (eds) *Building a Transnational Civil Society*, Basingstoke, Palgrave, pp. 241–59.

Drah, F.K. (1993) 'Civil Society and the Transition to Pluralist Democracy' in K. Ninsin and F.K. Drah (eds) *Political Parties and Democracy in Ghana's Fourth Republic*, Accra, Woeli Publishing Services, 72–115.

Duffield, M. (2001) *Global Governance and the New Wars*, London, Zed Books.

Duffy, R. (2006) 'Non-Governmental Organisations and Governance States: The Impact of Transnational Environmental Management Networks in Madagascar', *Environmental Politics*, 15 (5), 731–49.

Eade, D. and Lighteringen, E. (eds) (2001) *Debating Development*, Oxford, Oxfam.

Ebrahim, A. (2003) *NGOs and Organisational Change*, Cambridge, Cambridge University Press.

Edwards, M. (2000) *NGO Rights and Responsibilities*, London, The Foreign Policy Centre.

Edwards, M. (1999) 'Legitimacy and Values in NGOs and Voluntary Organisations: Some Sceptical Thoughts' in D. Lewis *International Perspectives on Voluntary Action*, London, Earthscan 1999, pp. 258–67.

Edwards, M. and Gaventa J. (eds) (2001) *Global Citizen Action*, Boulder, Lynne Rienner.

Engberg-Pedersen, P., Gibbon, P., Raikes, P. and Udshott, L. (eds) (1996) *Limits of Adjustment in Africa*, Oxford, James Currey.

Fox, J.A. and Brown, L.D. (eds) (1998) *The Struggle for Accountability: The World Bank, NGOs and Grassroots Movements*, London, MIT Press.

Fraser, A. (2005) 'Poverty Reduction Strategy Papers: Now Who Calls the Shots?', *Review of African Political Economy*, 104/5, 317–40.

Freres, C.L. (1999) 'European Actors in Global Change' in J. Grugel (ed.) *Democracy without Borders*, London, Routledge, pp. 42–56.

Friedrich Ebert Stiftung (2003) *Political Handbook and NGO Calendar*, Dar es Salaam, FES.

Friedrich Naumann Stiftung (2003) *Regional* Office *in Africa* 'The Basic Principles of Liberalism and Liberal Democracy', http://www.fnst.de/ausland/regional/e-saf.phtml.

Frimpong-Ansah, J.H. (1991) *The Vampire State in Africa: The Political Economy of Decline in Ghana*, Oxford, James Currey.

Fukuyama, F. (1991) 'Liberal Democracy as a World Phenomenon', *PS*, 24, 659–63.

Garland, E. (1999) 'Bushmen Building Civil(ised) Society in the Kalahari and Beyond', in J.L. Comaroff and J. Comaroff (eds) *Civil Society and Political Imagination in Africa*, London, University of Chicago Press, pp. 72–107.

Gaventa, J. (2001) 'Global Citizen Action: Lessons and Challenges' in M. Edwards and J. Gaventa (eds) *Global Citizen Action*, Boulder, Lynne Rienner, pp. 275–87.

Ghimire, K.B. (ed.) (2005) *Civil Society and the Market Question: Dynamics of Rural Development and Popular Mobilization*, Basingstoke, Palgrave.

Gibbon, P. (2001) 'Civil Society, Locality and Globalization in Rural Tanzania: A Forty-Year Perspective', *Development and Change*, 32, 819–44.

Gibbon, P. (ed.) (1995) *Liberalised Development in Tanzania*, Uppsala, Scandinavian Institute of African Studies.

Glenn, J. (2008) 'Global Governance and the Democratic Deficit: Stifling the Voice of the South', *Third World Quarterly*, 29 (2), 217–38.

Goodhart, M. (2005) 'Civil Society and the Problems of Global Democracy', *Democratization*, 12 (1), 1–21.

Goodin, R.E. (2003) 'Globalizing Justice' in D. Held and M. Koenig-Archibugi (eds) *Taming Globalization*, Cambridge, Polity Press, pp. 68–92.

Grant, J.A., McLean, S.J. and Shaw, T.M. (2003) 'Emerging Transnational Coalitions Around Diamonds and Oil in Civil Conflict in Africa' in M.G. Cohen and S. McBride (eds) *Global Turbulence: Social Activists and State Responses to Globalisation*, Aldershot, Ashgate 2002, pp. 124–39.

Grant, R.W. and Keohane, R.O. (2005) 'Accountability and Abuses of Power in World Politics', *American Political Science Review*, 99 (1), 29–43.

Grugel, J. (ed.) (1999) *Democracy without Borders*, London, Routledge.

The Guardian, Dar es Salaam (2007) 'Starbucks Coffee Deal with Ethiopia Hailed as Model', Business and Finance, 3 July: ii.

Hajnal, P.I. (2006) 'Civil Society, the UN and G7/8 Summitry' in J.J. Kirton and P.I. Hajnal (eds) *Sustainability, Civil Society and International Governance*, Aldershot, Ashgate, pp. 279–318.

HakiElimu (2005) *HakiElimu Annual Report 2005*, Dar es Salaam, HakiElimu.

HakiElimu (n/d) *What is HakiElimu?*, Dar es Salaam, HakiElimu.

HakiKazi Catalyst (2004) *Supporting the Right to a Say – A Key Factor in Reducing Poverty*, Arusha, HakiKazi Catalyst.

Hansen, H.B. and Twaddle, M. (1998) *Developing Uganda*, Kampala, Fountain.

Hearn, J. (2000) 'Aiding Democracy? Donors and Civil Society in South Africa', *Third World Quarterly*, 21 (5), 815–30.

Hearn, J. (2001) 'The "Uses and Abuses" of Civil Society in Africa', *Review of African Political Economy*, 28 (87), 43–53.

Held, D. and Koenig-Archibugi, M. (eds) (2003) *Taming Globalization*, Cambridge, Polity Press.

Hencke, D. (2004) 'Labour Members Fewest Since 1930s', *The Guardian*, Manchester, 27 July, 4.

Herbst, J. (1993) 'The Dilemmas of Explaining Political Upheaval: Ghana in Comparative Perspective' in J. Widner (ed.) *Economic Change and Political Liberalisation in Sub-Saharan Africa*, London, Johns Hopkins University Press, pp. 182–92.

Hoffmann, M.J. and Ba, A.D. (2005) 'Contending Perspectives on Global Governance' in A.D. Ba and M.J. Hoffmann (eds) *Contending Perspectives on Global Governance*, London, Routledge, pp. 249–87.

Holtom, D. (2007) 'The Challenge of Consensus Building: Tanzania's PRSB 1998–2001', *Journal of Modern African Studies*, 45 (2), 233–51.

Hoogvelt, A. (1997) *Globalisation and the Postcolonial World*, Oxford, Oxford University Press.

Howard, M. (2003) 'Best Get Used to War', *The Guardian*, Manchester, 13 January, 17.

Howell, J. and Pearce, J. (2001) *Civil Society and Democracy*, London, Lynne Rienner.

Husselbee, D. (2001) 'NGOs as Development Partners to the Corporates: Child Football Stitchers in Pakistan' in D. Eade and E. Lighteringen (eds) *Debating Development*, Oxford, Oxfam, pp. 127–44.

Igoe, J. and Kelsall, T. (2005) *Between a Rock and a Hard Place: African NGOs, Donors and the State*, Durham, North Carolina, Carolina Academic Press.

Igoe, J. (2005) 'Power and Force in Tanzanian Civil Society: The Story of the Barabaig NGOs in the Hanang Community Development Project', in J. Igoe and T. Kelsall (eds.) *Between a Rock and Hard Place: African NGOs, Donors and the State*, Durham, North Carolina, Carolina Academic Press, pp. 115–46.

Igoe, J. (2003) 'Scaling up Civil Society: Donor Money, NGOs and the Pastoralist Land Rights Movement in Tanzania', *Development and Change*, 34 (5), 863–85.

Igoe, J. (2004) *Conservation and Globalisation: A Study of National Parks and Indigenous Communities from East Africa to South Dakota*, London, Thompson Learning.

Imanishimwe, L. (2007) 'EU/Africa Trade Relations: Where is the Farmer in the Economic Partnership Agreements?', *Satnet News*, Fort Portal, Uganda, (10), August, 15.

Inglehart, R. (1999) 'Post-Materialism Erodes Respect for Authority, but Increases Support for Democracy' in P. Norris (ed.) *Critical Citizens: Global Support for Democratic Governance*, Oxford, Oxford University Press, pp. 236–51.

Inglehart, R. (1977) *The Silent Social Revolution*, Princeton, NJ, Princeton University Press.

Ishakanian, I. (2008) 'Democracy Promotion and Civil Society' in M. Albrow, H. Anheier, M. Glasius, M.E. Price and M. Kaldor (eds) *Global Civil Society 2007/8*, London, Sage, 58–85.

Izama, A. (2007) 'Save Mabira Stakes to be Raised', *Sunday Monitor*, Kampala, 26 August, 1–2.

Jacoby, T. (2005) 'Cultural Determinism, Western Hegemony and the Efficiency of Defective States', *Review of African Political Economy*, 105 (5), 215–33.

Jacobsen, H. (2001) 'My Father Never Read a Book, But He Knew from Television who Kenneth Tynan Was', *The Guardian*, G2, Manchester, 20 November, 6–7.

Jordan, L. and van Tuijl, P. (eds) (2006) *NGO Accountability: Politics, Principles and Innovations*, London, Earthscan.

Journalists Environment Association of Tanzania (JET) (n/d) *Some Basic Facts About JET*, leaflet, JET, Dar es Salaam.

Jubilee Debt Campaign (2008) *Unfinished Business: Ten Years of Dropping the Debt*, London, Jubilee Debt Campaign.

Jubilee South (2002) 'South-South Summit Declaration: Towards a Debt Free Millennium', in R. Broad (ed.) *Global Backlash: Citizen Initiatives for a Just World Economy*, Oxford, Rowman and Littlefield, pp. 275–81.

Kabarole Research Centre (KRC) (2007) *KRC Home Page*, http://www.krc.or.ug

Kajege, M. (2003) 'The Shortcomings of the NGO Bill' in Friedrich Ebert Stiftung *Political Handbook and NGO Calendar*, Dar es Salaam, FES, pp. 98–101.

Kaldor, M. (2003) *Global Civil Society: An Answer to War*, Cambridge, Polity Press.

Kaldor, M., Anheier, H. and Glasius, M. (eds.) (2003) *Global Civil Society*, Oxford, Oxford University Press.

Karlstrom, M. (1999) 'Civil Society and its Presuppositions: Lesson from Uganda', in J.L. Comaroff and J. Comaroff (eds) *Civil Society and Political Imagination in Africa*, London, University of Chicago Press, pp. 104–23.

Keane, J. (2003) *Global Civil Society*, Cambridge, Cambridge University Press.

Keane, J. (2001) 'Global Civil Society?' in Anheier, H., Glasius, M. and Kaldor, M. (eds) *Global Civil Society*, Oxford, Oxford University Press, pp. 23–47.

Keck, M.E. and Sikkink, K. (1998) *Activists Beyond Borders*, London, Cornell University Press.

Kelly, A. (2006) 'Anchors of Humanity Urged to Set Example', *The Guardian*, Manchester, 8 November, 3.

Kelsall, T. (2001) 'Donors, NGOs and the State: Governance and "Civil Society" in Tanzania' in O. Barrow and M. Jennings (eds) *The Charitable Impulse: NGOs and Development in East and North East Africa*, Oxford, James Currey, pp. 133–48.

Kennedy, P. (2008) 'The Power Game', *LSE Magazine*, Summer: 6–8.

Kirton, J.J. and Hajnal, P.J. (eds) (2006) *Sustainability, Civil Society and International Governance*, Aldershot, Ashgate.

Klein, N. (2003) 'Now Bush Wants to Buy the Complicity of Aid Workers', *The Guardian*, Manchester, 23 January, 16.

Knight, B. and Stokes, P. (1996) 'Self-Help Citizenship', *The Guardian*, Manchester, 3 October, 2.

Kraus, J. (1991) 'The Political Economy of Stabilisation and Structural Adjustment' in D. Rothchild (ed.) *Ghana: The Political Economy of Recovery*, London, Lynne Rienner.

Kreye, D.K. (1996) in S.C. Chew and R. Denemark *The Underdevelopment of Development*, Thousand Oaks, CA, Sage.

Kuhne, W. (1994) 'The Changing International Environment of African Pol-itics' in S. Brune, J. Betz and W. Kuhne (eds) *Africa and Europe: Relations of Two Continents in Transition*, Munster, German Overseas Institute, pp. 3–24.

Kwesiga, J.B. and Namisi, H. (2006) 'Issues in Legislation for NGOs in Uganda' in L. Jordan and P. van Tuijl (eds) *NGO Accountability: Politics, Principles and Innovations*, London, Earthscan, pp. 81–91.

Lawyers Environmental Action Team (LEAT) (2003) *Robbing the Poor to Give to the Rich*, http://www.leat.ortz/activities/buly/eir.submission

Laxer, G. and Halperin, S. (eds) (2003) *Global Civil Society and its Limits*, Basingstoke, Macmillan.

Lewis, D. (2002) 'Civil Society in African Contexts: Reflections on the Usefulness of a Concept', *Development and Change*, 33 (4), 568–86.

Lewis, D. (ed.) (1999) *International Perspectives on Voluntary Action*, London, Earthscan.

Lipschutz, R. (2005) 'Global Civil Society and Governability: Resistance, Reform or Resignation' in G. Baker and D. Chandler *Global Civil Society*, London, Routledge, pp. 148–70.

Lipschutz, R.D. (ed.) (2006) *Civil Societies and Social Movements*, Aldershot, Ashgate, pp. 407–29.

Logan, C.J., Muwanga, N., Sentamu, R. and Bratton, M. (2003) *Uganda Round 2 Afrobarometer Survey Report*, Washington, D.C., International Foundation for Electoral Systems.

Luckham, A.R. (1971) 'A Comparative Typology of Civil-Military Relations', *Government and Opposition*, Winter, 8–34.

Maina, W. (1998) 'Kenya: The State, Donors and the Politics of Democratization' in A. Van Rooy (ed.) *Civil Society and the Aid Industry*, London, Earthscan, pp. 134–67.

Majot, J. (2006) 'On Trying to do Good Well: Practising Participatory Democracy through International Advocacy Campaigns' in L. Jordan and P. van Tuijl (eds) *NGO Accountability: Politics, Principles and Innovations*, London, Earthscan, pp. 211–28.

Makumbe, J.M. (1998) 'Is there a Civil Society in Africa', *International Affairs*, 74 (2), 305–17.

Mbabazi, P. and Taylor, L. (2005) (eds) *The Potentiality of 'Developmental States' in Africa: Botswana and Uganda Compared*, Dakar, Codesria.

Mbilinyi, M. and Rusimbi, M. (2005) 'Tanzania: Is This a Pro-poor Gender-sensitive Budget?', *Review of African Political Economy*, 32 (106), 627–30.

McHenry, D. (1994) *Limited Choices: The Political Struggle for Socialism in Tanzania*, London, Lynne Rienner.

McKeon, N. (2005) 'The Farmers' Movement and the Market Question in Senegal' in K.R. Ghimire *Civil Society and the Market Question: Dynamics of Rural Development and Popular Mobilization*, Basingstoke, Palgrave, pp. 189–226.

Mercer, C. (2002) 'The Discourse of *Maendeleo* and the Politics of Women's Participation on Mount Kilimanjaro', *Development and Change*, 32, 101–27.

Michael, S. (2004) *Undermining Development: The Absence of Power Among Local NGOs in Africa*, Oxford, James Currey.

Migiro (1990) in H. Othman, I.K. Bavu and M. Okema (eds) *Tanzania: Democracy in Transition*, Dar es Salaam, Dar es Salaam University Press.

Mlama, P. (2002) 'Local Perspectives on Globalisation: The Cultural Domain' in J. Semboja, J. Mwapachu and E. Jansen *Local Perspectives on Globalisation: The African Case*, Dar es Salaam, Mkuki na Nyota Publishers, pp. 57–83.

Mmuya, M. and Chaligha, A. (1992) *Towards Multi-Party Democracy in Tanzania*, Dar es Salaam, Dar es Salaam University Press.

Monbiot, G. (2005) 'Thanks to Corporations, Instead of Democracy we get Baywatch', *The Guardian*, Manchester, 13 September, 27.

Morena, E. (2006) 'Funding the Future of the Global Justice Movement', *Development*, 49 (2), 29–33.

Museveni, Y. (1998) *Sowing the Mustard Seed*, Basingstoke, Macmillan.

Mutahi, P. and Kagwanja, P. (2008) 'Every Penny in Aid has a String of War on Terrorism Attached', *Daily Monitor*, Kampala, 13 August, 22.

Mvungi, S.C.A. and Mhina, A.K.L. (1990) 'Dodoma Urban: Searching for a People's MP' in H. Othman, I.K. Bavu and M. Okema (eds) *Tanzania: Democracy in Transition*, Dar es Salaam University Press, pp. 103–20.

Nanz, P. and Steffek, J. (2004) 'Global Governance, Participation and the Public Sphere', *Government and Opposition*, 39 (2), 314–35.

Ninsin, K. and Drah, F.K. (eds) (1993) *Political Parties and Democracy in Ghana's Fourth Republic*, Accra, Woeli Publishing Services.

Norris, P. (ed.) (1999) *Critical Citizens: Global Support for Democratic Governance*, Oxford, Oxford University Press.

Norris, P. (2002) *Democratic Phoenix*, Cambridge, Cambridge University Press.

O'Brien, R. (2006) 'Workers and the World Order: The Tentative Transformation of the International Union Movement' in R.D. Lipschutz (ed.) *Civil Societies and Social Movements*, Aldershot, Ashgate, pp. 407–29.

Oloka-Onyango, J., Kibwana, K. and Peter, C.M. (1996) *Law and the Struggle for Democracy in East Africa*, Nairobi, Claripress.

Osman, M. (2006) 'Western NGOs and Islam: How to Counter the Image of "Missionaries and Spies"', *Europe's World*, 1–3.

Ossewaarde, R. Nijhof, A. and Heyse L. (2008) 'Dynamics of NGO Legitimacy: How Organising Betrays Core Missions of INGOs', *Public Administration and Development*, 28, 42–53.

Othman, H., Bavu, I.K. and Okema, M. (eds) (1990) *Tanzania: Democracy in Transition*, Dar es Salaam, Dar es Salaam University Press.

Oxfam (2006) *You Have the Power to Change Minds*, Oxford, Oxfam.

Park, A., Curtice, J., Thompson, K., Jarvis, L. and Bromley, C. (eds) (2001) *British Social Attitudes: The Eighteenth Report*, London, Sage.

Pattie, C., Seyd, P. and Whiteley, P. (2003) 'Civic Engagement in Modern Britain', *Parliamentary Affairs*, 56, 616–33.

Peeler, J.A. (1998) *Building Democracy in Latin America*, London, Lynne Rienner.

Pharr, S.J. and Putnam, R.D. (eds) (2002) *Disaffected Democracies*, Princeton, NJ, Princeton University Press.

Pianta, M. (2001) 'Parallel Summits and Global Civil Society' in H. Anheier, M. Glasius and M. Kaldor (eds) *Global Civil Society*, Oxford, Oxford University Press, pp. 169–94.

Pinkney, R. (2005) *The Frontiers of Democracy*, Aldershot, Ashgate.

Pinkney, R. (2001) *The International Politics of East Africa*, Manchester, Manchester University Press.

Pommerolle, M.E. (2005) 'Leaders in the Human Rights Sector: The Paradoxical Institutionalisation of a Kenyan NGO' in J. Igoe and T. Kelsall *Between a Rock and a Hard Place: African NGOs, Donors and the State*, Durham, North Carolina, Carolina Academic Press, 93–113.

Prato, S. (2006) 'Funding NGOs: Making Good the Democratic Deficit/Interview with Stefano Prato', *Development*, 49 (2), 11–14.

Putnam, R.D. (2000) *Bowling Alone*, London, Simon and Schuster.

Putnam, R.D., Pharr, S.J. and Dalton, R. (2002) 'Introduction: What's Troubling the Trilateral Democracies' in S.J. Pharr and R.D. Putnam (eds) *Disaffected Democracies*, Princeton, NJ, Princeton University Press.

Raikes, P. and Gibbon, P. (1996) 'Tanzania 1986–94' in P. Engberg-Pedersen, P. Gibbon, P. Raikes and L. Udshott (eds) *Limits of Adjustment in Africa*, Oxford, James Currey, pp. 215–308.

Rawlence, B. (2005) 'NGOs and the New Field of African Politics: A case study from Zambia' in J. Igoe and T. Kelsall *Between a Rock and a Hard Place: African NGOs, Donors and the State*, Durham, North Carolina, Carolina Academic Press, 147–64.

Reitan, R. (2007) *Global Activism*, London, Routledge.

Rice, X. (2007) 'Factory May Destroy Natural Wonder', *The Guardian*, Manchester, 12 July, 16.

Rice, X. (2007) 'White Water Torrent to Die as Nation Gambles on Huge Nile Dam Project', *The Guardian*, Manchester, 31 May, 21.

Richter, I.K., Berking, S. and Müller-Schmid (eds) (2006) *Building a Transnational Civil Society*, Basingstoke, Palgrave.

Rosenau, J.N. (2005) 'Global Governance as a Disaggregated Complexity' in A.D. Ba and M.J. Hoffmann (eds) *Contending Perspectives on Global Governance*, London, Routledge, pp. 131–53.

Rothchild, D. (ed.) (1991) *Ghana: The Political Economy of Recovery*, London, Lynne Rienner.

Rugendyke, B. (ed.) (2007) *NGOs as Advocates for Development in a Globalising World*, London, Routledge.

Rylander, S. (1998) *Swedish Policy Towards Africa in the Twentieth Century*, Dar es Salaam, Economic and Social Research Foundation.

Sadoun, B. (2006) 'Donor Policies and the Financial Autonomy of Development NGOs', *Development*, 49 (2), 45–51.

Salamon, L.M. and Anheier, H. (1999) 'The Third World's Third Sector in Comparative Perspective' in D. Lewis *International Perspectives on Voluntary Action*, London, Earthscan, pp. 60–93.

Sayer, J. (2007) 'Risks and Rewards: NGOs Engaging the Corporate Sector' in B. Rugendyke (ed.) *NGOs as Advocates for Development in a Globalising World*, London, Routledge, pp. 127–55.

Scharpf, F.W. (2002) 'Interdependence and Legitimation' in S.J. Pharr and R.D. Putnam (eds) *Disaffected Democracies*, Princeton, NJ, Princeton University Press.

Scholte, J.A. (n/d) 'Africa in an Era of Globalisation', in Development Studies Association *Africa after 2005*, Bideford, Development Studies Association, pp. 6–11.

Scholte, J.A. (2004) 'Civil Society and Democratically Accountable Global Governance', *Government and Opposition*, 39 (2), 211–33.

Semboja, J., Mwapachu, J. and Jansen, E. (eds) (2002) *Local Perspectives on Globalisation: The African Case*, Dar es Salaam, Mkuki na Nyota Publishers.

Shaw, T. (2005) 'Uganda as an African "Democratic Developmental State"'? HIPC Governance at the Turn of the 21st Century' in P. Mbabazi and L. Taylor (eds) *The Potentiality of 'Developmental States' in Africa: Botswana and Uganda Compared*, Dakar, Codesria, pp. 33–43.

Shivji, I.G. (2002) 'Globalisation and Popular Resistance' in J. Semboja, J. Mwapachu and E. Jansen (eds) *Local Perspectives on Globalisation: The African Case*, Dar es Salaam, Mkuki na Nyota Publishers, pp. 101–18.

Sikkink, K. (2005) 'Patterns of Dynamic Multilevel Governance and the Insider-Outsider Coalition' in D. Della Porta and S. Tarrow (eds) *Transnational Protest and Global Activism*, Oxford, Rowman and Littlefield, pp. 151–73.

Sunseri, T. (2005) 'Something Else to Burn: Forest Squatters, Conservationists and the State in Modern Tanzania', *Journal of Modern African Studies*, 43 (4), 609–40.

Swedish International Development Agency (SIDA) (n/d) *What does SIDA do in Tanzania?*, http://sida.se/sida/jsp/sida.jsp?d.

Swedish International Development Agency (1998) *Partnership in Development: Sweden and Tanzania*, Dar es Salaam, Embassy.

Tandon, Y. (2003) 'NEPAD + Sap + Gats + DSB' in P. Bond (ed.) *Fanon's Warning: A Civil Society Reader on the New Partnership for Africa's Development*, Trenton, New Jersey, Africa World Press, pp. 59–63.

Tanzania Association of NGOs (TANGO) (2002) *Civil Society Brief*, Dar es Salaam, TANGO.

Tanzanian Affairs (1998) 'Tanzania and the Multi-National Agreement on Investment (MAI)', 60, May–August, London, 10–12.

Tanzanian Affairs (2002) 'The Air Traffic Control Saga', May–August, 72, 10–11.

Tanzanian Affairs (2008), January–April, 'Fight Against Corruption', 1–11.

Tanzania Gender Networking Programme (TGNP) (2004) *Gender Platform* 'Editorial', 2.

Tanzania Natural Resources Forum (TNRF) (2006) *Insights into Forestry, Governance and National Development: Illegal Logging in Southern Tanzania*, Arusha, TNRF.

Taylor, I. and Williams, P. (eds) (2004) *Africa in International Politics*, London, Routledge.

Thomas, C. (2004) 'The IFIs' Relations with Africa' in I. Taylor and P. Williams (eds) *Africa in International Politics*, London, Routledge, pp. 174–94.

Timms, D. (2004–5) 'A Mouse that Roars – How WDM Took on the GATS', *Action*, London, World Development (WDM), 8–10.

Tomlinson, B. (2002) 'Defending Humane Internationalism: The Role of Canadian NGOs in a Security-Conscious Era', *International Journal*, LVII (2), 273–82.

Tripp, A.M. (1997) *Changing the Rules: The Politics of Liberalization in the Urban Informal Economy in Tanzania*, London, University of California Press.

Tripp, A.M. (2000) 'Political Reform in Tanzania: The Struggle for Associational Autonomy', *Comparative Politics*, 32 (2), 191–214.

Turner, M. and Hulme, D. (1997) *Global Governance, Administration and Development*, Basingstoke, Macmillan.

Uganda Debt Network (2005) *About Uganda Debt Network*, http://www.udn.or.ug/about.html

United Nations Development Programme (UNDP) (2007) *Human Development Report 2007/2008*, Basingstoke, Palgrave.

United Republic of Tanzania (1992) *The Presidential Commission on Single Party or Multiparty Systems in Tanzania*, Dar es Salaam, Dar es Salaam University Press.

Van Donge, J.K. and Liviga, A.J. (1989) 'The 1985 Tanzanian Parliamentary Elections: A Conservative Election', *African Affairs*, January, 47–62.

Van Rooy, A. (ed.) (1998) *Civil Society and the Aid Industry*, London, Earthscan.

Vidal, J. (2007) 'Close Encounters', *The Guardian*, Manchester, 3 January, 9.

Vidal, J. (1998) 'Modem Warfare', *The Guardian*, Manchester, 13 January, 4.

Vincent, F. (2006) 'NGOs, Social Movements, External Funding and Dependency', *Development*, 49 (2), 22–8.

Wainwright, H. (2005) 'Civil Society, Democracy and Power: Global Connections' in H. Anheier, M. Glasius and M. Kaldor (eds) *Global Civil Society 2004/5*, London, Sage, pp. 94–119.

Wallace, T., Bornstein, L. and Chapman, J. (2007) *The Aid Chain*, Bourton on Dunsmore, Practical Acting Publishing.

Waltz, K. (1979) *The Theory of International Politics*, Reading, MA, Addison Wesley.

Warkentin, C. (2001) *Reshaping World Politics: NGOs, the Internet and Global Civil Society*, Oxford, Rowman and Littlefield.

Watt, D., Flanary, R. and Theobald, R. (1999) 'Democratisation or the Democratisation of Corruption? The Case of Uganda', *Commonwealth and Comparative Politics*, 47 (3), 37–64.

Whiteley, P. (2003) 'The State of Participation in Britain', *Parliamentary Affairs*, 56, 610–15.

Widner, J. (ed.) *Economic Change and Political Liberalisation in Sub-Saharan Africa*, London, Johns Hopkins University Press.

Wilkinson, R. (ed.) (2005) *The Global Governance Reader*, Abingdon, Routledge 2005.

Wood, A. (2000) 'What Role for Multilateral Institutions, Donors and NGOs in the New Framework for Poverty Eradication?' in B. Deacon (ed.) *Civil Society, NGOs and Global Governance*, Sheffield, Globalisation and Social Policy Programme Occasional Paper Number 7/200, pp. 45–61.

Woollacott, M. (2005) 'We are not Instruments of US Power', *The Guardian*, Manchester, 28 May, 24.

World Bank (1999) *Annual Report 1999*, Washington, DC, World Bank.

World Bank (1996) *Uganda: The Challenge of Growth and Poverty Reduction*, Washington, DC, World Bank.

World Bank (1998) *World Development Indicators*, Washington, DC, World Bank.

Youngs, R. (2004) *International Development and the West*, Oxford, Oxford University Press.

Zurn, M. (2004) 'Global Governance and Legitimacy Problems', *Government and Opposition*, 39 (2), 260–87.

Index